D1572714

Preachers of the Italian Ghetto

Preachers of the Italian Ghetto

EDITED BY

David B. Ruderman

UNIVERSITY OF CALIFORNIA PRESS

Berkeley   Los Angeles   Oxford

University of California Press
Berkeley and Los Angeles, California
University of California Press
Oxford, England
Copyright © 1992 by
The Regents of the University of California

Library of Congress Cataloging-in-Publication Data

Preachers of the Italian ghetto / edited by David B. Ruderman.
   p. cm.
   Includes bibliographical references and index.
   ISBN 0-520-07735-0 (alk. paper)
   1. Preaching, Jewish—Italy—History—16th century. 2. Preaching,
Jewish—Italy—History—17th century. 3. Judaism—Italy—
History—16th century. 4. Judaism—Italy—History—17th century.
5. Jewish sermons—History and criticism. 6. Rabbis—Italy—
Biography. 7. Moscato, Judah ben Joseph, ca. 1539–ca. 1593.
I. Ruderman, David B.
BM730.A4I87 1992
296.4′2′094509031—dc20
                                     91-31552
                                     CIP

Printed in the United States of America

1   2   3   4   5   6   7   8   9

The paper used in this publication meets the minimum requirements of American
National Standard for Information Sciences—Permanence of Paper for Printed Library
Materials, ANSI Z39.48-1984 ∞

For Tali
With Great Affection

CONTENTS

ILLUSTRATIONS

ONE

Introduction

David B. Ruderman

When in 1581 the English cleric Gregory Martin published his personal reflections on Rome, he singled out the Italian preachers whose activity he had observed:

> And to heare the maner of the Italian preacher, with what a spirit he toucheth the hart, and moveth to compunction, (for to that end they employ their talke and not in disputinge matters of controversie which, god be thanked, there needeth not) that is a singular joy and a merveilous edifying to a good Christian man.[1]

Father Martin's panegyric on the pleasure of listening to a moving sermon was surely not an atypical response to the phenomenon of preaching in the sixteenth and seventeenth centuries. As Hilary Smith remarks, the same scenario was reported all over Europe: "large congregations sitting (or standing) spellbound at the feet of a preacher who, by the sheer power of his eloquence and personal magnetism, was able to hold their attention for an hour or possibly longer."[2] Of course, the good friar meant Christian preachers and their sermons, those he seemed to encounter wherever he wandered in Rome: in the major churches, in the hospitals and convents, and even in the piazzas. There is no doubt that he also noticed a community of Jewish residents in the city of the popes during these meanderings. He acknowledges hearing "the voices of the holy preachers" in their regular weekly meetings with the Jews, exhorting them to convert to Christianity.[3]

One wonders if Father Martin could have also known that, besides that painful obligatory hour of Christian proselytizing to which the Jews of the Roman ghetto were subjected, they, too, willingly flocked to their own *predicatori* on Sabbaths and on special occasions. It was not uncommon for some curious Christians to be present in ghetto synagogues

בס"ד חלק ראשון על ה' ה'תורה
ספר שמו

אור הדרשנים

מורה באלבע הסימנים · מכל דברים וענינים ·

של מאמרי נאמנים · שילקוט בפנים שונים ·

מועיל לבחורים וזקנים · להקל טורח המציעים ·

ועוד מדליק לפניהם נרות · מלאכת הדרשות ·

מאירות · בחבור יפה ובאמירות · לעשות

דרשות יקרות · יפעת כמו של מעלת הרופא

מופהק דורש טוב לעמו · ברומא בכנסת ה'ה'

קאטלאני ורגוניסי י"ץ כמוהר"ר יעקב

בכמוהר"ר יצחק צהלון זצ"ל

לשם הבורא יגיענו לרויחה ·

הועתק על יד הבחור שלמה בלא"א יצחק ד"ד

קושטה עטיאש נרו בלונדרא שנת ה'תע"ז:

First page from Jacob Ẓahalon's *Or ha-Darshanim* (A Manual for preachers) (London, 1717). Ms. 1646:33. Courtesy of the Library of The Jewish Theological Seminary of America.

during the delivery of the sermon. The Jews, like the Jesuits Martin described, might have expounded in their own manner, of course, on "some good matter of edification, agreable to their audience, with ful streame of the plainest scriptures, and piked sentences of auncient fathers, and notable examples of former time, most sweetly exhorting to good life, and most terribly dehorting from al sinne and wickedness, often setting before them the paines of hel, and the joyes of Heaven."[4] Most probably, such a scenario was invisible to the pious Christian gentleman who, like many of his contemporaries, had little reason to intermingle with Jews in their own houses of worship, and who could not deem them worthy of his attention except as potential candidates for the baptismal font.

In reality, however, the period of the late sixteenth and seventeenth centuries was not only an age of the sermon for Catholics and Protestants but for Jews as well. Just as Christian preachers were increasingly committing their most effective homilies to print for an enthusiastic reading public, so their Jewish counterparts were similarly inclined to polish their oral vernacular sermons, to translate them into elegant Hebrew prose, and thus to satisfy the equally voracious appetite of their Hebrew reading public. In Italy, in Amsterdam, in the Ottoman empire, and in Eastern Europe, the Jewish preacher assumed a status unparalleled in any previous age, and the interest of a Jewish laity in hearing and reading sermons reached unprecedented heights.[5] This new role of the *darshan*, the Jewish counterpart to the "sacred orator," as mediator between Jewish elite and popular culture, effected through the edifying delivery and eventual diffusion of his printed sermons, undoubtedly closely approximates similar cultural patterns emerging throughout early modern Europe. Yet Jewish preachers and their sermons, particularly those emerging in the Italian ghetto, also reflect a cultural ambiance unique to Jews, emanating from the special characteristics of their cultural heritage and the specific circumstances of their social and political status in Italy.[6]

A book exclusively devoted to Jewish preachers and their sermons delivered in the Italian ghetto is surely a novelty even in our present day, one of dramatic proliferation of books on Jewish studies in Israel, the United States, and Europe. Indeed, with few exceptions, the historical study of Jewish homiletical literature in all periods, despite its centrality and pervasiveness within Jewish culture, is still in its infancy. Surely this deficiency follows the general pattern: the history of Catholic and Protestant preaching in early modern Europe still remains a relatively underdeveloped field. Whether the state of research on Jewish preaching is the same or worse is a matter of conjecture. What is clear, however, as Marc

Saperstein amply relates in his essay below, is that even the major Jewish sermon collections in print have not been adequately studied. Thousands of sermons still in manuscript, primarily in Hebrew but also in Italian, have been almost completely neglected, and historians have only infrequently utilized this material in reconstructing the social and intellectual world of Italian Jewry in this period.

This modest volume does not purport to correct these deficiencies. It considers only a handful of well-known Italian preachers, and only a small sampling of their prodigious literary corpus. But as a beginning, it highlights several salient features of Jewish preaching within the context of the Italian ghetto in the sixteenth and early seventeenth centuries, and it attempts to extrapolate from this context something more about the nature of the Jewish cultural ambiance in general. Before introducing the larger social and cultural context of Jewish life in the ghetto period, and before highlighting some of the major themes discussed in the essays below, a few words of explanation about the genesis of this project are in order.

The idea of this book grew out of an invitation I extended to three scholars in the field of Renaissance and Baroque Italian Jewish intellectual and social history to join me at Yale in a faculty seminar during the spring of 1990 on the subject of Jewish preachers of the Italian ghetto. Moshe Idel, Robert Bonfil, and Joanna Weinberg graciously accepted my invitation. Each of us decided to select a distinguished preacher of the late sixteenth or early seventeenth century and to explore the larger Jewish cultural landscape of his age from the vantage point of his sermons. We had all written considerably on this period but had rarely approached our subject exclusively from the perspective of sermons and their cultural setting, and we had never worked in concert. We agreed not to impose on our sessions any defined agenda; each researcher would decide independently which features of the sermons to stress, whether their content or form, or both; their connection to larger cultural issues, to Jewish-Christian relations, to popular culture, to the diffusion of kabbalah, and so on. Each of us presented an original paper in the seminar and engaged in a most stimulating and fruitful discussion with the others and with other invited Jewish historians and colleagues at Yale. In addition, I invited Marc Saperstein, the author of a recent volume on Jewish preaching, to offer a general overview of our subject from the comparative perspective of preaching in other Jewish communities. Finally, I asked Elliott Horowitz, another Jewish historian of early modern Italy, who had visited Yale during the previous year, to contribute a chapter on funeral sermons, a subject related to his own research. The results of this collective effort are now before the reader.

I.

The world inhabited by Jewish preachers and their congregations in the sixteenth and seventeenth centuries was a fundamentally different one from that of their immediate predecessors of the medieval and Renaissance periods. A new oppressive policy instituted by Pope Paul IV and his successors in the middle of the sixteenth century caused a marked deterioration in the legal status and physical state of the Jewish communities of the papal states and in the rest of Italy as well. Jews living in the various city-states of Italy suddenly faced a major offensive against their community and its religious heritage, culminating in the public incineration of the Talmud in 1553 and in restrictive legislation leading to increased impoverishment, ghettoization, and even expulsion. Jews previously had been expelled from the areas under the jurisdiction of Naples in 1541. In 1569, they were removed from most of the papal states, with the exception of the cities of Ancona and Rome. Those who sought refuge in Tuscany, Venice, or Milan faced oppressive conditions as well. The only relatively tolerable havens were in the territories controlled by the Gonzaga of Mantua and the Estensi of Ferrara.

The situation was further aggravated by increasing conversionary pressures, including compulsory appearances at Christian preaching in synagogues and the establishment of transition houses for new converts which were designed to facilitate large-scale conversion to Christianity. Whether motivated primarily by the need to fortify Catholic hegemony against all dissidence, Christian and non-Christian alike, or by a renewed zeal for immediate and mass conversion, spurred in part by apocalyptic frenzy, the papacy acted resolutely to undermine the status of these small Jewish communities in the heart of western Christendom.[7]

These measures stood in contrast to the relatively benign treatment of Jews by the Church and by secular authorities in Italy throughout previous centuries. Jewish loan bankers had initially been attracted to northern and central Italy because of the generous privileges offered them by local governments eager to attract adequate sources of credit for local businesses and, in particular, for small loans to the poor. As a result of the granting of such privileges to individual Jews in the thirteenth, fourteenth, and fifteenth centuries, miniscule Jewish communities grew up throughout the region, consisting of Jews who had migrated from the southern regions of Italy and of other immigrants from Provence, from Germany and eventually from Spain. The backbone of these communities was the entrenchment of successful loan bankers who had negotiated legal charters (*condotte*) for themselves and those dependent upon them, and who also carried the primary burden of paying taxes to the authorities. By the sixteenth century, Jewish merchants and artisans joined these communities, until eventually the moneylenders were no longer in the majority.[8]

In the relatively tolerant conditions of Jewish political and economic life until the mid-sixteenth century, the cultural habits and intellectual tastes of some Italian Jews were stimulated by their proximity to centers of Italian Renaissance culture. A limited but conspicuous number of Jewish intellectuals established close liaisons with their Christian counterparts to a degree unparalleled in earlier centuries. The most significant example of such Jewish-Christian encounter in the Renaissance took place outside of Florence in the home of the Neoplatonic philosopher Giovanni Pico della Mirandola. Out of a mutually stimulating interaction between Pico and his Jewish associates and a prolonged study of Jewish books emerged one of the most unusual and exotic currents in the intellectual history of the Renaissance, the Christian kabbalah. In an unprecedented manner a select but influential group of Christian scholars actively sought to understand the Jewish religion and its sacred texts in order to penetrate their own spiritual roots more deeply. Such a major reevaluation of contemporary Jewish culture by Christians would leave a noticeable mark on both Christian and Jewish self-understanding in this and later periods.[9]

The new cultural intimacy of intellectuals from communities of both faiths could not, however, dissipate the recurrent animosities between Jews and Christians even in the heyday of the Renaissance. In the fifteenth century, Franciscan preachers such as Bernardino da Siena and Antonino da Firenze openly attacked the Jewish loan bankers and their supposedly cancerous effect upon the local populace. Others, like Bernardino da Feltre, launched the drive to establish *monti di pietà*, public free-lending associations with the avowed purpose of eliminating Jewish usury in Italy altogether. Such campaigns often led to painful consequences for Jewish victims: riots, physical harassment, even loss of life, as in the case of Bernardino's most notorious incitement, his charge of Jewish ritual murder in the city of Trent in 1475. If there was a shelter from such disasters, it was the fragmented political nature of the Italian city-states along with the highly diffused and sparsely populated Jewish settlements throughout the region. Aggressive acts against Jews were usually localized and relatively circumscribed; the Jewish victims of persecution often found refuge in neighboring communities and even found ways to return to their original neighborhoods when the hostilities had subsided.[10]

By the middle of the sixteenth century, the new legislative measures affecting the conditions of Jewish life on Italian soil effectively altered this social and cultural climate to which Jews had grown accustomed. The most conspicuous transformation was the erection of the ghettos themselves, those compulsory Jewish quarters in which all Jews were required to live and in which no Christians were allowed to live. The word was probably first used to describe an area in Venice, supposedly because it had once been the site of a foundry (*getto*-casting), selected as early as 1515 as the compulsory residential quarter for Jews. With the passage of Pope Paul IV's infamous bill *Cum nimis absurdum* in 1555, the ghetto of Rome came into being, and similar quarters gradually spread to most Italian cities throughout the next century.[11]

The notion of the ghetto fit well into the overall policy of the new Counter-Reformation papacy. Through enclosure and segregation, the Catholic community would now be shielded from Jewish "contamination." Since Jews could more easily be identified and controlled within a restricted neighborhood, the mass conversionary program of the papacy could prove to be more effective, and the canon law could be more rigidly applied. The conversionary sermons to which Friar Martin had listened were an obvious manifestation of this new reality of concentrating larger numbers of Jews in cramped and restricted neighborhoods and of constantly harassing them materially and spiritually. Another was the severe economic pressure placed upon many Jewish petty merchants and artisans obliging them to compete fiercely for the diminished revenue available to them within their newly restrictive neighborhoods. Jewish loan banking activities also collapsed, with capital more readily available to Christians from other sources. While pockets of Jewish wealth and power were surely entrenched in ghetto society, a newly emerging class of impoverished Jews was conspicuously present, and a growing polarization of rich and poor became an inevitable consequence of the crowded, urbanized, and intense social settings of the new Jewish settlements.

Yet the ghetto also constituted a kind of paradox in redefining the political, economic, and social status of Jews within Christian society. No doubt Jews confined to a heavily congested area surrounded by a wall shutting them off from the rest of the city, except for entrances bolted at night, were subjected to considerably more misery, impoverishment, and humiliation than before. And clearly the result of ghettoization was the erosion of ongoing liaisons between the two communities, including intellectual ones. Nevertheless, as Benjamin Ravid has pointed out in describing the Venetian ghetto, "the establishment of ghettos did not . . . lead to the breaking of Jewish contacts with the outside world on all levels from the highest to the lowest, to the consternation of church and state alike."[12] Moreover, the ghetto provided Jews with a clearly defined place within Christian society. In other words, despite the obvious negative implications of ghetto sequestrations, there was a positive side: the Jews were provided a natural residence within the economy of Christian space. The difference between being expelled and being ghettoized is the difference between having no right to live in Christian society and that of becoming an organic part of that society. In this sense, the ghetto, with all its negative connotations, could also connote a change for the better, an official acknowledgment by Christian society that Jews did belong in some way to their extended community.

The notion of paradox is critical to Robert Bonfil's understanding of the ghetto experience in his recent writing on the subject.[13] For him, paradox, the mediating element between two opposites, represents a distinct characteristic of transitional periods in history, "a part of the structural transformation instrumental in inverting the medieval world and in creating modern views."[14] Most paradoxical of all is Bonfil's contention that the kabbalah, an object of Christian fascination in the Renaissance, became in this later period the most effective mediator between Jewish medievalism and modernity. It became "an anchor in the stormy seas aroused by the collapse of medieval systems of thought" and, simultaneously, "an agent of modernity."[15] In "conquering" the public sermon, in encouraging revisions in Jewish liturgy, in proposing alternative times and places for Jewish prayer and study, and in stimulating the proliferation of pious confraternities and their extra-synagogal activities, the kabbalah deeply affected the way Italian Jews related to both the religious and secular spheres of their lives. In fact, the growing demarcation of the two spheres, a clear mark of the modern era, constituted the most profound change engendered by the new spirituality.[16]

Along with religious changes went economic and social ones. The concentration and economic impoverishment of the ghetto that engendered an enhanced polarization between rich and poor appeared to facilitate a cultural polarization as well. For the poor, knowledge of Hebrew and traditional sources conspicuously deteriorated. For the rich, elitist cultural activities were paradoxically enhanced. They produced Hebrew essays, sermons, dramas, and poetry using standard baroque literary conventions.[17] They performed polyphonic music reminiscent of that of the Church,[18] entertained themselves with mannerist rhyming riddles at weddings and other public occasions,[19] and lavishly decorated their marriage certificates with baroque allegorical symbols.[20] The seemingly "other-worldly" kabbalist Moses Zacuto was capable of producing "this-worldly" Hebrew drama replete with Christian metaphors, as Bonfil mentions.[21] And ironically, despite the insufferable ghetto, some Jews, undoubtedly the most comfortable and most privileged, seemed to prefer their present status.[22]

In describing the ghetto era in such a manner, Bonfil strongly urges a reconsideration of the importance of the Renaissance era for Jewish cultural history. He claims that the beginning of incipient modernism was not the Renaissance, as earlier historians have thought, but the ghetto age, as late as the end of the sixteenth and throughout the seventeenth century. Moreover, Bonfil urges that one should view this later period not as a continuation of the Renaissance, "a mere blossoming [of Renaissance] trends after a long period of germination," but as a distinct era in itself, that of the baroque, and that this latter term, used primarily in a literary or artistic context, is also a relevant category in periodizing a unique and repercussive era in the Jewish experience.[23]

The full implications of Bonfil's revisionist position for the study of Jewish history have yet to be explored. Few historians have employed the term "baroque" in describing Jewish culture during the period from the end of the sixteenth century, and most of the contributors below are reticent to use it in this volume as well. Few are yet prepared (as is this writer) to deny any significance altogether to the Renaissance in shaping a novel and even modern Jewish cultural experience. In fact, Bonfil's emphasis on the sharp rupture and discontinuity engendered by the ghetto might be tempered by a greater emphasis of the lines of continutiy between the Renaissance and the post-Renaissance eras.[24] Be that as it may, Bonfil's novel emphasis opens the possibility for a fresh assessment of the ghetto experience with respect to Jewish-Christian relations, Jewish cultural developments, and the ultimate emergence of a modern and secularized temperment, with all its complexities, within the Jewish communities of early modern Europe.

II.

Bonfil's bold interpretation of the cultural experience of the Italian ghetto might serve as a useful backdrop for discussing some of the major themes presented in the essays below. Whether or not the conclusions of each, written from the perspective of one individual preacher and his pulpit, fully conform to Bonfil's synthesis, the latter at least offers us a theoretical framework in which to compare and assess the particular portraits sketched below, and to attempt to abstract from them some tentative conclusions about the Jewish preaching situation and its relationship to the larger cultural world from which it emerged.

Most of the questions posed by Marc Saperstein in his preliminary overview of Jewish preaching relate directly to the issues raised by Bonfil.[25] He asks whether the study of sermons might shed some light on the vitality or impotency of philosophical modes of thought among Italian Jews, on the degree of popularization of the kabbalah, or on the influence of Christian or classical modes of thought. He is interested in exploring the relationship between the content and style of Jewish and Christian preaching, and between Jewish preaching in Italy and in other Jewish communities. His agenda for further research includes a more thorough study of the education of preachers, the politics of preaching, and the function of the preacher as a social critic and social observer.

Many, if not all, of these questions are addressed in the subsequent essays. We first turn to the portrait of Judah Moscato (Mantua, c. 1530–c. 1593) offered by Moshe Idel, since Moscato's public career as preacher and rabbi preceded the other major figures included in this volume by several decades, certainly long before the official erection of the ghetto in Mantua in 1612, and even before the public atmosphere for Jews had severely worsened in this relatively tolerant center of Jewish life.[26] No doubt Moscato's extraordinary use of classical pagan and Christian sources and motifs in his sermons, utterly different from any other Jewish preacher whose sermons are known to us, including Figo, del Bene, or Modena, accounts for Idel's understanding of the preacher's achievement. Idel's acknowledgment of the impact of Renaissance culture on Jewish intellectual life, particularly that part nourished by kabbalistic thought, helps to explain his distinctive approach to Moscato as well.[27]

Idel begins his essay by surveying the history of the kabbalah on Italian soil with particular attention to Mantua. While pointing out the difficulty of establishing a consistent pattern of development within the cultural ambiance of Mantua during the sixteenth century, Idel defines two chief characteristics of the form this study took in this city and throughout Italy from the late fifteenth century through Moscato's lifetime and even beyond. First, kabbalah was no longer studied within the framework of schools and teachers as had been the case in Spain, but rather autodidactically through books, especially after the first printing of the *Zohar* in 1558–1560. Second, it was usually interpreted figuratively by both Jews and Christians, as classical pagan literature was received and interpreted during the Renaissance. It was thus correlated within the context of prevailing philosophical and humanist concerns.

According to Idel, Moscato was deeply affected by the syncretistic culture of the Renaissance and he interpreted kabbalistic sources to conform to contemporary non-Jewish patterns. In fact, his published collection of sermons is so replete with diverse quotations from Jewish and non-Jewish literature and so theologically complex that it is hard to imagine that its contents bear much resemblance to oral sermons delivered before an ordinary congregation of worshipers. Accordingly, Idel rules out the possibility of understanding Moscato's printed essays as actual sermons and considers them instead as "part of the literary legacy of Italian Jews," a legacy appreciated only by those with specialized knowledge in Jewish and Renaissance culture. In other words, Moscato's book of sermons offers no evidence of how he functioned as a preacher, as a mediator between high and low cultures, and it cannot be understood as a collection of real oral encounters in the same way as those of del Bene, Figo, or Modena.

Treating Moscato exclusively as an esoteric thinker, Idel provides two telling examples from his writing to illustrate how he attempted to discover a phenomenological affinity between Jewish and Hermetic sources, and how he even misinterpreted a kabbalistic source to conform to a view external to Judaism. Because of its "hermeneutical pliability," as Idel calls it, the kabbalah was divorced from its organic relationship with Jewish observance, treated as another form of speculative philosophy, and subsequently became for Moscato and others "the main avenue of intellectual acculturation into the outside world."[28] The hold of general culture was so powerful over this Jewish thinker that the kabbalah was reduced by him to a mere intellectual tile in the complex mosaic of late Renaissance thought.

Given Moscato's intellectual proclivities, Idel calls him a Renaissance, not a baroque, thinker, despite the fact that he lived in the second half of the sixteenth century. If there was any difference between his "Renaissance" style and that of a thinker like Yohanan Alemanno, the Jewish associate of Pico della Mirandola, who was active almost a century earlier, it was that by his day Moscato had become overwhelmed by the Renaissance. Unlike Alemanno, who had contributed independently to shaping Pico's thought, Moscato was strictly a consumer, albeit an enthusiastically creative one. In his case, the gravitational center of his thinking had shifted so that the Renaissance and not Judaism became the standard for evaluating truth. His compulsion to harmonize Jewish revelation with other disparate sources was markedly different from the later efforts of del Bene and Figo to separate Judaism from alien philosophies, to demarcate the secular from the sacred, and subsequently, to reassert the uniqueness of the Jewish revelation.

Robert Bonfil's contribution to this volume deals with the fascinating but generally neglected Judah del Bene, who flourished years after Moscato's death (Ferrara, 1615?–1678).[29] Bonfil undertakes the formidable task of comparing del Bene's scholarly essays in his published book *Kissot le-Veit David* with a sampling of his sermons still in manuscript. In comparing the way a profound thinker might address a wider public audience as opposed to intellectuals alone, Bonfil proposes to underscore the mediating function of the preacher, one who undertakes a negotiation at once between elite and popular culture, between his own desires and those of his audience, between conservation and innovation, between his imagination and reality, and between the Jewish and the non-Jewish world.

Bonfil illustrates how the style of del Bene's sermons skillfully obscures but nevertheless conveys the explicit messages of his scholarly tome. Although this preacher obstensibly stressed continuity and traditionalism, the discerning observer of his baroque use of metaphor might occasionally disclose a rupture or discontinuity with the past. Del Bene's use of the metaphor of a snake in one of his sermons, conveying both the evil and the positive attribute of discretion, might suggest his sensitivity to linguistic polyvalence as well as some conceptual affinity to Christian symbolism. More significantly, his seemingly conventional assault on "Greek science" in his sermons should not be taken at face value as the dogmatic pronouncement of an archtraditionalist. When such utterances are examined in the light of his statements in *Kissot le-Veit David*, del Bene emerges not as an opponent of all rational pursuits but as a staunch anti-Aristotelian. Like his hero Socrates, he strove to liberate his community from its servitude to false gods, meaning for him Scholastic metaphysics. By differentiating the illicit and arrogant claims of philosophy from the hypothetical but useful insights of natural science, del Bene reconsidered the whole structure of knowledge, as Bonfil puts it, realigning "Greek science" with divine revelation rather than rejecting the former altogether. Although he might sound superficially like a medieval preacher, in Bonfil's eyes he was manifestly modern. And by introducing the new through the mask of the old, he was functioning as a good preacher should, mediating between the one and the other. In adopting such a creative stance in his sermons, Bonfil further suggests, del Bene shared a common front with Jesuit clerics by defending traditional values while embracing the new opportunities offered by the sciences now deemed devoid of metaphysical certainty.

My essay on Azariah Figo (Pisa, Venice, 1579–1637) focuses on an epistemological realignment in the thought of this preacher which closely parallels that of Judah del Bene.[30] I argue here and elsewhere that science was a crucial element in the ghetto ambiance.[31] In an age of revolutionary advances in understanding the natural world, the ghetto walls could not and did not filter out the new scientific discourse just as they could not filter out so much else. When the gates of their locked neighborhood opened at the crack of dawn, young Jewish students were on their way to the great medical schools of Italy: Bologna, Ferrara, and especially Padua. For Jews, the medical schools were exciting intellectual centers offering them new vistas of knowledge, new languages, new associations, and, above all, new values. The communities which sent them to study were energized by their return. More than ever before, Jewish communities were led by men who could creatively fuse their medical and rabbinic expertise. Medicine had always been a venerated profession among Jews, but with greater exposure to a flood of printed scientific and medical texts in Hebrew and other languages as well as to the university classroom, Jews of the ghetto were even more sensitized to the importance of these subjects.

Although not known to be a doctor, Figo had more than a casual interest in medicine, as his sermons amply testify. Like his teacher Leon Modena, he seems to have had serious reservations about the kabbalah, for it played no apparent role in his homiletic presentation of Judaism. What is striking about his espousal of traditional values is his assumption that his listeners were enthusiastic about nature, and that their positive response should be fully tapped in teaching religious values. Precisely like del Bene, Figo was not an antirationalist but an anti-Aristotelian. From his perspective, physics was to be divorced from metaphysics, and subsequently Jews could comfortably dabble in the wonders of the natural world without feeling that such involvements threatened their allegiance to Judaism. The newly emerging alliance between religion and science in the mind of the rabbi meant that science dealt only with contingent facts while religion was empowered with the absolute authority to determine ultimate values.

Displaying the image of man as creator empowered to replicate nature, employing medical and natural analogies to preach ethics, and evoking the language of empiricism to underscore the veracity of the theophany at Sinai, Figo well grasped the mentality of his listeners and sought to translate his Jewish message into a language that they would fully understand and appreciate. In so doing, he revealed a remarkable kinship with those same Jesuit clerics, enthusiasts of science in their own right, who were proclaiming the majesty of God's creation before their own congregations not far beyond the ghetto gates.

Having considered three preachers up to now, the reader will surely be struck by the apparent contrast between the profile of Moscato on the one hand and those of del Bene and Figo on the other. Perhaps one way of understanding the mind-set of Moscato in relation to that of his younger contemporaries is to view them as representing two chronological stages in the structural development of Jewish thought in the late sixteenth and early seventeenth centuries. Still enamored of the web of Renaissance correlations and harmonies, to recall the language of Foucault's well-known description of Renaissance thinking,[32] Moscato had surely tread this path to its very limits. His was truly a revolt against the metaphysical certainty of the Aristotelian world view comparable to that of del Bene and Figo. He consistently sought meaning from a vast array of alternative sources: Plato, Pythagoras, other ancients, and even Church fathers. In so doing, he opened the flood gates to metaphysical uncertainty and lack of faith. Even the hallowed truths of Judaism were in doubt when juxtaposed with a bewildering assortment of other perceived truths and sources. Whether or not Moscato actually produced a single harmony in his own mind, it seems clear that such a message was unattainable to even the most persistent reader of his recondite prose. Such epistemological confusion could not easily be reduced to a mere sermon, to public teaching.

Del Bene's and Figo's negative or, at least, cool response to speculative kabbalah, their firm repudiation of the attempt to harmonize Judaism with alien thought, their separation of metaphysics from physics, and their desire to reclaim the priority and uniqueness of the Jewish faith surely represent a negative reaction to the kind of excesses associated with Moscato's intellectual enterprise (Idel would label them "Counter-Renaissance" types, borrowing Hiram Haydn's label[33]). Theirs was a novel attempt to redefine the Jewish faith from the perspective of the post-Renaissance world they now inhabited. And having rescued their religious legacy from such subordination to Renaissance culture as that exemplified by Moscato, they were anxious to restate its message clearly and unambiguously to their constituents. They could become effective preachers in a way Moscato could never be.

And what of Leon Modena (Venice, 1571–1648), perhaps the most illustrious Jewish preacher of his generation? Joanna Weinberg's essay returns us completely to the preaching situation, to the way Modena conceptualized the role of the preacher within Jewish society.[34] Weinberg eschews the temptation to label Modena's intellectual style—whether medieval, Renaissance, or baroque—and rather concentrates primarily on his homiletical art. Modena had actually defined his own style as a kind of compromise between the rhetorical extremes of Judah Moscato and the simpler language of Ashkenazic or Levantine rabbis, as Weinberg mentions. Even more telling is his "blending of the Christian sermon with the traditional Jewish homily," a fusion he engendered according to the model of one of the best-known Christian preachers of the Counter-Reformation, Francesco Panigarola.[35] Modena had acquired a copy of Panigarola's manual for preachers and apparently absorbed many of its prescriptions, as his own sermons fully testify. Panigarola's work attempted to define the relation of classical oratory and ecclesiastical preaching in mediating between the demands of the secular and the sacred. Modena saw himself in an analogous role within Jewish society. Like the Catholic preacher, he considered the sermon as epideictic oratory; he avoided excessive citations in favor of a refined and polished humanist style; and, as Weinberg's close analysis of his tenth published sermon illustrates, he closely followed the structural guidelines of Panigarola in presenting traditional rabbinic texts to his Jewish congregation. As Weinberg concludes, the preacher of the Counter-Reformation saw his sermons as an effective means of expressing views of the Church establishment. While Modena's function in the Jewish community was less formally defined, his preaching role bears a striking affinity to that of his Christian counterpart: "His consciousness of the responsibility of the preacher derived in no small measure from what he learned from his Christian neighbors."[36]

While Weinberg focuses more on Modena's preaching style than on the substance of his thought, her conclusions suggest clear analogies with the aforementioned portraits of del Bene and Figo. Whether or not his thoughts betrayed a Renaissance or a post-Renaissance consciousness, his self-image as a preacher was surely shaped along the lines of the Catholic model of the Counter-Reformation era. Like the two other Jews, he was teaching Judaism in a manner not so different from that of the Jesuit preachers only a short canal ride from the Venetian ghetto.

It is interesting to recall in this context that in an earlier essay Moshe Idel labeled Modena "a Counter-Renaissance" figure because of his attempt to disassociate Jewish faith from the kind of Renaissance interpretations of the kabbalah so characteristic of Moscato's thought.[37] Could Modena's attempt to distance himself from Moscato's homiletical style be more broadly understood as a critique of the latter's entire intellectual approach? Whatever the case, Modena adopted a fideistic position advocating a direct return to the sacred texts of Judaism; his critique of the kabbalah, which he defined as a Platonistic forgery, was "a natural consequence of this endeavor," as Idel put it.[38] Like del Bene and like Modena's own student Figo, he approved of the divorce of Aristotelian metaphysics from Judaism, and like them, he openly encouraged the Jewish study of the physical world and medicine.[39] Although Weinberg mentions and does not discount this interpretation, she prefers to focus here on Modena's mode of preaching. One wonders, however, whether Modena's preaching style might still be considered along with his ideals as a religious thinker and spokesman of Judaism. John O'Malley's pioneering study of the sacred orators of the papal court during the Renaissance is suggestive in this regard. His work reveals how the medium of the sacred orators and the papal messages were organically linked.[40] Similarly, Modena's preaching style, which Weinberg has so ably identified, might be integrated successfully with the emerging intellectual agenda common to the other preachers of the ghetto we have previously considered; that is, their attempt to break with the past and to steer Jewish faith on a new course, restructuring the relationship between the sacred and profane in a manner not unlike that of their Catholic colleagues.

Elliott Horowitz's treatment of Jewish funeral sermons breaks new ground in directions quite different from the other essays in this volume.[41] His study of the eulogies penned by the rabbis Samuel Judah Katzenellenbogen (Padua, 1521–1597), Abraham of Sant'Angelo (Bologna, 1530?–1584?) and Isaac de Lattes (Mantua, Venice, etc., d. c. 1570) attempts to explain the origins of the phenomenon of Jewish funeral sermons in Italy. He also concerns himself with two other "dominant themes in Italian Jewish life": the interaction between Ashkenazic, Sephardic, and native Italian Jewish religious traditions, on the one hand, and the debate over the proper use of the kabbalah in Jewish society, on the other.[42] Horowitz tentatively argues that the eulogy emerged from a confluence of two primary forces: the limited and belated impact of "the humanist revolution in funerary oratory inaugurated by Pier Paolo Vergerio in 1393," and the more substantial connection with Hispanic-Jewish traditions brought to Italy by Jewish immigrants from Provence or Spain.[43] The eulogy became a common phenomenon in the Italian Jewish community by the late sixteenth century among all Jews, including the Ashkenazic, and many were frequently published in sermon collections.

From close readings of several sermons delivered by the three rabbis, Horowitz considers the place of the eulogy in the social organization of the death ritual, the particular circumstances in which the sermons were delivered, and how the preacher shaped his words of the dead to fit the needs of his living audience, hoping to ingratiate himself through his well-chosen phrases. Horowitz also shows how citations from kabbalistic literature, including the recently published *Zohar*, were increasingly introduced into the public eulogy. As he indicates, after the controversial publication of the latter work in 1558–1560, the kabbalah lost much of its esoterism so that even intellectually conservative preachers like Katzenellenbogen had little hesitation in employing its language in their public sermons.[44]

Horowitz's preliminary conclusions regarding a subject hardly studied at all are difficult to link with the previous essays. Horowitz does confirm the observations of Bonfil and Saperstein about the kabbalah gradually "conquering" the public sermon by the late sixteenth century.[45] His concluding suggestion regarding the "mannerist" character of Modena's eulogy of Katzenellenbogen, so different from Katzenellenbogen's earlier one on Moses Isserles, might be meaningfully integrated with Weinberg's portrait of Modena as well as the other portraits in this volume, and might even suggest the possibility of a real shift in the style and substance of Jewish eulogies by the end of the sixteenth century. The subject obviously requires more investigation. This is also the case regarding the question of the origin of the Jewish eulogy in Italy. Although Horowitz minimizes the impact of the humanist model, one might ask whether the frequent use of the eulogy by such Catholic clergy as the aforementioned Panigarola during the Counter-Reformation has any bearing on the development of its Italian-Jewish counterpart in the same era.[46] It would be interesting to compare, for example, the structure of Panigarola's eulogy for Carlo Borromeo, published in 1585 in Rome, with those discussed by Horowitz.[47] To what extent do eulogies in the two faith communities "create" heroes, models of genuine Christian or Jewish living, and to what extent do these heroic images compare with each other? Funeral orations for popes and rabbis project ideal types to be appreciated and emulated by their listeners. A comparison of the two might reveal how the ideals of each community converge and diverge.

Finally, Horowitz mentions on several occasions that the eulogy was delivered within the setting of a Jewish pious confraternity.[48] To what extent was this practice common within the Christian community? How important were the confraternities in promoting the *laudatio funebris* as a part of the ritual organization of death? Horowitz has shown elsewhere how Jewish confraternities assumed the prerogative of managing the rituals of dying and mourning in a fashion similar to the Christian associations.[49] Could the diffusion of the eulogy be linked with this wider phenomenon? Horowitz's initial exploration of the Jewish eulogy invites future researchers to examine these and other questions further.

Not only this last essay but, to a great extent, all the others included in this volume merely scratch the surface of a largely untapped field. They do, however, suggest some of the possibilities for using the sermon as a means of penetrating the larger social and cultural setting of any religious community in general, and specifically of Jewish life in the ghetto age. They attempt to explore the spiritual ideals and pedagogic goals of religious leaders aspiring to uplift and educate their constituencies through their homiletic skills and strategies. They illuminate from varying perspectives the transformation of Italian Jewish culture in the late sixteenth and early seventeenth centuries, the adjustment of a beleaguered but proud minority to its ghetto segregation, the openness of Jews and their surprising appropriations of the regnant cultural tastes of the surrounding society, as well as the restructuring of thought processes, ritual practice, and social organization engendered by the new urban neighborhoods. Whether intended or not, the preachers of the Italian ghetto have left behind a richly textured panorama of some of the many faces of their dynamic and creative cultural universe. In the chapters that follow we hope to provide a partial but absorbing glimpse of that universe.[50]

NOTES

1. Gregory Martin, *Roma Sancta* (1581), ed. George B. Parks (Rome, 1969), pp. 70–71, quoted by Frederick J. McGinness in "Preaching Ideals and Practice in Counter-Reformation Rome," *Sixteenth Century Journal* 11 (1980): 124.

2. Hillary D. Smith, *Preaching in the Spanish Golden Age* (Oxford, 1978), p. 5. She also quotes on the same page, note 1, the evocative description of Benedetto Croce in his *I predicatori italiani del Seicento e il gusto spagnuolo* (Naples, 1899), p. 9: "chi puo ripensare al Seicento senza rivedere in fantasia la figura del *Predicatore*, nerovestito come un gesuita, o biancovestito come un domenicano o col rozzo saio cappuccino, gesticolante in una chiesa barocca, innanzi a un uditorio dia fastosi abbigliamenti." For a recent bibliography on Catholic preaching in early modern Europe, see the essay by Peter Bayley in *Catholicism in Early Modern Europe: A Guide to Research*, ed. John O'Malley, vol. 2 of *Reformation Guides to Research* (St. Louis, 1988), pp. 299–314.

3. See McGinness, p. 109. On the importance of obligatory sermons in fostering conversion to Christianity during this period, see Kenneth Stow, *Catholic Thought and Papal Jewry Policy 1555–1593* (New York, 1977), chap. 10, and the earlier works he cites, especially those of Browe and Hoffmann.

4. *Roma Sancta*, pp. 71–72, quoted by McGinness, p. 109.

5. There exists no comprehensive treatment of this phenomenon in recent scholarly literature. The best overview of Jewish preaching in general with ample references to the early modern period is Marc Saperstein, *Jewish Preaching 1200–1800: An Anthology* (New Haven and London, 1989). On Jewish preaching in Eastern Europe, see Jacob Elbaum, *Petiḥut ve-Histagrut: Ha-Yeẓirah ha-Ruḥanit be-Folin u-ve-Arẓot Ashkenaz be-Shalhe ha-Me'ah ha-16* (Jerusalem, 1990), pp. 223–247. On the Sephardic preacher, see Joseph Hacker, "The Sephardic Sermon in the Sixteenth Century" [Hebrew], *Pe'amim* 26 (1986): 108–127.

6. The scholarly literature on Italian Jewish preaching is also limited. See Robert Bonfil, *Rabbis and Jewish Communities in Renaissance Italy*, trans. from the Hebrew by Jonathan Chipman (Oxford, 1990), pp. 298–315; Joseph Dan, "An Inquiry into the Hebrew Homiletical Literature During the Period of the Italian Renaissance" [Hebrew], *Proceedings of the Sixth World Congress of Jewish Studies* (Jerusalem, 1967), division 3, pp. 105–110. Additional references are provided in the essays below.

7. See especially Stow, *Catholic Thought and Papal Jewry Policy*; idem, "The Burning of the Talmud in 1553 in the Light of Sixteenth-Century Catholic Attitudes Toward the Talmud," *Bibliothèque d'humanisme et Renaissance* 34 (1972): 435–459; Daniel Carpi, "The Expulsion of the Jews from the Papal States during the Time of Pope Pius V and the Inquisitional Trials against the Jews of Bologna" [Hebrew], in *Scritti in memoria di Enzo Sereni*, ed. Daniel Carpi and Renato Spiegel (Jerusalem, 1970), pp. 145–165 (reprinted with additions in Daniel Carpi, *Be-Tarbut ha-Renasans u-vein Ḥomot ha-Geto* [Tel Aviv, 1989], pp. 148–167); and David Ruderman, "A Jewish Apologetic Treatise from Sixteenth-Century Bologna," *Hebrew Union College Annual* 50 (1979): 253–276.

8. On Jewish life in Renaissance Italy, see the standard surveys of Cecil Roth, *The Jews in the Renaissance* (Philadelphia, 1959); Moses A. Shulvass, *Jews in the World of the Renaissance* (Leiden and Chicago, 1973); and Attilio Milano, *Storia degli ebrei in Italia* (Turin, 1963). See also Robert Bonfil, *Rabbis and Jewish Communities*; David B. Ruderman, *The World of a Renaissance Jew* (Cincinnati, 1981).

9. For a survey and interpretation of Jewish intellectual life in the Renaissance

with extensive bibliographical citations, see David B. Ruderman, "The Italian Renaissance and Jewish Thought," in *Renaissance Humanism: Foundations and Forms*, 3 vols., ed. Albert Rabil, Jr. (Philadelphia, 1988), vol. 1, pp. 382–433.

10. In addition to the references cited in note 8 above, see, for example, Léon Poliakov, *Jewish Bankers and the Holy See*, trans. M. L. Kochan (London, Henley, and Boston, 1977); Shlomo Simonsohn, *History of the Jews in the Duchy of Mantua* (Jerusalem, 1977); Umberto Cassuto, *Gli ebrei a Firenze nell'età del Rinascimento* (Florence, 1918; 1965); and Gaetano Cozzi, ed., *Gli ebrei e Venezia secoli XIV–XVIII* (Milan, 1987).

11. See Benjamin Ravid, "The Venetian Ghetto in Historical Perspective," in *The Autobiography of a Seventeenth-Century Venetian Rabbi*, ed. and trans. Mark Cohen (Princeton, 1988), pp. 279–283, and also his "The Religious, Economic, and Social Background of the Establishment of the Ghetti in Venice," in Cozzi, *Gli ebrei e Venezia*, pp. 211–259; Attilio Milano, *Il Ghetto di Roma* (Rome, 1964).

12. Ravid, "The Venetian Ghetto," p. 283.

13. Robert Bonfil, "Change in the Cultural Patterns of a Jewish Society in Crisis," *Jewish History* 3 (1988): 11–33. (Reprinted in David B. Ruderman, ed., *Essential Papers on Jewish Culture in Renaissance and Baroque Italy* [New York, 1992].) See also his "Cultura e mistica a Venezia nel Cinquecento," in Cozzi, *Gli ebrei e Venezia*, pp. 496–506.

14. Bonfil, "Change in Cultural Patterns," p. 13.

15. Ibid., p. 12.

16. Ibid., and in general, the entire essay.

17. See Bonfil's essay and Jefim Schirmann, "Theater and Music in Italian Jewish Quarters XVI–XVIII Centuries" [Hebrew], *Zion* 29 (1964): 61–111; and his "The Hebrew Drama in the XVIIIth Century" [Hebrew], *Moznayim* 4 (1938): 624–635. Both reprinted in Schirmann, *Studies in the History of Hebrew Poetry and Drama*, 2 vols. (Jerusalem, 1977), vol. 1, pp. 25–38; 44–94.

18. See Dan Harrán, "Tradition and Innovation in Jewish Music of the Later Renaissance," *The Journal of Musicology* 7 (1989): 107–130, reprinted in Ruderman, *Essential Papers*; Israel Adler, "The Rise of Art Music in the Italian Ghetto," in *Jewish Medieval and Renaissance Studies*, ed. Alexander Altmann (Cambridge, Mass., 1967), pp. 321–364.

19. See Dan Pagis, "Baroque Trends in Italian Hebrew Poetry as Reflected in an Unknown Genre," *Italia Judaica* (Rome, 1986), vol. 2, pp. 263–277 (reprinted in Ruderman, *Essential Papers*); and Pagis, *Al Sod Ḥatum* (Jerusalem, 1986).

20. Shalom Sabar, "The Use and Meaning of Christian Motifs in Illustrations of Jewish Marriage Contracts in Italy," *Journal of Jewish Art* 10 (1984): 46–63.

21. See Bonfil, p. 21, and Yosef Melkman, "Moses Zacuto's Play *Yesod Olam*" [Hebrew], *Sefunot* 10 (1966): 299–333.

22. Bonfil, pp. 16–18.

23. Ibid., p. 18 and throughout. For a discussion of the meaning of the Renaissance when applied to Jewish culture, see Ruderman, "The Italian Renaissance," cited in note 9 above. On previous uses of the term "baroque" in characterizing Jewish cultural history of the ghetto era, see Giuseppe Sermonetta,

"Aspetti del pensiero moderno nell'ebraismo tra Rinascimento e età barocca," in *Italia Judaica*, vol. 2, pp. 17–35; David B. Ruderman, *A Valley of Vision: The Heavenly Journey of Abraham ben Hananiah Yagel* (Philadelphia, 1990), pp. 65–68. On the notion of "Baroque" in general, see, for example, Frank J. Warnke, *Versions of Baroque: European Literature in the Seventeenth Century* (New Haven and London, 1963), and the additional references cited in Ruderman, p. 65, n. 192.

The participants in this volume, as the reader will notice, employ the terms "Renaissance," "post-Renaissance," "Counter-Renaissance," and "baroque" in describing Jewish cultural development in the late sixteenth and early seventeenth centuries in less than uniform ways. While I have attempted to clarify (and even to reconcile tentatively) their usages in this introduction, I am well aware that a lack of uniformity still remains. This situation seems unavoidable, however, given the present state of research and the differences in approach among the contributors and other scholars of this era. For further clarification of this issue of periodizing the "Renaissance" and "baroque" with respect to Jewish culture, see Ruderman, *Essential Papers*, especially the introduction, and compare Hava Tirosh-Rothschild, "Jewish Culture in Renaissance Italy: A Methodological Survey," *Italia* 9 (1990): 63–96.

24. In this regard, consider Moshe Idel's essay in this volume.

25. See below, pp. 22–40.

26. This situation is fully discussed in Simonsohn, *Mantua*. Idel's essay is found below, pp. 41–66. In designating Moscato the oldest of the preachers discussed below, I exclude those discussed collectively by Horowitz in his essay on eulogies. Given its special subject matter, I have treated this essay separately from the rest.

27. See, for example, his "The Magical and Neoplatonic Interpretations of the Kabbalah in the Renaissance," in *Jewish Thought in the Sixteenth Century*, ed. Bernard Cooperman (Cambridge, Mass., 1983), pp. 186–242, and his "Major Currents in Italian Kabbalah Between 1560–1660," *Italia Judaica*, vol. 2, pp. 143–162. Both essays have been reprinted in Ruderman, *Essential Papers*.

28. See below, p. 57.

29. See below, pp. 67–88.

30. See below, pp. 89–104.

31. For additional references, see Ruderman below, pp. 101–102, n. 1.

32. See Michel Foucault, "The Prose of the World," in *The Order of Things: An Archeology of the Human Sciences* (New York, 1970), pp. 17–50, first published as *Les mots et les choses* (Paris, 1966). This type of thinking characterized that of Moscato's Jewish contemporary, Abraham Yagel. On him, see David B. Ruderman, *Kabbalah, Magic, and Science: The Cultural Universe of a Sixteenth-Century Jewish Physician* (Cambridge, Mass. and London, 1988), especially chap. 4.

33. See Hiram Haydn, *The Counter-Renaissance* (New York, 1950), and compare Moshe Idel, "Differing Conceptions of Kabbalah in the Early 17th Century," in *Jewish Thought in the Seventeenth Century*, ed. Isadore Twersky and Bernard Septimus (Cambridge, Mass., and London, 1987), pp. 137–200, especially p. 174.

34. See below, pp. 105–128. For additional references to Modena's life and

thought, see the references in Weinberg's essay below, especially the work of Howard Adelman.

35. See below, p. 110.

36. See below, p. 122.

37. See the reference to his essay in note 34 above.

38. Ibid.

39. On this, see Ruderman, "The Language of Science as the Language of Faith," listed in my essay below, pp. 101–102, n. 1.

40. John W. O'Malley, *Praise and Blame in Renaissance Rome: Rhetoric, Doctrine, and Reform in the Sacred Orators of the Papal Court c. 1450–1521* (Durham, N.C., 1979).

41. See below, pp. 129–162.

42. See below, p. 131.

43. See below, pp. 131–135.

44. See below, p. 137.

45. See Bonfil, "Change in the Cultural Patterns," p. 12, and in his book, *Rabbis and Jewish Communities*, and see Saperstein below, p. 26.

46. On the Catholic eulogy during the Counter-Reformation, see McGinness, "Preaching Ideals and Practice," p. 125, and the bibliography cited there, especially Verdun L. Saulnier, "L'oraison funèbre au XVI$_e$ siècle," *Bibliothèque d'Humanisme et Renaissance* 10 (1948): 124–157.

47. See *Oratione Del. R. P. Francesco Panigarola . . . In morte, e sopra il corpo Dell' Ill. mo Carlo Borromeo* (Rome, 1585).

48. See below, pp. 135–137, 138, 141, 144.

49. Elliott Horowitz, "Jewish Confraternities in Seventeenth-Century Verona: A Study in the Social History of Piety," Ph.D. dissertation, Yale University, 1982, chap. 3.

50. My thanks to Benjamin Ravid and Marc Saperstein for reading a draft of this introduction and offering me their thoughtful comments.

TWO

Italian Jewish Preaching: An Overview

Marc Saperstein

On a day between Rosh Hashanah and Yom Kippur, probably in the year 1593, Rabbi Samuel Judah Katzenellenbogen of Padua delivered a eulogy for Judah Moscato. As befits the time of year, he began with a discussion of repentance, proceeding to argue that one of the primary functions of the eulogy was to inspire the listeners to repent. He went on to discuss the qualities of a great scholar: perfection of intellect and behavior and the capacity to communicate wisdom to others, both by capturing the listeners' attention with appealing homiletical material and by teaching them the laws they must observe, which are essential for the true felicity of the soul, even though most contemporary congregations do not enjoy listening to the dry halakhic content. At this point the printed text of his sermon reads, "Here I began to recount the praises of the deceased, and to show how these four qualities were present in him to perfection, the conclusion being that we should become inspired by his eulogy and allow the tears to flow for him, look into our deeds, and return to the Lord."[1]

This passage encapsulates for me something of the challenge and frustration of studying Italian Jewish preaching, and to some extent Jewish preaching in general. Here is a leading Italian rabbi eulogizing perhaps the best-known Jewish preacher of his century. We are given some important statements about the function of the eulogy, the proper content and structure of the sermon, the expectations and taste of the average listener. Then we come to the climactic point, where the preacher turns to Moscato himself. We expect an encomium of the scholarship and piety of Moscato and, what is more important for our purposes, a characterization of his preaching, an indication of his contemporary reputation, an evaluation from a colleague who apparently had a rather

שנים עשר דרשות

מדרשות החכם הכולל כמהרר

שמואל יודא נרו

בן הרב הגדול בישראל נודע שמו כמהרר מאיר זל
קצנאילנבוגן מקק פאדווה •

בתבות הסר זואן ברואגין בן האהרן אלוויזו ברואגית

פי נאמן כיעו אשר פורינן •

כתר שם טוב עולה

וויניציאה
עליד זואן דגארה סנת ושמח לפק •

con licentia de' Superiori.

Title page from Samuel Judah Katzenellenbogen's *Shneim-Asar Derashot* (Venice, 1594). Courtesy of the Library of The Jewish Theological Seminary of America.

different homiletical style. None of this is forthcoming. This climactic section of the eulogy is deemed unworthy of being recorded, presumably because of its specificity and ephemeral character. What for us (and perhaps for at least some of the listeners) is the most important content has been lost forever.

In *Kabbalah: New Perspectives*, Moshe Idel argues that even after the life work of Gershom Scholem and two generations of his disciples, the literature of Jewish mysticism is by no means fully charted: important schools may never have committed their doctrines to writing, significant works have been lost, certain texts may have arbitrarily been given undue emphasis at the expense of others no less important, and there is as yet no comprehensive bibliographic survey of the literature that does exist.[2] How much more is this true for Jewish sermon literature, which has had no Gershom Scholem to chart the way. The history of Jewish preaching in general, and that of Italy in particular, may best be envisioned as a vast jigsaw puzzle from which ninety percent of the pieces are missing and seventy-five percent of those that remain lie in a heap on the floor—and for which we have no model picture to tell us what the design should look like. Generalizations about trends or characteristics of the homiletical tradition are like speculations about the design of the puzzle based on individual pieces or small clusters that happen to fit together. And without a clear map of the conventions and continuities of the tradition, all assertions about the novelty or even the significance of a particular preacher or sermon are likely to be precarious and unfounded.

The magnitude of what we lack is astonishing. Leon Modena's *Autobiography* informs us that he preached at three or four places each Sabbath over a period of more than twenty years, and that he had in his possession more than four hundred sermons. Yet only twenty-one from the early part of his career were published, and the rest have apparently been lost.[3] When we think of the pinnacle of Italian Jewish preaching, Moscato is probably the name that comes first to mind. Yet a contemporary of Moscato's nominated David Provençal, the author of the famous appeal for the founding of a Jewish university, as "the greatest of the Italian preachers in our time." Like most of his other works, Provençal's sermons (if written at all) are no longer extant, leaving us no basis for evaluating the claim.[4] It does, however, give us pause to consider that our standard canon of important Italian Jewish preachers may be highly arbitrary.

The record before the sixteenth century is almost entirely blank: one manuscript by a mid-fifteenth-century preacher, Moses ben Joab of Florence, described and published in part by Umberto Cassuto more than eighty years ago.[5] We have no known extant sermon reacting to the popular anti-Jewish preaching of such Franciscan friars as Bernardino da Siena, John Capistrano, and Bernardino da Feltre; or to the notorious ritual murder charge surrounding Simon of Trent; or to the arrival on Italian soil of refugees from the Iberian peninsula; or to the exploits in Italy of the charismatic David Reubeni, including an audience with Pope Clement VII; or to the burning of the magnificently printed volumes of the Talmud in Rome and Venice; or to the arrest, trial and execution of former Portuguese New Christians who had returned to Judaism in Ancona and the attempted boycott of that port; or to the papal bull *Cum nimis absurdum* and the establishment of the Ghetto in Rome.

There can be little question that Jewish preachers alluded to, discussed, and interpreted these events in their sermons. Nor can it be doubted that the records of these discussions would provide us with precious insight into the strategies of contemporary Jews for accommodating major historical upheavals to their tradition and, conversely, for reinterpreting their tradition in the light of contemporary events. But it apparently did not occur to these preachers that readers removed in space and time from their own congregations would be interested in learning about events in the past, and they therefore had little motivation to write what they said in a permanent form.[6]

Much of the material that exists has yet to be studied. Isaac Ḥayyim Cantarini of Padua does not appear in any of the lists of great Italian preachers known to me. Yet he may belong in such a list; no one has ever taken a serious look at his homiletical legacy. He left behind what appears to be the largest corpus of Italian Jewish sermons in existence. The *Sefer Zikkaron* of Padua gives the number as "more than a thousand," and a substantial percentage of these are to be found in six large volumes of the Kaufmann manuscript collection in Budapest (Hebrew MSS 314–319), each one of them devoted to the sermons for a complete year between 1673 and 1682; there may be more such volumes as well. In many cases there are two sermons for each *parashah*, one delivered in the morning, the other at the *Minḥah* service. The sermons are written in Italian, in Latin letters, with Hebrew quotations interspersed.[7]

I once thought of looking through the volume containing the sermons for 1676–1677 to see if I could find any reaction to the news of the death of Shabbetai Ẓevi, but I soon realized the enormity of the task: that volume alone runs to 477 pages, and there is no guarantee that the preacher would have referred to the event explicitly as soon as the news reached his community. Needless to say, for someone interested in intellectual or social history during this period, not to mention the history of Jewish preaching or the biography of a many-talented man, these manuscripts may well repay careful study with rich dividends.

The first desideratum is therefore bibliographical: to compile a complete list of all known manuscripts of Italian sermons—let us say through the seventeenth century—to complement the printed works identified by Leopold Zunz and others. Then we need a data base that would include a separate entry for each sermon, including the place and approximate date of delivery, the genre (Sabbath or holiday sermon, eulogy, occasional, etc.), the main biblical verses and rabbinic statements discussed, the central subject or thesis, and any historical connection with an individual or an event. This would at least spread out all the known pieces of the puzzle on the table before us and facilitate the process of putting them together.

In addition to actual sermons, related genres need to be considered. Rabbi Henry Sosland has given us a fine edition of Jacob Zahalon's *Or ha-Darshanim*, a manual for preachers from the third quarter of the seventeenth century.[8] But the "Tena'ei ha-Darshan," written by Moses ben Samuel ibn Basa of Blanes, is no less worthy of detailed analysis.[9] Nor should the various preaching aids be overlooked: works intended to make the preacher's task easier by collecting quotations on various topics, alphabetically arranged, analogous to a host of such works written by Christian contemporaries.[10]

Once the material has been charted, we can define the questions that need to be addressed. Perhaps the most obvious deal with the sermons as a reflection of Italian Jewish culture, as documents in Jewish intellectual history. To what extent can we find in the sermons evidence for the continued vitality of philosophical modes of thought, for the popularization of kabbalistic doctrines, for the influence of classical motifs or contemporary Christian writings? As these are the questions that will be addressed most thoroughly in the following presentations, I will not pursue the theme further here.

What can we say about the native Italian homiletical tradition, and the impact of the Spanish tradition in the wake of the Sephardic immigration? We can outline the broad contours of the Spanish homiletical tradition as it crystallized in the late fifteenth century, and trace its continuity within the Ottoman Empire.[11] The manuscript sermons of Joseph ben Hayyim of Benevento, dating from 1515 until the 1530s, provide an example of preaching on Italian soil very much in the Spanish mold: a verse from the *parashah* and a passage of aggadah (often from the *Zohar*) as the basic building blocks, an introduction including a stylized asking of permission (*reshut*) from God, the Torah, and the congregation, followed by a structured investigation of a conceptual problem, sometimes accompanied by an identification of difficulties (*sefekot*) in the *parashah*.[12] But the paucity of Italian material from the fifteenth century and the first half of the sixteenth century makes it very difficult to delineate the process by which Spanish-Jewish preaching influenced home-grown models.

What is the relationship between Jewish and Christian preaching in Italy? I am referring not to a rehashing of the debate about the influence of Renaissance rhetorical theory,[13] but to an assessment of the more immediate impact of published Christian sermons and actual Christian preachers. Did the notorious conversionist sermons influence Jewish preaching style? Did conversionist preachers learn from Jewish practitioners the most effective ways to move their audiences?[14] Nor should we forget that Italian Jews did not always need to be coerced to listen to Christian preachers, as we learn from a passing reference to "educated Jews" (*Judei periti*) at a sermon delivered by Egidio da Viterbo in Siena on November 11, 1511.[15]

That Christians attended the sermons of Leon Modena is known to every reader of his *Autobiography*;[16] not as widely known is the passage in which he refers to his own attendance at the sermon of a Christian preacher,[17] and the fact that he owned at least one volume of Savonarola's sermons and an Italian treatise on "The Way to Compose a Sermon."[18] His letter to Samuel Archivolti describes the sermons in *Midbar Yehudah* as a blending of Christian and Jewish homiletics, and he uses the Italian terms *prologhino* and *epiloghino* to characterize the first and last sections of his discourses.[19] All of this bespeaks an openness to what was happening in the pulpits of nearby churches. Extremely important work has been done during the past two decades on various aspects of the history of Italian Christian preaching;[20] the task of integrating this with the Jewish material remains to be accomplished.

Another aspect of this subject relates to the use of Italian literature by Jewish preachers. Extravagant claims have been made; an *Encyclopaedia Judaica* article asserts that "Like Petrarch, Dante was widely quoted by Italian rabbis of the Renaissance in their sermons.[21] I do not know what evidence could support such a statement. The written texts contain few examples of Jewish preachers using contemporary Italian literature, and there is no reason to assume that such references would be eliminated in the writing, or that those who quoted Italian authors would be predisposed not to write their sermons. Nevertheless, those examples which do exist are instructive. Joseph Dan has discussed Moscato's citation of Pico della Mirandola which, though incidental to the preacher's main point, shows that there was apparently nothing extraordinary about using even a Christological interpretation for one's own homiletical purpose.[22]

More impressive are stories used by Leon Modena. The allegory he incorporates into a sermon on repentance, in which Good and Evil exchange garments so that everyone now honors Evil and spurns Good, is presented as one he "heard," probably from a Christian or from a Jew conversant with Christian literature. Another story, used in the eulogy for a well-known rabbinic scholar, tells of a young man who tours the

world to discover whether he is truly alive or dead. The answer he re-
ceives from a monk is confirmed in a dramatic dialogue with the spirit
of a corpse in the cemetery. Modena attributes this story explicitly to a
"non-Jewish book." While I have still not succeeded in identifying the
direct source of the story, it certainly reflects the late medieval and Renaissance preoccupation with death and dying that produced not only the
various expressions of the *danse macabre* motif but a host of treatises
on good living and good dying, including dialogues involving a non-
threatening personification of Death.[23]

What do we know about the training of preachers? For no other country is there such ample evidence for the cultivation of homiletics as an
honorable discipline in the paideia as there is for Italian Jewry. The
kinds of evidence range from the exemplary sermon of Abraham Farissol
dating from the early sixteenth century to the letters of Elijah ben Solomon ha-Levi de Veali almost three hundred years later.[24] There seems
to have been a special emphasis on students accompanying their teacher
to listen to sermons delivered during religious services, especially on
major preaching occasions. In addition, preaching was actually taught in
the schools.[25] Public speaking and the delivery of sermons was to be
part of the curriculum in David Provençal's proposed Jewish college in
Mantua.[26] The preaching exercises in which Modena participated when
he was no older than ten do not seem to have been unusual.[27] The
delivery of a sermon by a precocious child may well have had the effect
that the playing of a concerto by a young prodigy would have had in
the age of Mozart. But the actual mechanism for instruction—whether
printed collections of sermons were studied and sermons by noted
preachers were critiqued, what written guidelines for the preparation of
sermons were used in the schools—remains to be fully investigated.

A work like *Medabber Tahapukhot* by Leon Modena's grandson Isaac
provides dramatic evidence of the tumultuous politics of the pulpit. Indeed, the ways in which the selection of preachers for various occasions
could reveal a hierarchy of prestige, unleashing bitter quarrels, is one of
the central subjects of the book.[28] Conflicts over the limits of acceptable
public discourse—what content could and could not properly be addressed from the pulpit—were part of the same cultural milieu that
produced the battles over the printing of the *Zohar* and the publication
of de' Rossi's *Me'or Einayim*.[29] Sometimes these issues were directed to
legal authorities who issued formal responsa, but in addition to evoking
decisions from the scholarly elite, they reflect problems in the sensibilities
and tastes of the listeners in the pews. A full range of such nonsermonic
texts is necessary for an adequate reconstruction of the historical dynamic of Italian Jewish preaching.

A final set of questions relates to the writing and printing of sermon collections. Although sermons were undoubtedly delivered in the vernacular throughout the Middle Ages, Italy seems to have produced the first texts of Jewish sermons actually written in a European vernacular language.[30] Why did some Jewish preachers begin to write in Italian in the late sixteenth and seventeenth centuries? What does the transition from Hebrew to Italian in Hebrew characters (Dato) to Italian in Latin characters (Cantarini) reveal about contemporary Jewish culture? Despite the new linguistic variety in the manuscripts, however, printed collections remained in Hebrew. The number of such books published in Venice between 1585 and 1615, by both Italian and Ottoman preachers, is an astounding indication of public demand for this kind of literature. Modena decided to prepare a selection of his sermons for print in the hope that the proceeds would help ease his financial pressures, although in this, as in so many other pecuniary matters, he was apparently disappointed.[31]

In addition to the economics of sermon publishing, the format seems worthy of attention. While most collections of Spanish and Ottoman sermons are arranged in accordance with the weekly *parashah*, most Italian collections are not. We have relatively few ordinary Sabbath sermons, particularly in print; most of them are for special Sabbaths, holidays, occasions in the life cycle or the life of the community. Yet there is abundant evidence that weekly preaching on the *parashah* was the norm throughout Italy. Could there have been a conscious avoidance of the Sephardic format in these published collections? We have no answer as yet.

I turn now to a more detailed discussion of certain aspects of Italian preaching. Among other roles, the preacher appears as a guardian of moral and religious standards, and therefore as a critic of the failings of his listeners. Frequently this was just the kind of material the preacher would omit when writing his words for publication, assuming that readers in distant cities would have little interest in the local issues he had addressed.[32] But some of this social criticism has been preserved. If we are careful to distinguish generalized complaints, the commonplaces of the genre of rebuke that recur in almost every generation, from attacks that target a specific, concrete abuse, we may find clues to the stress lines within Jewish society, clues that become more persuasive when the sermon material is integrated with the contemporary responsa literature.[33]

The proper assessment of the sermonic rebuke is not always obvious. I am not quite certain what to make of the accusation, made by both Samuel Katzenellenbogen and Jacob di Alba, that among those who leave the synagogue after the *Tefillah* and who therefore miss the sermon are congregants who hurry to return to their business affairs.[34] Can they be

talking about Jews who engage in work on the Sabbath after attending
only part of the Saturday morning service? This would be a violation so
serious that one wonders why any rabbi would focus on the much more
trivial offense of missing the sermon or insulting the preacher.

Is this particular rebuke then merely a rhetorical device used to dis-
credit those who walk out early by suggesting to the remaining congregation that the exiters *might* be going to work? If so it could not be used to
prove that serious Sabbath violation was actually occurring, but only that
the possibility of such violation was plausible enough for the listeners
not to dismiss the suggestion as absurd. Or could the entire passage be
referring not to the Sabbath but to the weekday morning service? If this
is the case, it would be evidence of a very different dynamic: the cultivation of the practice of a daily *"devar Torah,"* and the resistance on the
part of Jews who were committed enough to attend the service, but re-
sented the homiletical accoutrement as an imposition on their time. As
with the Moscato eulogy, Katzenellenbogen leads us to the brink of something rather important but fails to give us quite enough to use it with
confidence.

Other passages of rebuke are more straightforward. Cecil Roth wrote
that "the employment of adventitious aids to female beauty was a perpet-
ual preoccupation of Renaissance [Christian] preachers and moralists,
and it is certain that Jewish women followed (or anticipated) the general
fashion."[35] He provided no documentation for this, or for the subsequent assertion that "in Italy generally no sort of ornament was more
common than false hair, generally blond, . . . and the wealthy Jewess
was able to keep abreast of fashion simply by remodeling her wig."[36]
Sixteenth-century Jewish literature reveals the concern of Jewish moralists with this practice.

In a sermon for the Sabbath of Repentance, Katzenellenbogen turns
to the women in the congregation and raises a rather sensitive issue.
Women, says the preacher, must heed the moral instruction of the religious authorities even when they do not like it. The example chosen to
illustrate the point is one in which the preacher claims the women of
his city are particularly susceptible to failure: the prohibition against
revealing their hair or adorning themselves with a Gentile wig that is
indistinguishable from their own hair. "In all the Ashkenazi communities, for generations, our ancestors have protested that women must not
wear even a silk ribbon that has the color of hair"; the preacher refers
here to a lengthy legal decision of his in which he argued against authorities who permitted these practices. But this is not, as Roth would suggest,
simply a matter of Jewish women being influenced by their surroundings. Katzenellenbogen argues that the fashions of Jewish women are
particularly scandalous "in a place where the Gentile women are accus-

tomed to cover their hair, and the nuns strictly prohibit adorning themselves with a wig." The function of the Christian environment is not merely to serve as a source of seduction; the preacher uses his Christian neighbors as a rhetorical goad to bring the listeners back to their own tradition.[37]

Preachers were also moved to condemn what they considered to be a deterioration of sexual mores. Israel Bettan cited a passage by Azariah Figo condemning the practice (perhaps more widespread in Italy than in other countries?) of recreational gazing at women, both married and single, "an indulgence that must inevitably lead to graver offenses."[38] But this is at most a minor infraction of the traditional code of Jewish norms. A far more serious charge is leveled by Figo elsewhere:

> From then [the destruction of the second Temple] until now, the first two of these sins, namely idolatry and murder, have ceased from the people of Israel. Thank God, there are no reports of a pattern or even a tendency to commit these two sins among our nation—except as a result of compulsion, or in a rare individual case. But the third sin, sexual immorality (*gillui arayot*), has not been properly guarded against. Jews have violated the rules in these sinful generations in various ways, engaging in all kinds of destructive behavior publicly, out in the open, without any shame or embarrassment.[39]

Unlike the more concrete condemnations by the preachers in Prague 150 years later,[40] this passage remains too vague to be of much value to the social historian, although listeners in the audience may well have thought of specific examples. Nevertheless, the contrast drawn between what the preacher does not consider to be a real problem in his community (the attraction of Christianity, crimes of violence) and what he does (the more serious kind of sexual sins), and the claim that such behavior is tacitly condoned by many Jews, may point to a genuine sense of breakdown in the core of the traditional Jewish ethos.[41]

Financial arrangements also had the potential to create deep conflicts. With considerable power, Azariah Figo addressed the complex problem of impermissible loans. The poor are forced to seek loans from the rich, who "devour their flesh with several forms of clear-cut, open interest." Even worse, in his eyes, is that the sense of sinfulness about such forbidden arrangements has been lost. "If a group of Jews were to be seen going to a Gentile butcher and were then seen publicly eating pig or other forbidden meat, they would be stoned by all, although this entails only one negative prohibition, for which the punishment is lashes. Yet here we see those who lend money on interest, which involves six transgressions for the lender, as well as others for the borrower, the guarantor, the witnesses, and the scribe, and all are silent."[42]

Like the passage about sexual immorality cited above, this reflects a
serious gap between the values of the community and those of its religious leadership. The prevalent social norms deem the dietary laws to
be crucial to Jewish identity even though from a legal standpoint they
do not entail the most serious of sins. Taking interest from a fellow
Jew has more serious legal consequences, but ordinary Jews consider it
innocuous. Those who are aware of the prohibition, we are told, show
deference to the tradition by hypocritical attempts to avoid the appearance of transgression, through ruses such as an arrangement by which
the creditor may live in an apartment without rent. As for the *cambio*
(exchange contract), some may be permissible, but many others are totally forbidden, so that even the well-intentioned merchant may unwit-
tingly err. "My quarrel with them, is this," the preacher concludes: "Why
don't they consult with experts in these matters, who can provide them
with proper guidance?"[43] The passage is extremely rich, revealing the
frustrations of religious leaders in the face of economic and social forces
they are unable to control.

In addition to areas of major conflict, the sermons may reveal aspects
of the norms of social life and mentality. Wedding sermons must surely
reflect the attitude of the preacher toward women and marriage. The
earliest Italian preacher whose sermons are preserved, Moses ben Joab
of mid–fifteenth-century Florence, speaking at a betrothal celebration
of a certain Abraham of Montalcino, delivered himself of what reads
today like a misogynistic diatribe, but must have seemed to him like
a conventional assessment of woman's limitations and perils. He then
proceeds,

> What can a man do who wants to find himself a wife? All around him are
> "brokers of sin," who find something good to say about those who have
> no merit. Today they tell him one thing, tomorrow another, until their
> combined efforts wear him down. In order to lead him into their trap, they
> tell him, "This woman who is coming into your home will bring some
> dowry!" . . . Whoever escapes from the snares of these people like an ener-
> getic bird or deer, and finds himself a decent woman, has indeed "found
> something good."

The use of the occasion of a betrothal celebration to incorporate into a
religious discourse an attack against the prevailing standards of marriage
brokers shows that Italian preachers, though frequently ponderous, were
not without humor.[44]

A passage in a sermon by Katzenellenbogen gives us a glimpse of
child-rearing practices that might be related to the burgeoning scholarly
literature on attitudes toward children and private life. At issue is an
aggadic statement (B. Ḥag. 3a) that small children should be brought to

hear sermons, even though they cannot understand them. But this is obvious, the preacher says: if the small children were left home alone, their parents would stand impatiently and resentfully during the sermon, not listening to what was being said but wishing it would end, afraid that their children might be harmed. Thus, "even if parents were not commanded to bring their pre-school children, they would bring them of their own accord out of fear lest they be harmed if they are left at home with no adult around." The preacher does not address the problem of concentrating on the sermon if the infant or toddler is present in the synagogue, but we have here a rather moving indication of concern for the welfare of small children left without adult supervision.[45]

The fact that Italian preachers such as Katzenellenbogen and Modena made eulogies a significant component of their relatively small selection of published sermons may well have solidified the prestige of that genre as a written text. No consideration of Jewish attitudes toward death and beliefs about the afterlife can claim any semblance of respectability unless it is based on a thorough study of this literature. Though often stylized and filled with conventions and commonplaces, the eulogies also reveal the texture of interpersonal relationships: the feelings of a student for his teacher (or the teacher for a young student), the bonds of genuine friendship, the pain at the loss of a member of the immediate family.[46] No branch of Jewish homiletical literature is more deserving of systematic study.

I must mention one other kind of occasional preaching. Not infrequently, the sermon was used as a vehicle to raise funds for a worthy cause. Each community supported the central institutions of Jewish life through a system of self-imposed taxation, and there were standard funds for freewill offerings. But there were also unusual cases that warranted a special appeal from the pulpit. The causes deemed worthy of such special appeals reflect the shared values of the society, and the arguments used to convince the listeners give point to a consensus about the expectations of responsibility in Jewish life. In addition, these arguments exhibit one aspect of the rhetorical arsenal at the preacher's disposal.

For example, Moscato devoted a significant part of a sermon for the holiday of Sukkot to an appeal on behalf of the impoverished sick. He notes that this has been "imposed upon me by the [lay] leaders of our people to make known in public their suffering, for their numbers and their need are greater than usual." After dwelling on the importance of charitable giving and the special claim of the impoverished sick, he moves on to other exegetical material, but later in the sermon reminds the listeners that he expects their pledges. The entire solicitation section is an integral part of the sermon, crafted with no less artistic sophistication than the rest.[47]

Katzenellenbogen delivered a eulogy for R. Zalman Katz of Mantua "in the public square of the ghetto . . . for all the synagogues were closed because of the plague," a circumstance repeated several generations later (in 1657) when Jacob Zahalon preached from the window balcony of a private home to Jews standing in the street below.[48] At this time, when "the line of judgment is stretched out against us," donations to charity are a traditional safeguard from harm. The eulogy ends with a direct appeal:

> There is no need to dwell at length on these matters, for I know that your excellencies are not unaware of the great power of this mitzvah of charitable giving, particularly at this perilous time. But I beseech your excellencies to contribute speedily as much as you can, in accordance with the needs of the hour. And I will be the first to perform this mitzvah; see my example and do likewise.[49]

In this dramatic gesture, the preacher establishes a model not only for the congregation of listeners, but for subsequent fund-raisers as well.

Even in more normal times, the eulogy was apparently an occasion for appeals on behalf of needy members of the family of the deceased. Leon Modena excelled in this, as in so many other areas. His *Autobiography* reports that as part of his eulogy for a friend in 1616, he exhorted the congregation to take up a collection to provide a dowry for the orphaned daughter. Five hundred ducats were raised, about twice Modena's own maximum annual income, though lower than the dowries he was able to provide for his own daughters, which were by no means high. The achievement was unusual enough to be taken as a model for emulation by Christian preachers, who would say on their days of penitence, in inspiring their audiences to charity, "Did not one Jew in the ghetto raise five hundred ducats with one sermon to marry off a young girl?"[50] Unfortunately, he left no known written record of the eloquence of his appeal.

The Days of Awe were often an occasion for pulpit-inspired philanthropy. Azariah Figo devoted part of his sermon on the second day of Rosh Hashanah in 1643 to a collection for the impoverished Jewish community of Jerusalem; forced to pay an enormous tax, they had sent emissaries to all the communities of the Diaspora. Figo's thematic verse is actually only a strategically chosen phrase wrenched from its syntactical context: *Ha-makom ha-hu Adonai yireh* (Gen. 22:14). This expresses both the unique providential relationship with the holy city and the hope that "God will see the affliction of that place, and bring it healing and recovery through the extraordinary kindness and generosity of your excellencies, as befits the sanctity of the place and of this time." The practice of emergency appeals for the land of Israel on the Days of Awe was not an innovation of the past generation.[51]

I hope this sketchy introduction to the riches and challenges of Italian Jewish preaching will serve to whet the appetite for the subsequent presentations by my colleagues. It is a topic about which much more could be said, but I am already chastened by one of the wisest sentences Leon Modena ever wrote: "In all of the congregations of Italy where I have preached, I never heard anyone complain that the sermon was too short, only that it was too long."[52]

NOTES

1. Samuel Judah Katzenellenbogen, *Shneim-Asar Derashot* (Jerusalem, 1959; reprint of Warsaw, 1876 ed. [for a reason that escapes me, the Warsaw edition identified the author as "MaHaR I Mintz," leading to confusion with the fifteenth-century Talmudic scholar R. Judah Mintz]), p. 21b (page references are to the "Arabic" numerals). See also p. 58a, a eulogy for R. Joseph Karo: "After that I went into a recounting of the praise of the deceased *ga'on*," and p. 61a, a eulogy for R. Zalman Katz of Mantua: "After that I began to recount the praise of the deceased *ẓaddik*." Despite its elliptic character, the eulogy for Karo contains some important historical information. See Robert Bonfil, *Ha-Rabbanut be-Italyah bi-Tekufat ha-Renesans* (Jerusalem, 1979), p. 194. That the elimination of material about the deceased from the written eulogy was not unique to Katzenellenbogen can be seen from Azariah Figo's eulogy for Abraham Aboab, *Binah le-Ittim* (Warsaw, 1866), sermon 75, p. 122c: "I spoke at length on some other such aspects of his personal behavior; I have not written it at length."

2. Moshe Idel, *Kabbalah: New Perspectives* (New Haven, 1988), pp. 18–21.

3. Mark Cohen, ed., *The Autobiography of a Seventeenth-Century Venetian Rabbi* (Princeton, 1988; henceforth *Autobiography*), pp. 95, 102. In July of 1991, Dr. Benjamin Richler, of the Institute of Microfilmed Hebrew Manuscripts in Jerusalem, informed me of the recent discovery of a manuscript of sermons apparently by Leon Modena.

4. Abraham Portaleone, epilogue to *Shiltei Gibborim* (Jerusalem, 1970), p. 185c. JTS MS Rab 172 was a collection of sermons written "by one of the scholars from the Provençal family in Mantua," and acquired by Leon Modena in Venice in 1595. While some are not without interest, they do not seem to be the work of a master preacher of Moscato's rank, and there were many other members of the family who could have written them.

5. Umberto Cassuto, "Un rabbino fiorentino del secolo XV," *Rivista Israelitica* 3 (1906): 116–128, 224–228; 4 (1907): 33–37, 156–161, 225–229.

6. For a general discussion of the tendency to omit historical references from sermon texts prepared for publication, or to refer to events in a general manner that assumes knowledge by the listener but raises problems for the historian, see my *Jewish Preaching 1200–1800* (New Haven, 1989), pp. 80–84 and the passage

by Azariah Figo cited on p. 86. See also the historical events mentioned by the fifteenth-century preacher Moses ben Joab of Florence in Cassuto, "Un rabbino fiorentino," *Rivista Israelitica* 3 (1906): 117–118, and his statement cited in *Jewish Preaching 1200–1800*, p. 18.

7. On Cantarini, see Zalman Shazar, *Ha-Tikvah li-Shenat HaTak* (Jerusalem, 1970), especially pp. 13–15, 18. Another massive manuscript (376 folios) of sermons that, to my knowledge, has not been studied is by Samuel ben Elisha Portaleone: British Library Add. 27, 123. Eliezer Nahman Foa, a disciple of Menahem Azariah of Fano, left four manuscript volumes entitled "Goren Ornan" (Mantua M. 59; Jerusalem Institute for Microfilmed Hebrew Manuscripts 842–845), but these are closer to homiletical commentaries than actual sermons. The only extant collection of Jewish sermons larger than Cantarini's from before the nineteenth century are the manuscripts of Saul Levi Morteira of Amsterdam.

8. Henry Sosland, *A Guide for Preachers on Composing and Delivering Sermons: The OR HA-DARSHANIM of Jacob Zahalon* (New York, 1987).

9. Columbia University MS X893 T15 Q; the text was written in Florence in 1627. See Bonfil, *Ha-Rabbanut*, p. 192; Sosland, *Guide*, pp. 82–83n.

10. Examples from Italy include "Kol Ya'akov" by Jacob ben Kalonymos Segal (Columbia University MS X893 J151 Q; see Bonfil, *Ha-Rabbanut*, pp. 192–193; Sosland, *Guide*, pp. 83–84n), Leon Modena's "Beit Lehem Yehudah," an index to *Ein Ya'akov* (see *Autobiography*, p. 226), and Jacob Zahalon's alphabetical index to *Yalkut Shimoni* (see Sosland, *Guide*, pp. 73–76). For other such preacher aids by Jews, see *Jewish Preaching 1200–1800*, pp. 16–17, 286.

11. See *Jewish Preaching 1200–1800*, pp. 66–78.

12. Joseph ben Hayyim of Benevento, Parma Hebrew MS 2627 (De' Rossi, 1398).

13. Israel Bettan, *Studies in Jewish Preaching: Middle Ages* (Cincinnati, 1939), p. 196; Isaac Barzilay, *Between Reason and Faith* (The Hague and Paris, 1967), pp. 168–169; Isaac Rabinowitz, *The Book of the Honeycomb's Flow* (Ithaca, 1983), pp. liv–lx; Alexander Altmann, "Ars Rhetorica as Reflected in Some Jewish Figures of the Italian Renaissance," in *Jewish Thought in the Sixteenth Century*, ed. Bernard Cooperman (Cambridge, Mass., 1983); Sosland, *Guide*, pp. 105–107, n. 14, all emphasize the citations of classical rhetoricians by Jewish writers. Joseph Dan, *Sifrut ha-Musar ve-ha-Derush* (Jerusalem, 1975), pp. 190–197 argues that Moscato's sermons should be seen more in the context of the internal Jewish homiletical tradition. I tend to agree with Dan; see the example of continuity in *Jewish Preaching 1200–1800*, pp. 71–72. [Cf. Moshe Idel's essay in this volume.—Ed.]

14. On the forced conversionary sermon in Italy, see S. W. Baron, *A Social and Religious History of the Jews*, 18 vols. (Philadelphia, New York, 1952–1983), vol. 14, pp. 50–51, 323–324, n. 47; Kenneth Stow, *Catholic Thought and Papal Jewry Policy* (New York, 1977), pp. 19–21. I am not aware of any study of the actual rhetorical techniques of these sermons.

15. Ingrid D. Rowland, "Egidio da Viterbo's Defense of Pope Julius II, 1509 and 1511," in *De Ore Domini: Preacher and Word in the Middle Ages*, ed. Thomas Amos, Eugene Green and Beverly Kienzle (Kalamazoo, Mich. 1989), pp. 250, 260. Cf. Isaac Arama's description of Spanish Jews impressed by the sermons

of Christian preachers and demanding a higher level from their own rabbis: introduction to *Akedat Yizḥak*, trans. in *Jewish Preaching 1200–1800*, p. 393.

16. *Autobiography*, pp. 96, 117. See *Jewish Preaching 1200–1800*, pp. 26, 51, n. 19, and Isaac min ha-Levi'im, *Sefer Medabber Tahapukhot*, ed. Daniel Carpi (Jerusalem, 1985), p. 80. For Montaigne's description of a Jewish sermon he heard in Italy, see *Jewish Preaching 1200–1800*, p. 9.; for Giordano Bruno's praise of a contemporary Jewish preacher, see Cecil Roth, *The Jews in the Renaissance* (Philadelphia, 1959), pp. 36, 342.

17. In the Church of San Geremia: *Autobiography*, p. 109; see also his letter cited by Yosef Yerushalmi, *From Spanish Court to Italian Ghetto* (New York, 1971), pp. 353–354.

18. *Modo di comporre una predica*, by Panigarola (Venice, 1603); see Clemento Ancona, "L'inventario dei beni di Leon da Modena," *Bolletino dell'istituto di storia della società e dello stato veneziano* 10 (1967): 265–266. I am grateful to Howard Adelman for bringing this article to my attention. Modena himself claims to have written a work called *Matteh Yehudah* "on how to compose a well-ordered sermon" (Sosland, *Guide*, p. 82, n. 1). [See Joanna Weinberg's essay in this volume.—Ed.]

19. See *Jewish Preaching 1200–1800*, pp. 411–412.

20. Examples of book-length studies include John O'Malley, *Praise and Blame in Renaissance Rome* (Durham, N.C., 1979); Roberto Rusconi, *Predicazione e vita religiosa nella società italiana: Da Carlo Magno alla controriforma* (Turin, 1981); Carlo Delcorno, *Exemplum e letteratura: Tra Medioevo e Rinascimento* (Bologna, 1989); Daniel Lesnick, *Preaching in Medieval Florence: The Social World of Franciscan and Dominican Spirituality* (Athens, Ga. 1989); B. T. Paton, *Custodians of the Civic Conscience: Preaching Friars and the Communal Ethos in Late Medieval Siena* (Oxford, 1989). There have also been monumental editions of sermons by the greatest preachers, such as Bernardino da Siena's *Prediche volgari sul Campo di Siena 1427*, 2 vols. (Milan, 1989).

21. Joseph Sermoneta, "Dante," *Encyclopaedia Judaica*, vol. 5, p. 1295. This was apparently based on Cecil Roth's assertion that "Any person with the slightest pretext to education was familiar with Dante and with Petrarch. Rabbis quoted them in their sermons" (*The Jews in the Renaissance*, p. 33; note the addition of "widely" in the *EJ* statement). But Roth does not provide a single example of a sermon in which either Dante or Petrarch was quoted. For a more balanced treatment of Jewish knowledge of Italian literature, which does not address its use in sermons, see Moses Shulvass, *The Jews in the World of the Renaissance* (Leiden, 1973), pp. 230–231.

22. Joseph Dan, "Iyyun be-Sifrut ha-Derush ha-Ivrit bi-Tekufat ha-Renesans be-Italyah," *Proceedings of the Sixth World Congress of Jewish Studies* (Jerusalem, 1973), division 3, p. 108. [But compare Moshe Idel's essay below.—Ed.]

23. For the stories of Modena, see *Midbar Yehudah* (Venice, 1602), pp. 15a, 76b–77a; Saperstein, "Stories in Jewish Sermons (The 15th–16th Centuries)," in *Proceedings of the Ninth World Congress of Jewish Studies* (Jerusalem, 1986), division 3, pp. 105–106; *Jewish Preaching 1200–1800*, pp. 98–99, 342–343. The literature on Christian attitudes toward death in the fifteenth and sixteenth centuries is enormous; see Alberto Tenenti, *Sense de la mort et amour de la vie* (L'Harmattan,

1983, from the Italian ed. of 1957); Jean Delumeau, *Sin and Fear: The Emergence of a Western Guilt Culture* (New York, 1990, from the French ed. of 1983). While the idea that this world was the "land of the dead" was something of a topos (e.g. Delumeau, pp. 352–353, 459), Modena's story is different from most in that it does not use the macabre (involving the putrefaction of the corpse), or the theme of *memento mori*, but simply the claim that death is true life as its summons to renunciation of this world. Cf. Innocenzo Ringhieri's *Dialoghi della vita e della morte* (Bologna, 1550), set in a cemetery, in which Death serves as a guide to eternal bliss (discussed by Tenenti, pp. 270–271).

24. David Ruderman, "An Exemplary Sermon from the Classroom of a Jewish Teacher in Renaissance Italy," *Italia* 1 (1978): 7–38. Robert Bonfil, "Shteim-Esrei Iggerot me'et R. Eliyahu b'R. Shelomoh Raphael ha-Levi (de Veali)," *Sinai* 71 (1972): 167, 184–185.

25. Simḥah Assaf, *Mekorot le-Toledot ha-Ḥinukh be-Yisra'el.* 4 vols. (Tel Aviv, 1930–1950), vol. 2, pp. 157, 177.

26. See the text in Assaf, vol. 2, p. 119, paragraph 12, translated in Jacob Marcus, *The Jew in the Medieval World* (New York, 1965), p. 386.

27. *Autobiography*, pp. 85–86; see also *Jewish Preaching 1200–1800*, pp. 405–406.

28. For example, *Medabber Tahapukhot*, pp. 48–50, 62–63, 74–76, 78–79, 82–83, 104–106.

29. David Kaufmann, "The Dispute about the Sermons of David del Bene of Mantua," *Jewish Quarterly Review* 8 (1895–1896): 513–527. See also the responsa of Leon Modena on philosophical and kabbalistic content in sermons, in *Jewish Preaching 1200–1800*, pp. 406–408.

30. The manuscript sermons of Mordecai Dato; see Robert Bonfil, "Aḥat mi-Derashotav shel R. Mordekai Dato," *Italia* 1 (1976): 1–32; *Jewish Preaching 1200–1800*, p. 41 (and the reservation in n. 41).

31. *Autobiography*, pp. 101–102, 209 n.r, and the letter translated in *Jewish Preaching 1200–1800*, p. 411. In his introduction to *Midbar Yehudah*, Modena speaks of a glut of sermon collections on the market that diminishes their value in the eyes of potential buyers (pp. 3a–b, cited in Israel Rosenzweig, *Hogeh Yehudah Mi-keẓ ha-Renesans* [Tel Aviv, 1972], p. 45).

32. See the examples cited in *Jewish Preaching 1200–1800*, p. 22.

33. See my discussion of the methodological issues in "Sermons and Jewish Society: The Case of Prague," in a volume to be published by the Center for Jewish Studies, Harvard University, and edited by Bernard Cooperman.

34. See *Jewish Preaching 1200–1800*, p. 52 and n. 23.

35. Roth, *The Jews in the Renaissance*, p. 48.

36. Cf. Thomas Izbicki, "Pyres of Vanities: Mendicant Preaching on the Vanity of Women and Its Lay Audience," in *De Ore Domini*, pp. 211–234, esp. pp. 215–216, 219 on hairstyles and false hair.

37. *Shneim-Asar Derashot*, p. 9b; see also Gedaliah Nigal, "Derashotav shel Shemu'el Yehudah Katzenellenbogen," *Sinai* 36 (1971–1972): 82. For other examples of Christian behavior used by Jewish preachers as a model worthy of emulation, see my "Christians and Jews—Some Positive Images," in *Christians*

Among Jews and Gentiles, ed. George Nickelsburg (Philadelphia, 1986) (*Harvard Theological Review* 19, nos. 1–3 [1986]: 236–246).

38. *Binah le-Ittim*, 64, p. 93d; see Bettan, p. 237. A different sermon (13, p. 47b), in which Figo complains about the same common phenomenon, goes a step further by noting a rationale intended to justify the practice from traditional sources:

> Let them not heed deceitful chatter (cf. Exodus 5:9) which claims, "On the contrary, by this they increase their merit by subduing the erotic impulses [aroused]," like those who said, "Let us go on the road leading by the harlots' place and defy our inclination and have our reward." (B. AZ 17a–b)

Figo concedes that traditional ethical theory recognizes a great merit in overcoming the temptation to sin, which might lead some to conclude that arousing the temptation might play a positive religious role. But "in this generation of ours, with our sins, this is not the way"; the motivation of the young men is not pure, their purpose is only to see what they can see; the practice must therefore be condemned.

39. *Binah le-Ittim*, 48, p. 43b.

40. See my "Sermons and Jewish Society" (above, n. 33).

41. Needless to say, such passages from sermons need to be integrated with other types of literature, especially the contemporary responsa, before responsible conclusions about actual Jewish behavior (as opposed to the consciousness of the religious leadership) can be drawn.

42. *Binah le-Ittim*, 10, p. 33d; cf. Bettan, p. 239.

43. *Binah le-Ittim*, 10, p. 33d. On the complexity of the legal issues relating to the *cambio*, see Stephen Passamaneck, *Insurance in Rabbinic Law* (Edinburgh, 1974). For fifteenth- and sixteenth-century Italian Christian moralists and preachers and their distrust of "letters of exchange" as an attempt to camouflage illicit interest-bearing loans, see Delumeau, *Sin and Fear*, pp. 224–225; for the earlier period, see Lesnick, *Preaching in Medieval Florence*, pp. 119–121.

44. Cassuto, "Un rabbino fiorentino," *Rivista Israelitica* 4 (1907): 226–227. The last sentence alludes to Prov. 18:22, "One who has found a wife has found something good," frequently used as an ornament on Italian marriage contracts. The elements of humor and wit in Italian Jewish preaching (and in Jewish preaching in general) deserve careful study.

45. *Shneim-Asar Derashot*, p. 10a. The study of Jewish child-rearing practices (as distinct from more formal Jewish education) and their relationship with those of contemporary Christian neighbors (for example, whether the conclusions of Phillippe Ariès and his critics have any relevance to the Jewish family) has hardly begun. Pertinent to this passage would be Ariès's claim of a shift in the early modern period from a rather careless indifference toward the child to a regimen involving constant surveillance (*Centuries of Childhood: A Social History of Family Life* [New York, 1962, from the French ed. of 1960], pp. 94–97).

46. For example, Modena's eulogy for his mother delivered at the end of the thirty-day mourning period (*Midbar Yehudah*, pp. 51a–55a); see also Penina Nave, *Yehudah Aryeh mi-Modena, Leket Ketavim* (Jerusalem, 1968), pp. 143–144. Katzenellenbogen indicates that the prevalent taste considered it inappropriate to discuss in a eulogy the closeness of personal friendship between the preacher and

the deceased, but he defends his decision to do so anyway (*Shneim-Asar Derashot,* pp. 30a–31a). For recent studies of Italian Christian eulogies, see John McManamon, *Funeral Oratory and the Cultural Ideals of Italian Humanism* (Chapel Hill, N.C., 1989) and the articles by McManamon and Donald Weinstein in *Life and Death in Fifteenth-Century Florence,* ed. Marcel Tetel, Ronald Witt, and Rona Geffen (Durham, N.C., 1989), pp. 68–104. [see Elliott Horowitz's essay below.—Ed.]

47. Judah Moscato, *Nefuzot Yehudah* (Warsaw, 1871), sermon 36, pp. 97c–98a, 99d.

48. See Sosland, *Guide,* p. 26.

49. *Shneim-Asar Derashot,* p. 63b.

50. *Autobiography,* pp. 109, 41–42.

51. *Binah le-Ittim,* pp. 13d–14a. Cf. the Florentine preacher Jacob di Alba, *Toledot Ya'akov* (Venice, 1609), p. 85a:

> We might say, *How lonely does she sit* (Lam. 1:1): the city of God that descended to earth and *became like a widow* sitting on the ground, bereft of all distinction. But with regard to taxes and exactions, they perform a creation *ex nihilo* upon her; she is *great among the nations, a princess among the states* (Lam. 1:1), for she has existed only so that taxes might be taken from her, making something out of nothing. So it is, in our sins, at present: Jerusalem must pay many kinds of taxes, and if they did not send emissaries from various places, the inhabitants would not be able to endure.

52. Modena, *She'elot u-Teshuvot Ziknei Yehudah,* ed. Shlomo Simonsohn (Jerusalem, 1957), p. 126. The context is a halakhic question sent to him asking whether it was permissible for a preacher to turn over an hourglass on the Sabbath to time the sermon so that it would not be a burden on the congregation. For the use of the hourglass by Christian preachers, see *Jewish Preaching 1200–1800,* p. 38, n. 33.

THREE

Judah Moscato: A Late Renaissance Jewish Preacher

Moshe Idel

I.

One of the great challenges of Jewish cultural history is to properly understand the transmission and transformation of the medieval Jewish heritage in the Renaissance period. Renaissance thought was a highly eclectic and artificial configuration of disparate religious and philosophic traditions of the ancient and medieval past, brought together under a single intellectual roof conceived to be a universal and ancient theology called *prisca theologia*. The latter did not constitute a single overarching theory of knowledge like the great medieval *summae*, but rather a simultaneous disclosure of a vast variety of systems juxtaposed each against the other in order to determine a hidden affinity among them all. Within this new synthesis, the kabbalah was assigned an honorific place by both Christian and Jewish intellectuals.

Important treatises on the kabbalah were brought to Italy in the late fifteenth and sixteenth centuries by Spanish Jewish intellectuals who were heirs to a tradition of collecting and elaborating upon a body of ancient mystical lore that can be traced back to at least the thirteenth century. Despite the great attraction this material held for both Christians and Jews, few could understand its content accurately. This was so not only because of the highly symbolic language of much of this literature, but because it was composed in an entirely different spiritual ambiance, as part of the activity of small groups who employed idiosyncratic terminology in order to convey traditions they had received, innovations they had innovated, or experiences they had experienced. The well-known episode of the sixteenth-century Safed kabbalist, Isaac Luria, who

41

ספר נפוצות יהודה

דרושים לכל חפציהם נקבצו באו מיד דורש טוב לעמו ה"ה הגאון

כמהר יהודה יצ"ו בכ"הר יוסף מוסק"אטו זלה"ה רוחו הוא קבצם וידו חלקה
אותם למספר חמשים ושנים זכר לדבר בן נתן לנו וסימן טוב לדבר אנא
ה' הצליחה נא ואתה תחזה דמות דיוקנם חקוקה תחת כנפי ספורו
אשר יקדים לחבר ולקשר אותם על ידי חלקי אמריו
יתלכדו ולא יתפרדו :

ולמען לא יחסר כל בו הדפסנו ל"ח מאמרי חז"ל ומקראי קדש שעליהם תמוך מלת
המחבר לחדש דבר כענינס בכל דף ודף במספרם
כמשפט •

ואת ועוד אחרת לוה כנופע באפדרונכת בו יוסף ווינרס כל
מעוות ותקונו אבלו עס מורלת
הדף וספאנול וספורס •

כתר שם טוב עולה

זואן דגארה   נרפס על יד

פה ויניציאה שנת אשמח לפ"ק

Con licentia d'Superiori.

spent entire days trying to fathom the meaning of certain passages of the classic book of the *Zohar*, well illustrates this fact, one still not fully appreciated even by modern scholarship.[1]

The problem of understanding the Spanish kabbalistic corpus was even greater in Italy. The new students of the kabbalah in Italy in the early 1480s had to overcome the reticence, sometimes even the hostility, of an earlier generation of Italian Jews who had focused primarily on medieval forms of Jewish philosophy.[2] This younger generation of men like Yohanan Alemanno, David Messer Leon, or Abraham de Balmes, also had to study the complex kabbalistic writings without any authoritative guidance or any institutionalized curriculum, as had been the case in Spain.[3] In addition, they faced an even greater "handicap." These new kabbalists had been exposed, to a certain degree, to both medieval philosophy and humanistic culture prior to their encounter with kabbalistic literature. This training could, and, in fact, did affect their reading of religious sources that derived from so different a manner of thinking.[4] Understandably, they experienced considerable difficulties in reading Zoharic passages, and they felt more comfortable with philosophical expositions of the kabbalah.[5]

When Judah Ḥayyat, a conservative Spanish kabbalist, arrived in Mantua about 1495, he was appalled by the kind of books students of the kabbalah were studying. He compiled the first index of texts he thought should be prohibited, and in its place, proposed his own preferred list.[6] He was particularly incensed by the novel speculative interpretations of the kabbalah that had taken root on Italian soil where individuals studied on their own, without the support and anchor of kabbalistic conventicles, as had been the case previously in Spain and later in Safed. Ḥayyat's negative reaction was the result of this complex encounter between two different cultures: that of the more open environment of Italian Jews with that of the more particularistic and conservative tendencies of Spanish kabbalists.

Assuming Ḥayyat's testimony to be reliable in characterizing the state of kabbalistic studies in Mantua in the 1490s, and I see no reason to doubt it, does it suggest a pattern or tradition of study found particularly in Mantua well into the next century, including the period in which Judah Moscato [c. 1530–c. 1593], the subject of our study, lived? A rapid survey of several Mantuan authors and their sixteenth-century writings illustrates the formidable problem of arriving at any simple conclusions.

In the middle of the sixteenth century, the Mantuan kabbalist, Berakhiel Kafmann (b. 1485), attempted to harmonize kabbalah and philosophy as did some of his older contemporaries, by labeling kabbalah an "inner philosophy."[7] Despite this general approach in his only extant book, the *Lev Adam*, however, he surprisingly neglected to mention any precursors in Mantua, including the most illustrious Mantuan student of the kabbalah, Yohanan Alemanno.

But neither is there any mention of Kafmann's work in *Nefuẓot Yehudah*, the collection of sermons of Judah Moscato. Moscato nevertheless copied lengthy quotations from him and even praised him extensively in his later commentary on Yehudah Halevi's *Kuzari*.[8] At about the same time, the *Sefer Mekor Ḥayyim*, the super-commentary of the fourteenth-century Castilian Jewish thinker, Samuel ibn Zarza, on Abraham ibn Ezra's biblical commentary, was printed in Mantua in 1559. Despite its strong speculative concerns, and despite Moscato's keen interest in ibn Ezra, I could find no trace of this work in Moscato's writing.

Other examples are forthcoming to illustrate the problem of facilely characterizing the intellectual ambiance of sixteenth-century Mantua. In 1558, the *Ma'arekhet ha-Elohut*, a systematic and speculative exposition of some trends in thirteenth-century Kabbalah, was published in Mantua. In the fourteenth century, it had been interpreted in a relatively Aristotelian manner by the Italian kabbalist, Reuven Ẓarfati.[9] At the end of the fifteenth century in Mantua, Judah Ḥayyat criticized this commentary and composed his own, entitled *Minḥat Yehudah*, based almost exclusively on pure kabbalistic sources, the *Zohar* and the *Tikkunei Zohar*. We might assume that Ḥayyat's act was an expression of his allegiance to the anti-philosophical trend of Spanish kabbalah, but such an assumption is too simplistic. Despite his sharp denunciation of Ẓarfati's commentary, Ḥayyat was actually influenced by it and even quoted it extensively.[10] When the 1558 edition of the *Ma'arekhet ha-Elohut* appeared, the publishers decided to include larger sections of Ẓarfati's commentary, notwithstanding the explicit statement of one of them, Emanuel Benvienito, that he opposed Ẓarfati's philosophical orientation in interpreting kabbalah.[11] In the end, however, only the most "pernicious" passages of Ẓarfati's text were purged and the rest was printed with Benvienito's apparent approval. And precisely in the same period, Judah Moscato saw fit to quote Ḥayyat's antiphilosophical commentary in his own work on the *Kuzari*,[12] although the thrust of the commentary with its heavy emphasis on Zoharic theosophy and theurgy is not reflected at all in Moscato's thinking.

These examples amply illustate the danger of extrapolating from the intellectual ambiance of a specific locale a particular and consistent intellectual direction of an individual writing there. In our specific case, it would be hazardous to characterize the nature of Moscato's thinking solely on the basis of several contemporaneous works printed in his city, including the much disputed printing of the *Zohar*.[13] Indeed, as we shall soon see below, restricting Moscato's intellectual horizons to these Jewish writings alone might even distort a proper account of his intellectual posture.

In lieu of reducing Moscato's thought to the sum total of ideas and books in a certain place and time, let us widen our investigation to consider the larger social background of two public controversies that took place in Mantua in the decade preceding his death and in the decade following it. The first controversy, in which Moscato was moderately involved,[14] arose from the publication of Azariah de' Rossi's historiographical work, the *Me'or Einayim*. The author's employment of critical methods in determining matters of Jewish chronology, a rather skeptical approach regarding the veracity of rabbinic legends, and an exhaustive use of non-Jewish sources provoked a critical reaction from several conservative rabbis in northern Italy.[15] The second controversy took place around 1597 regarding the sermons of the young rabbi David Del Bene.[16] He was accused of introducing mythological motifs (in fact, the only specific example adduced by his accusators was a reference to Santa Diana), and of interpreting the Jewish tradition in an allegorical manner. Though Moscato had died five years earlier, David Del Bene's son, Yehudah Assael Del Bene, mentioned Moscato's name as the source of inspiration for David's fine rhetoric, insinuating that David's indiscretions were somehow attributable to Moscato.[17]

In both cases, the authors were criticized but not excommunicated. Azariah continued to hold his views; Del Bene implicitly recanted, restrained himself from interpreting the Jewish tradition in the manner of his earlier years, and was eventually nominated to become a communal rabbi. Second, both controversies took place in the same place and roughly in the same time period, indicating a wider issue than the mere idiosyncratic opinions of two Mantuan Jewish authors. The few extant documents of the Del Bene affair indicate that the preacher attracted large audiences,[18] and his more conservative critics were obliged to listen indignantly, but silently, to his preaching.[19] Further, as Robert Bonfil has suggested, the rabbinic manifesto which attempted to restrict the circulation of de' Rossi's provocative book met with limited support; the most important rabbinic authorities preferred a more moderate and quiet response.[20] Consequently, although both controversies were provoked by relatively extreme opinions, they seem to have been tolerated by the majority of the community, since only a minority openly opposed them.

In light of these two events, it is easier to understand the penetration of Renaissance motifs into Moscato's sermons. In comparison to his two contemporaries, he appears to have responded more moderately to Renaissance influences, retaining a strong sense of Jewish identity without becoming "out of fashion." At the same time, the stimulus of Renaissance culture surely helped to shape his "selective will"[21] in passing over recently published Hebrew books printed in Mantua in favor of motifs and ideas taken directly from his Christian environment. Common to the two controversies and to Moscato's enterprise in particular is an effort to make sense of the Jewish past, as Robert Bonfil has formulated it,[22] either through a new historical interpretation, in the case of de' Rossi, or by a "modern" figurative recasting of rabbinic aggadah, as in the case of Moscato and Del Bene. Accordingly, we should conclude that the appropriate context of Judah Moscato's thinking should be located not merely in the library of available Hebrew books in Mantua in his time but also, and, in my opinion, more importantly, in the dynamic interaction between ideas and their social settings, something which is less easily reconstructed and even less definitively demonstrated.

II.

Judah Moscato's two books have not attracted the attention of most scholars who deal with the history of the kabbalah. His book of sermons, the *Nefuẓot Yehudah*,[23] has been treated mostly in the context of homiletical literature[24] with little interest in the work's actual ideas. Moscato's commentary on the *Kuzari*, called the *Kol Yehudah*,[25] has been virtually ignored. We shall be concerned here mostly with Moscato's sermons, not for their literary achievement (an area outside my specific scholarly competence), but as a testimony to the author's ideas and as reflections of the Jewish intellectual ambiance in Mantua during the second half of the sixteenth century. My neglect of the literary aspect of his writing does not indicate a lack of appreciation for its literary significance; Joseph Dan has convincingly shown that Moscato's sermons were indeed masterpieces of Jewish homiletical creativity.[26]

I am, however, skeptical about the possibility that these difficult texts were ever delivered as sermons in any synagogue, at least in the Hebrew form we possess. There is presently a scholarly dispute regarding the language that served Italian Jewish preachers in the sixteenth century.[27] Robert Bonfil assumes that it was exclusively Italian,[28] while Joseph Dan asserts that it was both Hebrew and Italian.[29] Dan insists, however, in the particular case of Moscato, that his printed sermons were "undoubtedly" delivered in Hebrew.[30] This assumption implies that in their present form, Moscato's sermons closely approximate what he presented in the synagogue. According to Dan, the sermons themselves supply both direct and indirect indications of the fact that he spoke Hebrew.

It seems to me, however, that Dan neglected an important aspect of the sermons in reaching such a conclusion: the complex nature of their content. Should we assume that so many difficult and sometimes highly obscure passages (even difficult for Israeli graduate students in Jewish thought!) could possibly have been presented by a preacher orally to a largely unlearned audience? Could his congregation have understood what he was talking about? This may represent no great obstacle for one who assumes that the Lurianic kabbalah, a highly complex theosophy in its own right, became the accepted theology of Judaism shortly after Moscato's death.[31] But it appears more reasonable to assume that only a very few Jewish intellectuals were capable of grasping the presentation of so many diverse sources adduced and manipulated by Moscato in so sophisticated a manner, and even fewer could have followed an oral exposition of the same material as it has reached us in print.

Moscato's sermons should accordingly be treated as part of the literary legacy of Italian Jewish culture, providing reliable evidence of intellectual developments not always fully documented in other sources. And being written documents prepared by the author for publication, they have a different objective, at least from the perspective of the social group to whom they were addressed, than sermons delivered in the synagogue.

Thus, for example, when Moscato quotes Pico della Mirandola's commentary on Benivieni's *Songs of Love*, regarding the son of God, we might properly assume that by the middle of the sixteenth century, some Jewish writers were more willing to cite medieval and Renaissance Christian authors than were their counterparts a century earlier, and even more so than were their counterparts of the Middle Ages.[32] This is different, however, from concluding that it was plausible for a preacher to deliver such material from the pulpit of his synagogue! When David Del Bene introduced allegorical or figurative interpretations of Greek mythologies into his sermons some years later, a controversy immediately erupted, providing us a precious indication of the limits of Jewish tolerance during the sixteenth century. The more natural locus for close interaction between the two religions was in written and learned documents rather than in public forums. The fact that Moscato's implicit comparison of an ontological interpretation of the divine son with the view of the ancient Jewish sages passed with little notice, while Del Bene's innocent remarks exploded into a public debate, suggests the correctness of my assumption.

III.

How can we describe Moscato's general cultural attitude? There are at least three possible responses: (1) he was still deeply influenced by medieval thought, though traces of Renaissance influence are also detectable in his writing, the view of Herbert Davidson;[33] (2) he was fully aware of Renaissance culture, but, at the same time, remained a proud Jew deeply

contemptuous of Christological interpretations, and was essentially unaf-
fected by external influences in the shaping of his own views, the position
of Joseph Dan;[34] or (3) he was deeply affected by Renaissance culture
and it left a noticeable imprint on the essential character of his thought.[35]
The first two responses were formulated primarily on the basis of an
examination of the eighth sermon in Moscato's collection.[36] In what follows, I shall attempt to argue in favor of the third response, based on my
own analysis of the same sermon as well as material found in sermon
thirty-one. My main argument is that two different Hermetic views stemming from Renaissance sources informed the exegesis of the Jewish material in each of the two sermons. I would like to emphasize that these
views are not only quoted, a fact that is undeniable in any case, but, I
believe, they also constitute the hermeneutic *grille* for the speculative
interpretations of these sermons.

The eighth sermon is the shortest and one of the most accessible of
the entire collection. It is also the most frequently quoted in modern
research.[37] It deals with the origin of the garment of light, which, according to the Midrash, was used by God to wrap the world when he created
it. Taking as his starting point the Midrashic text in *Bereshit Rabbah*,[38]
Moscato describes the nature of the first creature, then mentions the
general affinity between the view of Plato and the ancient Jewish sages.[39]
He asks rhetorically if such an affinity can be found in this specific case.
In response to his own question, he quotes an unnamed Platonic source
that states that the first creature was designated as "His son, blessed be
He." How are we to understand this citation? For Joseph Dan, it represents "a clear and unequivocal" reference to Jesus Christ and indicates
Moscato's negative attitude toward Christological interpretations.[40] Such
a reading is questionable, however. Let us examine the source more
closely. Moscato describes the first emanation as follows:

> By the emanation of the aforementioned cause,[41] God, blessed be He, not
> only created everything, but He also created them in the most perfect way
> possible. And it [the cause, this first emanation] is called, in the words of
> the Platonists and other ancient sages [by the name of]: "His son, blessed
> be He," as the wise Yoan[42] Pico Mirandolana[43] testified in his small tract
> on celestial and divine love. And I was aroused by this to reflect that per-
> haps the sage among all men [Solomon] had intended this when he said:
> "Who has ascended heaven and come down . . . Who has established all
> the extremities of the earth? What is his name or his son's name if you
> know it?" (Proverbs 30:4)[44]

Moscato, following Pico,[45] attributes the appellation of the first emanation as son to the ancient, implicitly pagan, philosophers. Since "Jesus"
or "Christ" is not mentioned explicitly, nor is it implied, there is no reason

to regard this appellation as Christological. This discussion is rather part of the well-known enterprise of Pico to discover correspondences between Christian and pagan theological views, without assuming the ancient pagans were Christians, even hidden ones. Who were these ancient pagans? Pico, in his *Commento*, mentions the names: "Mercurio Trimegisto e Zoroastre," surely not Christians for either Pico or Moscato.

The Hebrew phrase "*Beno Itbarakh*" should be translated, as we do above, as "His son, Blessed be He," where "He" stands for God, not the son. Pico translates this phrase simply as "figliuolo di Dio," namely, the son of God. Interestingly enough, Pico is careful not to introduce a Christological understanding of this Hermetic or Zoroastrian "son." In fact, he explicitly cautions that people should not confuse this son with the one designated by "our theologians" as the son of God. The Christian "son" shares the same essence as the father and is equal to him, but this "son" of the ancient philosophers, in contrast, is created and not equal to God.[46] If Pico himself refrained from Christianizing the pagan notion, and had even cautioned against such an identification,[47] Moscato would have had no religious inhibitions about using the term "son." The intellectual context for this usage was aptly described by Harry A. Wolfson: "In the history of philosophy an immediate creation of God has been sometimes called a son of God. Thus Philo describes the intelligible world, which was an immediate creation of God and created by Him from eternity."[48]

In addition to this ancient usage, Wolfson also mentions that Leone Ebreo and Azariah de' Rossi, contemporaries or near-contemporaries of Moscato, and even Spinoza, also used it in a similar fashion. Unfortunately, Wolfson missed the quotations of Pico and Moscato above, as well as an additional manuscript source worth citing in this context. Its importance is threefold: it supplies a medieval addition to Wolfson's list, which could otherwise be interpreted as merely the influence of Philo on two Jewish thinkers who lived in the Renaissance period; it illustrates that this philosophical definition of "son" is not as unusual as we might imagine; and it helps clarify the passage from Moscato's sermon, the subject of our inquiry. Rabbi Levi ben Abraham, a well-known and controversial figure of late thirteenth-century Provence, wrote the following in his *Liviyat Ḥen*:

> "Tell me what is His name" [Proverbs 30:4] because granted that His essence is incomprehensible but to Him, [His] name is written in lieu of Himself. "What is the name of His son?" [30:4] hints at the separate intellect that acts in accordance to His command, who is Metatron, whose name is the name of his Master,[49] and he [Metatron] also has difficulty in under-

standing His true essence [*Amitato*] and in conceptualizing it [*Leẓayer ma-huto*] . . . the [separate] intelligences are called His son, because of their proximity to Him, and because He created them without any interme-diary.[50]

This medieval text clearly demonstrates how the separate intellect can be described as the son of God, as Pico and Moscato describe it, without any Christological connotation. Moreover, Moscato, unlike Pico, uses the same quotation from Proverbs found in Levi ben Abraham's discussion. This may be a sheer coincidence since *Liviyat Ḥen* was not a well-known text. Whatever the case, Moscato might have learned of this usage from this or from another still unidentified source.

Before concluding our discussion of the "son" passage, let us consider Azariah de' Rossi's usage in his *Me'or Einayim*, a text, we will recall, written in Mantua several years before Moscato had reached his prime. The two certainly knew of each other; Moscato even quoted de' Rossi, in his *Kol Yehudah*. De' Rossi writes: "It is merely a manner of terminology whether it is called son or emanation or light or *sefirah* or idea as Plato cleverly puts it."[51]

Again in this instance, "son" has no Christological association but is merely one of those terms which describe the first entity. I am not sure that Philo was the origin of de' Rossi's view here, as Wolfson seems to imply. Despite de' Rossi's acquaintance with Philo,[52] his reference to Plato and the term "idea" suggests that Pico might have been his direct source. Be that as it may, Moscato's sermon, like de' Rossi's comment, far from being in conflict with Christianity, was in concert with a Neoplatonic Hermeticism currently in fashion during the Renaissance period. In demonstrating how the rabbinic usage of the term correlated with Hermetic and Neoplatonic concepts, Moscato was engaged in a positive rather than a negative polemical enterprise.

What then is the significance of Pico's and subsequently Moscato's special usage of the concept of son? Both authors contributed to the philosophical discussion of the idea of "son" not so much under the influence of Philo but under the influence of Renaissance Hermet-icism,[53] and both thinkers subscribed to the "extradeical" version of the Platonic ideas in their interpretations.[54] While Pico consciously avoided identifying the philosophical notion of "son" with a theological one, Mos-cato was less reticent: he proposed the identification of "son" with the Torah itself.[55] In this instance at least, Moscato, and not Pico, facilitated a rapprochement between ancient theology and his own religion.

In this context let me raise Davidson's assumption that Moscato is merely a medieval thinker, despite his occasional Renaissance blandish-ments. Admittedly, quoting Pico does not certify Moscato as a Renaissance thinker. Pico himself quoted ancient and medieval opinions. To capture what is new in Pico, and consequently in Moscato, we need to consider more than their ideas; we must observe the peculiar manner or the structure in which these ideas were presented, or in the words of Cassirer, their dynamical interaction.[56]

Pico was called the *dux concordiae* by Marsilio Ficino, an epithet that epitomizes his special approach. In the *Commento* passage, the search for concordance is obvious: Plato, Hermes Trismegistus, and Zoroaster were all unanimous in designating the first creature by the term "son." This open or sometimes hidden affinity between the ancients underlies Pico's philosophical enterprise as part of the general direction of the more comprehensive *prisca theologia*.[57] The same search for correspondence informs Moscato's approach. Neither Pico nor Moscato claimed historical filiation between the ancients and the truths of their own traditions. When Moscato indicated in his sermon that "the views of Plato are approaching the view of our sages," he was not arguing, as he had done elsewhere, that Plato was actually influenced by priests or prophets. He was, instead, interested in discovering a phenomenological affinity between historically disparate religious and philosophical ideas. As such, Moscato's approach here is different from the common assumption of medieval and Renaissance Jewish thought that Plato had actually adopted Jewish concepts.[58] Moscato implicitly recognized an independent source of truth belonging to Plato and the ancient philosophers, and consequently chose to compare it with the Jewish one. If Plato was a mere "offspring" of rabbinic sapience, what would be the sense of such a comparison? From this perspective, Moscato comes closer to Pico than to any of his Jewish medieval and Renaissance predecessors.[59] As he had done in another case where he rejected Aristotle's alleged Jewish roots,[60] he also did not insist here on the view that what is good must be Jewish.

Interestingly enough, Moscato refrains from adducing kabbalistic sources in this context, texts which were certainly available to him.[61] In his *Theses*, Pico had mentioned that *ḥokhmah*, the second *sefirah* of the kabbalists, was identical with the Christian son.[62] Either Moscato was unaware of this text or was reluctant to mention so blatant a Christological reading of a Jewish text.

I reiterate my original point. Given its complexity and the confusion it engenders even among modern scholars, I wonder whether such an exposition of the correspondence between the Jewish view of primordial light, the Torah's light, and the Platonic and pagan views of the created son could actually have been presented within a synagogue sermon! On the contrary, Moscato would surely have avoided such an oral discussion. As he himself acknowledged elsewhere in a partially apologetic and revealing passage:

Let it not vex you because I draw upon extraneous sources. For to me, these foreign streams flow from our own Jewish wells. The nations of the earth derived their wisdom from the sages. If I often make use of information gathered from secular books, it is only because I know the true origin of that information. Besides, I know what to reject as well as what to accept.[63]

In his discussion of the son, writing for a discerning audience of readers who could appreciate his perspective, he accordingly found no reason to exercise any censorship in quoting Pico's provocative statement.

                                     IV.

Moscato's sermons reveal his general knowledge of and attitude toward the kabbalah. He occasionally quoted kabbalistic passages, especially from the *Zohar*, which, as we have mentioned, was already in print. Yet these citations in themselves do not indicate that he was very interested in, or able to decode accurately the intricacies of, Zoharic mythical and symbolic thought. Rather he seems only superficially to have absorbed this mythological material in a manner reflecting more the spirit of Italian Jewish culture in the sixteenth century than that of its original authors. The parallel emergence of Greek mythology and Spanish kabbalistic mytho-theosophy constitutes a very significant development in the consciousness of Italian Jewry of Moscato's era. Both literatures were subjected to the same strategy by Jewish readers: figurative interpretation. It started, mainly insofar as Greek astral mythology is concerned, with Leone Ebreo's *Dialoghi d'Amore*, and it continued in more moderate forms throughout the next century, including instances in Moscato's own writing. The figurative, allegorical interpretation of the kabbalah is found in the writing of Yohanan Alemanno at the end of the fifteenth century, and continues well into the seventeenth century. Moscato was one of the few Italian Jewish thinkers interested in both bodies of literature and he used both their mythologies in his own writing.

As an example, I would like to present Moscato's treatment of the nature of God found in a lengthy sermon called *The Divine Circle*. There is no doubt that this is one of the most important sermons in the collection, not only because of its length and richness, but because its major theme reappears in another sermon[64] and in his later work, the commentary on Judah Ha-Levi's *Kuzari*.[65] Because of the diversity of citations and the sermon's length, we shall confine our analysis to a partial presentation of the main simile: the image of the center and the circle. We begin with Moscato's presentation of the kabbalists' view of the first *sefirah*:

See how the sages of truth [Ḥakhmei ha-Emet, namely the kabbalists] revealed to us the meaning of this circle. Sometimes they draw the *sefirah* of *keter* as an entity, surrounding and encompassing the other *sefirot* from without, but sometimes they [draw it] in the center as a point within a circle. And I found the following statement in the book *Sha'arei Ẓedek* [of Joseph Gikatilla, 1248–c. 1325]: "*Keter* encompasses all the *sefirot* and that is why it is called *soheret*, derived from the word *sehor sehor* [roundabout]. *Malkhut* is called *dar* [resides],[66] since it serves as the residence of the Lord."[67]

According to Moscato, there are two different descriptions of the *sefirah keter*: it is sometimes symbolically referred to as a circle, while, at other times, as the point that is the circle's center. Moscato was certainly accurate regarding the first description. The ten *sefirot* are often pictured as ten concentric circles, the first and most comprehensive being *keter*, the last and the center being *malkhut*. In rare instances does one find the inverse description: *keter* is at the center and *malkhut* is at the extremity. However, I am not acquainted with any kabbalist who describes the first *sefirah* as both the circle and the center. Later in the same sermon, Moscato interprets the relationship between the last *sefirah*, *malkhut* (also referred to as *atarah*, diadem), and "God," apparently alluding to the *sefirah tiferet*, as that of the circle to its center.[68] The author understood Israel's encircling God by means of a diadem as hinting at the simile of the center and the circle.

The juxtaposition of two divergent views found in different sources is not unusual in kabbalistic literature, certainly not in the harmonizing atmosphere of the sixteenth century. Prima facie, here was merely another exercise in kabbalistic associative creativity. The primary incentive for such associations, however, was to establish a more systematic structure of kabbalistic theology by integrating two disparate positions, to reconstruct an alleged lost unity. Thus, for example, Moses Cordovero, Moscato's earlier contemporary, proposed a synthesis of two earlier theories of the nature of the *sefirot*, one that maintained that they were part of the divine essence, and one that maintained that they were instruments or vessels of divine activity. Cordovero argued that two different types of *sefirot* existed, each closely related to the other.

In contrast, Moscato juxtaposed two different kabbalistic views in order to advocate a third, namely, that the same entity can be defined as being both the circle and the center. What is surprising is that Moscato overlooked a rather common kabbalistic representation of the relationship between one of the lower seven *sefirot* and the other six as that between the center of the circle and six extremities of the circle's circumference. This view was widespread from the end of the thirteenth century,[69] and it was reiterated by several older contemporaries of Moscato in Safed. Even a diagram of this representation can be found in print in one of the kabbalistic texts Moscato might have known: Elijah de Vidas's *Reshit Ḥokhmah*.[70] Moscato nevertheless apparently ignored what is, perhaps, the closest kabbalistic parallel to his definition of God.

Instead, Moscato found an illustration of his idea of the center and the circle in a different source:

> And the letters of the Tetragrammaton hint at it: the *yod* represents a point as its shape is like a point, whereas the *he* and *vav* allude to a circle since they are circular numbers, as Abraham Ibn Ezra stated in his commentary on Exodus [32:1]. I shall also invoke the verse: "They shall praise Your name in a dance [maḥol]" [Psalm 149:3], this term being derived literally and semantically from the term *ḥozer ḥalilah* [literally, "turns around"].

The strongest and most authoritative name of God, the Tetragrammaton, is exploited to extrapolate the idea of center and point, again in a rather artificial way. The letter *yod*, because of its form, stands for the center, whereas the two other letters represent the circle, since their numerical equivalents, five and six, are circular numbers, namely, their square value ends with the same figure: twenty-five and thirty-six. Moscato puts together the shape of one letter with a certain numerical property of two others in order to confirm his view. However, the tendentious nature of this interpretation becomes obvious when we observe that the letter *yod* also stands for a circular number, ten, as Abraham ibn Ezra had pointed out. Moscato conveniently ignored this simple fact to illustrate his image of the center and the circle.

What was his reason for so artificial a reading? The answer lies in the definition of God mentioned in a source he immediately cites: "In Mercurio Trimegisto it is written that the Creator, blessed be He, is a perfect [or complete][71] circle,[72] whose center is everywhere and whose circumference is nowhere."[73]

After adducing this view of Hermes Trismegistus, Moscato exclaims: "See how wonderful is this matter that something that is neither a center nor a circumference is, at the same time, both a center and a circle." Only at this point, and not earlier, following the quotations of ibn Ezra and the kabbalists, does Moscato express his strong emotion. Moscato was citing a well-known definition of God that recurs in Christian pseudo-Hermetic sources from the twelfth century on.[74] To judge from his Italianate spelling of Hermes Trismegistus, it appears that Moscato quoted an Italian source. Whatever the source, we should point out that the same definition was adumbrated earlier in the same sermon:

> The term *makom*[75] is proper to Him, blessed be He, either under the aspect of point or under that of circle. Under the aspect of circle it is proper [to use the term *makom*] because of the resemblance to the supernal circumferent [sphere] which is the locus of everything that is placed within it. Under the

aspect of point it is proper because of the resemblance to the center that is like the locus of the supernal sphere, which is not surrounded by anything outside it.[76]

A preliminary observation is necessary regarding the terminology of this citation, as well as that of the pseudo-Hermetic passage. Moscato does not use the Hebrew equivalent for the Latin *sphera* that occurs in all Christian citations of the above definition. This is especially evident in the last quote, where the supernal sphere is mentioned explicitly, but only as part of a simile, while the author really had a circle in mind. This was done apparently in order to facilitate the interpretation of the aforementioned Hebrew texts that use the metaphors of circle and center, but not sphere. We might then assume that Moscato adapted the non-Jewish source to the Hebrew texts and created a new version of the pseudo-Hermetic definition of God. He resorted to the image of the circle rather than the sphere because the *sefirot* were depicted as circles and points.

Moscato similarly does not mention the idea of infinity as it relates to the sphere mentioned in the Christian texts, but substitutes the idea of perfection. This change might be explained by the fact that he related his analysis to the *sefirot* (that is, the finite aspect of the Divine known to human beings) and not to the *ein-sof* (the infinite aspect of the Divinity unknown to human beings). Why he ignores the concept of *ein sof* when referring to the concept of God's infinity in the pseudo-Hermetic source is not clear.

We can approach Moscato's passages simply as an interesting discussion, albeit ignored until now, of a well-known pseudo-Hermetic definition of God. Moscato's integrative effort of combining these two kinds of sources was facilitated by their common origin in Neoplatonism, a medium whereby spiritual entities were interpreted through imagery derived from geometry.[77] Such Plotinian images, ultimately stemming from Empedocles and Plato, underwent several transformations in the Middle Ages and influenced both the kabbalah and this pseudo-Hermetic source. Yet Moscato's integration of the two definitions in two disparate theological corpora is unique. It provides a striking illustration of the significant contribution of Hebrew sources to the study of Western ideas, sources usually unexploited in most contemporary scholarship.

What is more pertinent for our discussion, however, is the fact that the concept Moscato chose to employ in his description of the first *sefirah* came directly from the pseudo-Hermetic source. Moscato's reading of the kabbalistic source was not organic, based on the internal development of the text, nor originating from the privileged position of the Jewish tradition. Rather it was guided by the adoption of a view external to

Judaism, a view considered important enough by Moscato to impose its meaning on certain rabbinic, philosophic, and kabbalistic passages. Was this done consciously? Did Moscato actually believe that the Jewish sources reflected the same view as that in the Hermetic definition? This is a crucial question, which is, at the same time, a very difficult one to answer. What seems to be strange in this case is Moscato's utter failure to mention the idea frequently expressed elsewhere in his sermons that the Jewish sources inform the external ones. Perhaps he intentionally modified the Jewish texts to fit the non-Jewish one. But such a conclusion would appear unwarranted for an author who probably believed that all the Hebrew sources he marshalled for making his parallels surely fit his interpretation. Indeed, in the same sermon Moscato declares: "We shall be called the priests of the Lord by our attribution of the simile of the point and circle to the glory of the splendor of God,[78] blessed be He."[79]

This identification of the believers in the pseudo-Hermetic definition of God with His priests surely illuminates the author's sense of the Jewishness of the position he had presented. Why he believed as he did, however, is a question that transcends a strictly philological analysis of the text; it requires a wider examination of the larger context of Moscato's cultural milieu.

V.

A tentative response to the above question might be that the general culture in which Moscato lived was so powerful, and the intricacies of his Hebrew sources were so great, that we may suppose he inadvertently misinterpreted a Hebrew text in order to fit a pattern familiar to him from the study of non-Jewish thought. This answer, which, prima facie, seems to be rather implausible, is based on the assumption that there were few experts in the kabbalah in sixteenth-century Italy, and that they generally avoided the most formidable kabbalistic text, the book of the *Zohar*. This appears to be the reality from the end of the previous century well into the next century, even after the *Zohar* was published in 1558 both in Cremona and Mantua, since no Italian kabbalist in the sixteenth century ever wrote a commentary on the *Zohar*. In Safed, in contrast, such commentaries in the second half of the sixteenth century were most common. Even at the beginning of the seventeenth century, the mythological and symbolic aspects of the *Zohar* still remained elusive to most Italian students of kabbalah. Like the medievals who had struggled to understand the anthropomorphic expressions of the Bible and Midrash through the exegetical technique of figurative interpretation, they similarly labored to make sense of the kabbalah, which they viewed as an extension of Midrash.

Despite the impact of newly arrived Spanish kabbalists in Italy after 1492, both Jewish and Christian kabbalists continued to engage themselves in a certain type of mystical philosophy and hermeneutics rather than in a theurgical lore emphasizing the centrality of Jewish ritual activity. This dichotomy between the kabbalah in Italy and that of Safed seems to be generally reflected even in the writing of Mordecai Dato, Moscato's friend who studied for several years in Safed with Moses Cordovero. And even after Moscato's death, the dichotomy seems to have remained more or less evident. When Lurianic kabbalah reached Italy from Safed, it was absorbed and reinterpreted in accordance with the more speculative frame of mind of the Italian kabbalists.

This phenomenon, of course, is not entirely new. In thirteenth- and fourteenth-century Spain, several students of the kabbalah interpreted it philosophically. Their guiding principles, however, were mediated through Jewish philosophy, which had derived them, for the most part, from Arabic Aristotelian or Neoplatonic philosophies. It is only very rarely that we find a Spanish kabbalist who directly used Scholastic terminology to interpret Jewish mystical lore.

Not so in Italy, where the use of Scholastic concepts was not generally mediated by an already established Jewish form of Scholastic philosophy. Italian Jews, from the thirteenth century on, freely borrowed concepts and motifs from Christian theology and medieval Latin literature. By the sixteenth century, Italian kabbalists similarly borrowed from Christian theological sources. They, and those inclined to kabbalistic study like Moscato, functioned as did the medievals in freely appropriating non-Jewish thought into the study of Jewish texts. Moreover, in the Renaissance and post-Renaissance periods, the kabbalah, because of its theological and hermeneutical pliability, became the main avenue of intellectual acculturation into the outside world. Its affinities with Neoplatonism and Pythagoreanism facilitated a reciprocal interaction between Jewish and Christian ideas. Thus kabbalah in Italy simultaneously developed in two ways: it absorbed Neoplatonic and Hermetic elements related to its own concepts, and it either ignored, suppressed, or reinterpreted its more theurgical and theosophic elements by means of speculations recently imported from non-Jewish sources.

Our brief analysis of Moscato's treatment of kabbalistic sources illustrates how Italian culture often shaped the way Jewish thinkers interpreted the kabbalah on its arrival from Spain or the Ottoman empire. Moscato's appropriation of the pseudo-Hermetic definition of God and his adaptation of Jewish sources to it reflect a much wider phenomenon of assimilation reflected in this period in a wide variety of fields: science, historiography, literature, art, and music. Eschewing the theurgical views so characteristic of Spanish kabbalistic treatises, he concerned himself

with speculative and ethical issues. Thus, when Samuel Judah Katzenellenbogen referred to Moscato's achievement in a sermon of his own, he
mentioned, in a veiled critique of Moscato himself, that people "spurn
the substantial food that nourishes and strengthens,[80] and hanker after
the delicacies, the sweet tidbits that titilate the palate but leave the body
unfed."[81] This more conservative rabbi of Padua and Venice clearly
understood that his distinguished colleague had entangled himself in
aesthetic and theological concerns at the expense of halakhic ones.

The main processes shaping Moscato's attitude toward the Jewish tradition, as discussed here on a very small scale, parallel those involved in
any kind of strong cultural hermeneutics.[82] In his case, they include:
(1) suppression of the theurgical approach of the Zoharic kabbalah; (2)
emphasis upon speculative elements in Jewish literature more in conso-
nance with Renaissance views; and (3) absorption of non-Jewish ideas
which inform an already distorted presentation of Jewish texts. In principle, these were important contributions of the Christian Renaissance
hermeneutic *grille* (to use Couliano's phrase once again) in interpreting
Hebrew texts and ideas.

The approach I am advocating does not fit the portrayal of the proud
and contemptuous Moscato who looked down on the achievements of
the Renaissance; nor does it confirm the marginality of Renaissance
thought for Italian Jews. If there are instances where a superiority complex is expressed by Jews in this period, this "assertion of superiority can
be a sign of weakness and decline," as Robert Bonfil has felicitously
formulated it.[83]

Indeed, my examination of the reception of the kabbalah by Italian
Jewish authors of the late sixteenth century confirms for me another of
Bonfil's conclusions regarding the shift of moods within Italian Jewish
culture. A century earlier, during the Renaissance, Jews were more creative and culturally assertive; by Moscato's day, their culture had become
more derivative and dependent on the larger milieu than before.[84] By
the late sixteenth century, the Christian Renaissance had left its strong
and pervasive imprint on its Jewish minority. The Jews participated in
this cultural experience more by imitation than by creative assertion.
With the arrival of Cordoverian and later Lurianic forms of kabbalah in
Italy by the 1580s, new ideas circulated among some Jewish intellectual
circles, infusing some vitality into a weakened and declining Jewish intel-
ligentsia. Only then was kabbalah more widely recognized as a major
religious force by a significant elite group among Italian Jews.[85]

The intense study of kabbalah by both Jews and Christians in Italy,
and the philosophical, mainly Neoplatonic, interpretation of this lore, a
feature of the Renaissance period, provoked a reaction—a Jewish counter-Renaissance in the seventeenth century—whose major expression

was a sharp critique of the kabbalah. A silent negative response to the mythological-kabbalistic-Hermetic amalgam of Moscato's sermons, and perhaps to the Renaissance cultural tastes of Mantuan Jews in general, can be found in the sermons of Leon Modena, who, even in his youth, had retreated from the enthusiastic reception that kabbalah and Renaissance culture had been given in previous generations.[86]

NOTES

Many thanks to the editor, Prof. David Ruderman, whose careful reading of this study and suggestions for improvement contributed substantially to its final form.

1. See Meir Benayahu, ed., *Toledot Ha-Ari* (Jerusalem, 1967), pp. 319–320.

2. See Moshe Idel, "The Magical and Neoplatonic Interpretations of Kabbalah in the Renaissance," in *Jewish Thought in the Sixteenth Century*, ed. Bernard D. Cooperman (Cambridge, Mass., 1983), pp. 218–219.

3. Cf. Solomon Schechter, "Notes sur Messer David Léon," *Revue des études juives* 23 (1892): 126. It should be mentioned that in contemporary Spain the study of Kabbalah was part of the curriculum of some *yeshivot*; see Joseph Hacker, "On the Intellectual Character and Self-Perception of Spanish Jewry in the Late Fifteenth Century" [Hebrew], *Sefunot* 2, no. 17 (1983): 52–56.

4. See Moshe Idel, "Between the Concept of *Sefirot* as Essence or Instrument in the Renaissance Period," [Hebrew] *Italia* 3 (1982): 91 and note 16.

5. Ibid., pp. 89–90.

6. See Moshe Idel, "The Study Program of R. Yohanan Alemanno" [Hebrew], *Tarbiẓ* 48 (1979): 330–331.

7. See Moshe Idel, "Major Currents in Italian Kabbalah between 1560–1660," *Italia Judaica* (Rome, 1986), vol. 2, pp. 248–249.

8. See e.g. *Kol Yehudah* (Warsaw, 1880), book 4, section 86, fol. 63a. The profound influence of the "Divine Chapters," as Moscato calls Kafmann's book, is an issue that should preoccupy any serious study of Moscato's thought.

9. See Ephraim Gottlieb, *Studies in the Kabbala Literature*, ed. Joseph Hacker [Hebrew] (Tel Aviv, 1976), pp. 357–369.

10. See e.g. *Sefer Ma'arekhet ha-Elohut* (Mantua, 1558), fol. 61b.

11. Ibid., fol. 3b–4a.

12. See e.g. *Kol Yehudah*, book 3, fol. 71b; book 4, fols. 24ab, 64a.

13. See Isaiah Tishby, *Studies in Kabbalah and Its Branches* [Hebrew] (Jerusalem, 1982), vol. 1, pp. 79–130.

14. See David Kaufmann, "Contributions à l'histoire des luttes d'Azariah de'Rossi," *Revue des études juives* 33 (1896): 81–83.

15. See Robert Bonfil, "Some Reflections on the Place of Azariah de' Rossi's *Meor Einayim* in the Cultural Milieu of the Italian Jewish Renaissance," *Jewish Thought in the Sixteenth Century*, pp. 23–48.

16. See David Kaufmann, "The Dispute about the Sermons of David del Bene of Mantua," *Jewish Quarterly Review* o.s. 8 (1896): 513–524; and see Robert Bonfil's essay in this volume.

17. Ibid., p. 516, n. 3.

18. Ibid., pp. 518–519.

19. Ibid., p. 518.

20. Bonfil, "Some Reflections," pp. 28–29.

21. See Ioan P. Couliano, *Eros and Magic in the Renaissance*, trans. M. Cook (Chicago, London, 1987), p. 21.

22. Bonfil, "Some Reflections," p. 36.

23. In the following, I use the edition of Warsaw, 1871.

24. See below, note 29.

25. I use the Warsaw 1880 edition.

26. See note 29 below.

27. See the detailed presentation of the two views and the pertinent bibliography in Marc Saperstein, *Jewish Preaching, 1200–1800: An Anthology* (New Haven, London, 1989), pp. 39–43.

28. Robert Bonfil, *Rabbis and the Jewish Communities in Renaissance Italy* (Oxford, 1990), pp. 301–302: "Throughout this period Jewish sermons were delivered in Italian as was the practice in the Christian milieu."

See also the evidence related to a sermon of Shlomo Molkho delivered in Mantua, which was attended not only by Jewish adults but by Christians and children as well, a definitive proof that Spanish or Italian was the language of the sermon; cf. Saperstein, ibid., p. 51, n. 19, and Moshe Idel, "An Unknown Sermon of Shlomo Molkho" [Hebrew], in *Exile and Diaspora, Studies in the History of the Jewish People Presented to Prof. Haim Beinart*, ed. Aaron Mirsky, Abraham Grossman, Yosef Kaplan (Jerusalem, 1988), p. 431; there is still further evidence that each time Molkho preached in Rome princes and priests and a multitude of people attended, again a convincing indication of the language of his sermons. See also the text printed in A. Z. Aescoli, *Jewish Messianic Movements* [Hebrew], 2d ed. (Jerusalem, 1987), p. 409. Another bit of evidence, found in a neglected manuscript of Rabbi Jacob Mantino, regarding the use of Italian as the language of preaching at the middle of the sixteenth century, will be discussed elsewhere. From the evidence related to the sermons of David del Bene in Mantua, it seems reasonable to assume that they were also delivered in Italian; see Kaufmann, "The Dispute," p. 518.

29. See Joseph Dan, "The Sermon *Tefillah ve-Dim'ah* of R. Judah Moscato" [Hebrew], *Sinai* 76 (1975): 209–232; idem, "The Homiletic Literature and Its Literary Values" [Hebrew], *Ha-Sifrut* 3 (1972): 558–567.

30. *Encyclopaedia Judaica* (Jerusalem, 1971), vol. 12, col. 358: "It is possible that Moscato preached both in Hebrew and in Italian. . . . However, the sermons collected in *Nefuzot Yehudah* were undoubtedly delivered in Hebrew."

31. See Joseph Dan, "No Evil Descends from Heaven," in *Jewish Thought in the Sixteenth Century*, p. 103. Dan asserts that Cordovero's and Moscato's thought had created a gap between theology and the communal and personal experience of Jews, and this gap was overcome by the Lurianic myth at the beginning of the seventeenth century. However, I assume that, in any case, Moscato's views were understood only by the very few, and those of Luria by even fewer persons. Whether mythical Lurianism prevailed at the beginning of the seventeenth century in Italy or not is an issue still to be proven. See also below note 85.

32. See Shlomo Pines, "Medieval Doctrines in Renaissance Garb? Some Jewish and Arabic Sources of Leone Ebreo's Doctrines," in *Jewish Thought in the Sixteenth Century*, p. 390.

33. See his "Medieval Jewish Philosophy in the Sixteenth Century," in *Jewish Thought in the Sixteenth Century*, pp. 106–145, especially pp. 130–132.

34. *Hebrew Ethical and Homiletical Literature* [Hebrew] (Jerusalem, 1975), pp. 191–193. The same ideas were repeated again in his "An Inquiry into the Jewish Homiletic Literature of the Renaissance Period in Italy" [Hebrew], *Proceedings of the Sixth World Congress of Jewish Studies* (Jerusalem, 1977), division 3, pp. 105–110.

35. See e.g. Israel Bettan, *Studies in Jewish Preaching* (Cincinnati, 1939), p. 192, where he describes Moscato as "a child of the Renaissance." More recently this view was also embraced by R. Bonfil. I take this view as well. On the general influence of Renaissance culture on the Jews see David B. Ruderman, "The Italian Renaissance and Jewish Thought," in *Renaissance Humanism: Foundations and Forms*, 3 vols., ed. A. Rabil, Jr. (Philadelphia, 1988), vol. 1, pp. 382–433. As against these emphases regarding the influence of the Renaissance see the view of Dan, *Hebrew Ethical and Homiletical Literature*, p. 183, where he expresses the opinion that the Renaissance influence on Jewish literature was peripheral.

36. Fols. 21c–22b.

37. In addition to Dan's opinions related to this sermon, note 34 above, see also Isaac E. Barzilay, *Between Reason and Faith, Anti-Rationalism in Italian Jewish Thought 1250–1650* (The Hague, Paris, 1967), p. 173; Alexander Altmann, "Ars Rhetorica as Reflected in Some Jewish Figures of the Italian Renaissance," *Jewish Thought in the Sixteenth Century*, pp. 19–20. Although all of these scholars are aware of Moscato's quotation from Pico, none of them undertake a comparison of Moscato's sermon with Pico's *Commento*.

38. *Bereshit Rabbah*, vol. 3, p. 4, ed. J. Theodor and H. Albeck (Jerusalem, 1965), p. 19. For a detailed analysis of the meaning of this Midrashic text as hinting at emanation and its reverberation in kabbalah see Alexander Altmann, "A Note on the Rabbinic Doctrine of Creation," *Journal of Jewish Studies*, 6/7 (1955/1956): 195–206.

39. On this issue in medieval Jewish texts see Moshe Idel, "The Journey to Paradise" [Hebrew], *Jerusalem Studies in Folklore* 2 (1982): 7–16.

40. Dan, *Hebrew Ethical and Homiletical Literature*, p. 193. Dan's assumption that Moscato's reference to a Christological concept should automatically be construed as negative is unfounded. See e.g. the moderate attitude toward Christology of Moscato's contemporary, Solomon Modena, in David B. Ruderman, "A Jewish Apologetic Treatise from Sixteenth-Century Bologna," *Hebrew Union College Annual* 50 (1979): 265.

41. *Alul.* The very use of this term shows that it is a created, non-divine being to which Moscato refers. It should be mentioned that the question of the origin of Pico's view of the "first creature" is rather complex. The concept that the first created entity is an intelligible creature that includes in itself all the forms of existence is reminiscent of Rabbi Isaac ibn Latif's view of *nivra rishon*. As I have proposed elsewhere, Pico was acquainted with the major work of ibn Latif, *Sefer*

Sha'ar ha-Shamayim, where the above phrase recurs. See Moshe Idel, "The Throne and the Seven-Branched Candlestick: Pico della Mirandola's Hebrew Source," *Journal of the Warburg and Courtauld Institutes* 40 (1977): 290–292. Moscato does use the term *alul rishon,* which though conceptually identical to *nivra rishon,* differs from it terminologically. In his later work, *Kol Yehudah,* however, he quotes ibn Latif extensively, including texts wherein the term *nivra rishon* is mentioned; see e.g. book 4, 25, p. 49a, which does not refer to the topic of our sermon. On the history of ibn Latif's concept see Sarah O. Heller Willensky, "The 'First Created Being' in Early Kabbalah and Its Philosophical Sources" [Hebrew], in *Studies in Jewish Thought,* ed. S. O. Heller Willensky and Moshe Idel (Jerusalem, 1989), pp. 261–275. See also below note 46; Pico's *prima creatura* is a perfect translation of ibn Latif's term.

The fact that Moscato uses the term *alul* and not *nivra* suggests that initially he was better acquainted with Pico's views than with ibn Latif, and only later did the writings of the thirteenth-century kabbalist come to his attention.

42. Dan, in his analysis of this text, used a late and unreliable edition, Lemberg, 1859, where there is what I assume to be a printing error, and in lieu of "*Yoan,*" "*Yoel*" is printed, a shift easily understandable to readers of Hebrew. On the basis of this change Dan (*Hebrew Ethical and Homiletical Literature,* p. 192) decided that Moscato wanted to Judaise Pico. Though this may have been the intention of the unknown late Polish proofreader, it was not Moscato's. As we shall see immediately below, at least in this context Moscato refrains from Judaizing pagan authors.

43. This spelling is found also in Moscato's *Kol Yehudah,* book 4, 3, p. 11b. Here we find another reference to Pico's *Commento,* which is worthy of a detailed discussion in its own right.

44. Fols. 21c–21d.

45. *Commento sopra una canzona d'amore di Girolamo Benivieni,* chap. 4, in *Opera Omnia* (Basle, 1557), vol. 1, p. 899.

46. See ibid.:

> Questa prima mente creata, da Platone e così dalli antichi philosophi Mercurio Trimegista e Zoroastre è chiamato hora figluolo de Dio, hora mente, hora Sapientia, hora ragione Divina. . . . Et habbi ciascuno diligente advertentia di non credere che questo sia quello che de nostri Theologie è ditto figluolo di Dio, imperochè noi intendiamo per il figluolo di Dio una medesima essentia col padre, à lui in ogni cosa equale, creatore finalmente e non creatura, me debbesi comparare quello che Platonici chiamano figluolo di Dio, al primo e più nobile angelo da Dio prodotto.

There are some significant *variae lectionum* between this edition and that printed by Eugenio Garin, *De Hominis Dignitate,* . . . (Florence, 1942), pp. 466–467. In many respects Garin's version seems to be closer to Moscato's; the most important of them is that in lieu of the phrase "prima mente creata" Garin's version has "prima creatura." See above note 41.

On this text see Chaim Wirszubski, *Pico della Mirandola's Encounter with Jewish Mysticism* (Cambridge, Mass., and London, 1989), pp. 198–200. Wirszubski adduced a very interesting parallel to the passage in the *Commento* from one of Pico's *Theses* where the *filius Dei* of Mercurio, namely Hermes Trismegistus, is mentioned together with Zoroaster's *paterna mens,* Parmenides' *sphera intelligibilis,*

Pythagoras' *sapientia* and, according to Wirszubski's very plausible reconstruction, with the Kabbalistic *Metatron*, without even mentioning the Christian theological view. On Kabbalistic speculations concerning the "divine son" see Yehuda Liebes, "Christian Influences in the Zohar," *Immanuel* 17 (1983/1984): 51–59.

47. See Wirszubski, pp. 198–199.

48. *The Philosophy of Spinoza: Unfolding the Latent Processes of His Reasoning* (New York, 1969), vol. 1, p. 243.

49. *B. Sanhedrin,* 38b.

50. Ms. Vatican 192, fol. 76a; Ms. Munich 58, fol. 153a. On this treatise see Colette Sirat, "Les differentes versions du *Liwyat Hen* de Levi ben Abraham," *Revue des études juives* 122 (1963): 167–177. On Abraham Abulafia's understanding of Son, Metatron and separate intellect and that of one of his followers, the anonymous author of *Sefer ha-Zeruf,* see Wirszubski, *Pico della Mirandola's Encounter,* pp. 213–234. See the early Hebrew version of this discussion in Chaim Wirszubski, *Three Studies in Christian Kabbala* (Jerusalem, 1975), pp. 53–55.

51. *Me'or Einayim, Imrei Binah,* chap. 3, p. 101.

52. On this issue see Joanna Weinberg, "The Quest for Philo in Sixteenth-Century Jewish Historiography," *Jewish History, Essays in Honor of Chimen Abramsky* (London, 1988), pp. 171–172.

53. See *Poimandres* 1, 12–13ff. I have already pointed out that Hermetic influences on Jewish literature are found in a long series of texts in the Middle Ages, most of them, or perhaps all of them, through the intermediary of Arabic sources. See Moshe Idel, "Hermeticism and Judaism" in *Hermeticism and the Renaissance, Intellectual History and the Occult in Early Modern Europe,* ed. Ingrid Merkel and Allen G. Debus (London, Toronto, 1988), pp. 59–76. Jewish authors living in the Renaissance, however, like Isaac Abravanel, Moscato, de' Rossi, and Abraham Yagel, were influenced by Hermetic literature translated by Marsilio Ficino. Characteristically enough, de' Rossi intended to translate some portions of the Hermetic corpus into Hebrew. I assume that the Jewish interest in Hermetic writings has something to do not only with the Renaissance passion regarding this literature but also with the feeling corroborated by some modern studies that there is a certain similarity between Jewish and Hermetic ideas. See the pertinent bibliography in my aforementioned article.

54. For the history of this concept see Harry A. Wolfson, "Extradeical and Intradeical Interpretations of Platonic Ideas," in *Religious Philosophy* (Cambridge, Mass., 1965), pp. 27–68; and see also Idel, "The Magical and Platonic Interpretations," pp. 223–227.

55. On Torah as the intellectual universe see Moshe Idel, *Language, Torah and Hermeneutics in Abraham Abulafia* (Albany, 1989), pp. 29–38.

56. Ernst Cassirer, "Some Remarks on the Question of the Originality of the Renaissance," *Journal of the History of Ideas* 4 (1943): 49–56; Couliano, *Eros and Magic,* p. 12.

57. I propose to see in Pico and Ficino the Renaissance founders of a multilinear conception of religious and philosophical truth, an issue to be elaborated in my forthcoming treatment of the topic. For the time being see the bibliography mentioned by Wirszubski, *Pico della Mirandola's Encounter,* p. 198, n. 41.

58. The great majority of Renaissance Jews adhered to the medieval, unilinear conception of *prisca theologia*. See Moshe Idel, "Kabbalah and Philosophy in Isaac and Yehudah Abravanel" [Hebrew], in *The Philosophy of Leone Ebreo*, ed. M. Dorman and Z. Levi (Tel Aviv, 1985), pp. 73–112, especially pp. 84–86.

59. This conclusion holds also in the case of Abraham Yagel, Moscato's younger contemporary; see David B. Ruderman, *Kabbalah, Magic, and Science: The Cultural Universe of a Sixteenth-Century Jewish Physician* (Cambridge, Mass., and London, 1988), pp. 139–160; idem, *A Valley of Vision: The Heavenly Journey of Abraham ben Hananiah Yagel* (Philadelphia, 1990), pp. 23–68.

60. See his *Kol Yehudah*, book 2, fol. 76a. I shall discuss this passage in an appendix to my aforementioned study of the concept of *prisca theologia*.

61. See note 50 above.

62. See Wirszubski, *Pico della Mirandola's Encounter*, p. 199; idem, *Three Studies in Christian Kabbala*, p. 56.

63. Sermon 5. Cf. the translation of Bettan, *Studies in Jewish Preaching*, pp. 201–202. This statement should be compared with de' Rossi's plan to write an introduction to a proposed translation of two of the most important portions of the Hermetic corpus, there distinguishing between the holy and the profane. If the term profane stands for the "magical" part of Hermeticism, as Weinberg proposes, then de' Rossi concurs with Moscato's reticence in elaborating upon magic and theurgy. See Weinberg, "The Quest for Philo," n. 56. This awareness of the need for selectivity insofar as the pagan material is concerned shows that we are dealing with a moderate reception of Renaissance culture in both cases. On moderate adoption of the Renaissance among Jews see Moses A. Shulvass, "The Knowledge of Antiquity among the Italian Jews of the Renaissance," *Proceedings of the American Academy for Jewish Research* 18 (1948/49): 299.

64. Sermon 3, fol. 9c.

65. *Kol Yehudah*, book 4, 25, pp. 50a, 53ab.

66. *Dar* stems from the root *dur*, which is related to both the idea of dwelling and to the idea of circularity. Since God is defined as a circle, the last *Sefirah* was described, using the terminology of Joseph Gikatilla, the author of *Sha'arei Ẓedek*, as the circle where the *sefirah* of *tiferet*, the Lord, dwells in residence. See also below note 78.

67. *Nefuẓot Yehudah*, p. 80a.

68. Ibid., p. 81a; see also below note 78.

69. See Joseph Gikatilla's *Commentary on Ezekiel's Chapter on the Chariot*, Ms. Cambridge, Dd, 3, 1, fol. 22a.

70. *Reshit Ḥokhmah, Sha'ar ha-Kedushah*, chap. 2 (Jerusalem, 1984), vol. 2, p. 30, where the text of Gikatilla is quoted. This book was printed in Venice in 1579.

71. *Shalem.* In the Latin definitions, when the *sphera* is qualified, the terms *infinita* or *intelligibile* are used, but not the term perfect; however there are instances where the term *sphera* is not qualified.

72. In Hebrew *iggul*, literally circle, though in most of the Christian sources the parallel term is *sphera*, a sphere. The occurrence of the circle in lieu of the sphere may be related to the Neoplatonic definition of the circle as the figure

which has all the points of the circumference at an equal distance from the center. This definition is explicitly transferred by Moscato to God; see *Nefuẓot Yehudah*, p. 79d.

73. Ibid., p. 80a.

74. See C. Baumkehr, ed., *Das pseudo-hermetische Buch der XXIV Philosophorum* (Muenster, 1937), p. 208; D. Mahnke, *Unendliche Sphaere und Allmittelpunkt* (Halle, 1937); Chaim Wirszubski, "Francesco Giorgio's Commentary on Giovanni Pico's Kabbalistic Theses," *Journal of the Warburg and Courtauld Institutes* 27 (1974): 154; Georges Poulet, *Les Metamorphoses du cercle* (Flammarion, 1981), pp. 25–69; Frances A. Yates, *Giordano Bruno and the Hermetic Tradition* (London, 1964), p. 247 and n. 2; Alexander Koyre, *From the Closed World to the Infinite Universe* (New York, 1958), pp. 18, 279 n. 19, and Edgar Wind, *Pagan Mysteries in the Renaissance* (New York, 1967), pp. 227–228; Karsten Harries, "The Infinite Sphere: Comments on the History of a Metaphor," *Journal of the History of Philosophy* 13 (1975): 5–15.

75. The designation of God as place is a topos in ancient Jewish texts; see Ephraim E. Urbach, *The Sages, Their Concepts and Beliefs*, trans. I. Abrahams (Jerusalem, 1979), vol. 1, pp. 66–89; Brian P. Copenhaven, "Jewish Theologies of Space in the Scientific Revolution: Henry More, Joseph Raphson, Isaac Newton and Their Predecessors," *Annals of Science* 37 (1980): 489–548; Moshe Idel, "Universalization and Integration: Two Conceptions of Mystical Union in Jewish Mysticism," in *Mystical Union and Monotheistic Faith: An Ecumenical Dialogue*, ed. M. Idel and B. McGinn (New York, London, 1989), pp. 33–50.

76. *Nefuẓot Yehudah*, p. 79b. See also p. 79c where God is referred to as the absolute space which is, at the same time, the center and the circle.

77. On the images of the circle in Renaissance writings see Pines, "Medieval Doctrines," pp. 338–390; Barzilay, *Between Faith and Reason*, p. 175; and Moshe Idel, "The Sources of the Circle Images in *Dialoghi d'Amore*" [Hebrew], *Iyyun* 28 (1978): 156–166.

78. The Hebrew form *kevod tiferet* is unusual; Perhaps it stands for two *sefirot*: *malkhut* as *kavod* or glory, and *tiferet*, as a designation of the homonymous *sefirah*. Such an explanation may reflect the relationship between the two *sefirot* as circle and center respectively, as we have already seen above, note 66.

79. *Nefuẓot Yehudah*, p. 81b.

80. Namely halakhah. The feeling that there is an overemphasis on the aggadah at the expense of halakhah is interesting because it confirms the preoccupation with making sense out of the ancient legends on the part of Moscato's other contemporaries, de' Rossi and David del Bene. It should be mentioned that many of the sixteenth-century Italian kabbalists and intellectuals were interested in kabbalah more as a speculative, spiritual enterprise and as a way to understand the aggadic corpus, than as an interpretation of the halakhic *dromenon*. This distancing between the two major topics, which were presented as a unity in the *Zohar*, and the preference for the *aggadic* part of Judaism, betrays an influence of the Renaissance. On the general context of this disentanglement of theurgy, closely related to halakhah, from theosophy, see Moshe Idel, *Kabbalah: New Perspectives* (New Haven, London, 1988), pp. 262–264.

On halakhah and aggadah as codes of Jewish culture and the need to integrate them, see Zipora Kagan, *Halacha and Aggada as a Code of Literature* [Hebrew], (Jerusalem, 1988).

81. Cf. Bettan, *Studies in Jewish Preaching*, p. 226.

82. Cf. Couliano, *Eros and Magic*, p. 12.

83. "Some Reflections," p. 34 (where he also mentions Moscato), and p. 38.

84. "Major Currents in Italian Kabbalah," pp. 261–262. See also Ruderman, *Kabbalah, Magic, and Science*, pp. 159–160. This conclusion corroborates Isaiah Sonne's general thesis as to the paramount importance of a strong cultural environment for the development of Jewish Italian culture; see his *ha-Yahadut ha-Italkit, Demutah u-Mekomah be-Toledot Am Israel* (Jerusalem, 1961); Isadore Twersky, "The Contribution of Italian Sages to Rabbinic Literature," *Italia Judaica* (Rome, 1983), pp. 398–399.

85. The question of the dissemination of kabbalah in Italy since the late sixteenth century and especially at the beginning of the seventeenth century is still unresolved. See Robert Bonfil, "Halakhah, Kabbalah and Society, Some Insights into Rabbi Menahem Azariah da Fano's Inner World," in *Jewish Thought in the Seventeenth Century*, ed. Isadore Twersky and Bernard Septimus (Cambridge, Mass., 1987), pp. 39–61, especially p. 61, and his "Change in the Cultural Patterns of a Jewish Society in Crisis: Italian Jewry at the Close of the Sixteenth Century," *Jewish History* 3 (1988): 18–19, where he speaks of the isolation of the Kabbalists—in my opinion mainly the Lurianic Kabbalists—from the general public. However, the deep impact of the Cordoverian kabbalah in Italy was not overpowered by the later arrival of the Lurianic, especially Sarugian, kabbalistic systems; see Isaiah Tishby, *Studies in Kabbalah and Its Branches* [Hebrew] (Jerusalem, 1982), pp. 177–203; see also note 31 above.

86. See Moshe Idel, "Differing Conceptions of Kabbalah in the Early 17th Century," *Jewish Thought in the Seventeenth Century*, pp. 137–200, especially pp. 168, 173–174.

FOUR

Preaching as Mediation Between Elite and Popular Cultures: The Case of Judah Del Bene

Robert Bonfil

I.

Scholarly research bears more than one sign of vanity. The biblical author of Ecclesiastes already noted the link between tireless human curiosity and the ultimate vanity of discovery. Like any other vain pursuits, scholarly research follows fashion. The choice of the subject of this essay may well be considered a typical example of that fact. After centuries of oblivion, scholars have recently noticed Judah Assael Del Bene from very different standpoints. For some, Del Bene provides an example of the peculiar tension between rationalism and antirationalism which is supposedly immanent in Jewish culture. As such he represents a typical throwback to a centuries-old medieval posture within the baroque context of the seventeenth century. He personifies the Jewish way of resisting outside seduction toward acculturation and ultimate self-efface-ment.[1] For others, Del Bene represents instead one of the most vivid manifestations of the inception of modernity within Italian Jewish culture. He thus emerges as a prototype of an organic assertion of Jewish cultural self-consciousness within the spirit of the epoch.[2] In either case then, the figure of Del Bene is one with strong resonances in our own epoch, so intensely characterized by "baroque" manifestations and perplexities. A Rabbi in Ferrara, where he enjoyed the prominent social and cultural status inherited by his father David, Del Bene was undoubtedly a representative of the Jewish establishment in the age of the ghetto.

Title page from Judah Assael Del Bene's *Kissot le-Veit David* (Verona, 1646). Courtesy of The Beinecke Rare Book and Manuscript Library, Yale University.

It was in this capacity that Rabbi Judah ascended the synagogue pulpit and addressed his audience. He thus performed one of the most typical mediating functions in Jewish society. Assuming that preaching is an expression rooted in society's perception of its social identity, an individual appointed by society to perform such an activity is always a mediator.[3] The preacher's sermon is intended to mediate between different categories of thought underlying different life experiences. A preacher is expected to mediate between elite culture and popular culture. A synagogue sermon must be noticed and understood by the learned rabbis sitting in the first row as well as by the uneducated sitting in the back. This is perhaps the most difficult of the preacher's tasks. A preacher also mediates between his own desires and aspirations and those of his audience. He must instill knowledge and values that in his view are at least partially lacking in his audience, yet he must accomplish this without creating the impression that he is preaching something his audience is not a priori ready to accept. For his audience, the preacher must perform a function one might characterize as retrieving lost knowledge and values rather than innovating. In other words, a preacher is expected to mediate between the already known and the unknown; between conservation and innovation that occasionally might even be revolution; between the old and the new. Moreover, a preacher mediates between what his audience actually knows to be, and what it would, at least overtly, aspire to be; between actual reality and wishful thinking. Thus a preacher is supposed to warn and castigate, yet within limits already well defined and accepted by the audience. He is supposed to say in a captivating manner what everyone might otherwise hear from his own conscience. Should the preacher overlook these limits, he very likely might be dismissed. Within Jewish society, one may reasonably add a special component to this particular dimension. As Jewish society does not exist in a void, but rather in permanent interaction with the non-Jewish environment, a Jewish preacher may reasonably be expected to mediate between the Jewish universe of thought and values and the non-Jewish one. From this vantage point, the preacher's mediating function would then most likely be one between reception and rejection of external standards and values. In accomplishing his moralistic function, the preacher might, of course, primarily warn about such dangers as those inherent in nourishing oneself on Gentile culture or in questioning the stability of the traditional sociocultural structures of the Jewish community. As we shall see, however, there is much more to it than that.

In any case, the homiletical product of a preacher may allow the historian to detect the inception of change within a conservative society. Comparative analysis of sermons with what we know of learned elite culture might also allow us to perceive the limits of the mediating activity of the preacher, what he thought fit to include as well as what he preferred to exclude. Should we be lucky enough to be able to extend this comparative analysis beyond the field of what the preacher actually preached to his audience, and consider as well what the audience received and internalized, we would surely gain a deeper understanding of the different forces at work in the making of cultural change. Unfortunately, a set of all these elements together is very rarely at our disposal. Records of sermons that were actually delivered are nonexistent. Preachers did not yet read their speeches and, at least within Jewish society, people could not take notes because preaching almost always took place when writing was ritually forbidden. As is well known, what remains are only literary versions of sermons, as elaborated by the preacher himself *post eventum*, or shorthand records, written down by listeners after the holiday was over, on the basis of what they were able to store in memory. To the best of my knowledge, we do not possess more than one record of the same sermon. Yet we are usually relatively rich in material illuminating the preacher's learned culture or his social environment, often both.

Del Bene's preaching within seventeenth-century Italian Jewish society presents a rare opportunity to carry out a comparative analysis of this kind. In addition to his printed book of essays, *Kissot le-Veit David* (Verona, 1646), the cultural legacy of this rabbi includes the record of some sermons, written down by one relatively educated listener, Israel ben Abraham Ha-Kohen, in a manuscript entitled *Yessodato be-harerei Kodesh*,[4] which might be translated as "Its Foundation is in the Mountains of Holiness" (cf. Ps. 87:1) and where one may perhaps detect a baroque predilection for the antithesis between metaphorical depth and no less metaphorical heights, similar to Giovan Battista Marino's typical oxymora.[5] In his brief introduction, Ha-Kohen informs the reader that, once the Sabbath or holiday was over, he gathered his notes from the sermons he was able to remember of preachers he was fortunate enough to have heard speak. Most sermons recorded by Ha-Kohen were delivered by Rabbi Peletiah Monselice. Two were delivered by Rabbi Eliezer David Del Bene, father of Judah,[6] and the remaining fourteen by Judah.[7] In contrast to Monselice's sermons, which follow the weekly readings of the Torah systematically, most of Del Bene's sermons were delivered during holidays or on Saturdays preceding or following major holidays. It would therefore not be unreasonable to suppose that these were precisely the occasions on which Ha-Kohen left his country residence in order to enjoy the holiday in the more exciting atmosphere of Ferrara. Future research will undoubtedly elucidate this point more clearly. If proved, it would indeed strengthen the importance of Ha-Kohen's annotations as evidence for the mediation between elite urban culture and the popular culture more characteristic of the countryside.

To be sure, the use of Ha-Kohen's records confronts us with very serious methodological problems. For instance, how can we distinguish between what Del Bene effectively said and what Ha-Kohen reports that he said? This is not only a question of hermeneutics. In fact, Ha-Kohen frequently inserts his own comments into the text. How can we be sure that he always remembered to mark his words faithfully? Moreover, his Hebrew text very rarely records samples of the Italian terminology adopted by the preacher, who obviously preached in the vernacular.[8] Ha-Kohen apologizes for resorting to Italian words in cases where he felt absolutely unable to render the preacher's virtuosic puns properly in Hebrew.[9] Yet, notwithstanding this piece of conventional *captatio benevolentiae*, he apparently felt quite confident with his capacities. Ha-Kohen's records provide us with a very valuable piece of evidence.

As far as form is concerned, Del Bene's sermons were still constructed according to the standard scheme of synagogue preaching, deeply rooted in ancient Jewish homiletical tradition no less than in medieval university practice. They began with a "theme," that is a biblical verse, taken from the Torah reading of the day, together with a rabbinic saying, the relationship of which to the opening biblical verse seemed extremely difficult to grasp. The preacher was then to engage in detailed exegetical exposition in order to link the two cogently, constantly taking advantage of his hermeneutical effort to convey to the audience his didactic, indeed ideological message.[10] Such a rhetorical model was particularly fitting for the taste of Del Bene's time, which made the unexpected discovery of meaning an ideal of life no less than a source of aesthetic pleasure attained through stylistic virtuosity. The use of language was to the preacher what brush and colors were to the painter, building materials to the architect, observation of elements and plants to the natural philosopher, dissection of dead corpses to the doctor, or travelling to the adventurer and explorer. In his way, the preacher was to meet the challenge of shaping a wonderful new world on the familiar old foundations. Because of his basic function as mediator between opposites and of unraveler of enigmatic textuality, the preacher embodied the aspirations of the epoch perhaps more than many others. Students of Del Bene's literary style, as well as of his theory of style,[11] have come to the conclusion that baroque obscurity of style was indeed one of the things of which Del Bene was most proud.[12] In the introduction to *Kissot le-Veit David*, he even says that publication suffered considerable delay because of the difficulty of finding printers able to understand his plays on words, in order not to "rectify" what seemed to them to be erroneous! On the technical and formal level, Del Bene's praise of obscurity led to a dizzying display of dual meanings which may recall the baroque theory of meta-

phor, according to which metaphor represents the proper way of grasping the multiple facets of reality.

People might then have disagreed as to what constitutes the most
authentic eloquence. Should it be primarily style or content, the
preacher's ability to *epater le bourgeois* or his ardent commitment to a just
cause? Yet no one would have denied the importance of style in delivering striking antitheses and amazing paradoxes leading to a proper hermeneutic synthesis and unraveling of meaning.[13] We should then expect
to find this feature in Del Bene's sermons as well. To be sure, much
of such virtuosity must have been lost in his actual delivery to general
audiences. In reading Ha-Kohen's records, one can scarcely identify the
characteristically intricate style of *Kissot le-Veit David*. Was that a consequence of the conscious choice of the preacher, who opted for intelligibil-
ity at the expense of rhetoric, or was it the previously mentioned inability
of the listener to grasp the depths of the preacher's thought? The answer
is probably somewhere in between. Del Bene's actual ability to translate
his learned sensibility into a popular sermon must ultimately be read
between the lines of Ha-Kohen's notebook. In what follows I will present
two examples of how that process of mediation may have taken place
and some conclusions we may possibly draw from them.

II.

I am the snake. I am the snake of reason.

ERNEST HEMINGWAY, *A FAREWELL TO ARMS*

The first example is taken from the sermon delivered during the time
of the weekly reading of *Va-yehi* (Gen. 47:28–50:26).[14] On that occasion
Del Bene elaborated on the relationship established between Dan and
the serpent in Jacob's blessing to his sons (Gen. 49:16–17). He attempted
to reconcile the basic ambivalence between the idea of the snake, considered almost universally in the Judeo-Christian tradition as a symbol of
temptation and evil, with the presence of good beyond evil. On the surface, the dichotomy between good and evil appears to remain intact.
Good is eschatologically projected into messianic times, while evil is located in actual reality. Superficially, everything apparently fits inherited
medieval mythology; the structural antinomies are expected to be turned
upside down only in messianic times. Yet, if we are allowed to draw
conclusions from some vernacular insertions into Ha-Kohen's Hebrew
text, we might infer more: beyond the stereotypic messianic inversion of
present antinomies, the keynote of that sermon is an amazing, indeed
puzzling ambivalence, rich with insights. Ha-Kohen was in this case perfectly right in feeling himself incapable of reproducing the polyvalence

of the lofty language used by the preacher. At the beginning of the sermon, Ha-Kohen presents the biblical figure "Dan is a serpent" (Gen. 49:17) accompanied by the vernacular *giudizio e discrezione*, that is "judgment and discretion." It is as if the preacher quite clearly stated that if the idea of judgment is conveyed by the name of Dan (associated in Hebrew with the root *din*, meaning justice and related activities), then the serpent should also convey the idea of discretion, that mental attitude through which we express the correct judgments and proper distinctions that lead to behavior characterized by prudence and moderation. All this, the preacher hints, is also to be found in the Hebrew root *naḥash*, which conveys the meaning of divining, of knowing what is unknown to others, besides denoting the word "snake."

It is difficult to decide whether Del Bene openly indicated to his audience the linguistic polyvalence inherent in the Hebrew words in his sermon or not. In order to do this, he might have had to presuppose in his audience a degree of Hebrew knowledge deeper than the one he sadly described in his learned book of essays.[15] Yet the knowledge of Hebrew required to understand Del Bene's statements was not, after all, so extensive. A rudimentary mastery of Hebrew might have been sufficient to capture the preacher's basic message. It would be unwise to pronounce definitive judgment before we learn more about the cultural level of Ferrarese Jewry in Del Bene's time. Unfortunately, notwithstanding its importance, the history of the Jews in Ferrara is still waiting for its historian. This caveat aside, we may assume that since ha-Kohen does not elaborate on this point, Del Bene most likely did not elucidate the polyvalence. Ha-Kohen was sufficiently capable of understanding such a linguistic excursus, if in fact Del Bene had offered it to his audience. We should, therefore, infer that he did not. If this was the case, at least on the linguistic level, the preacher's mediation between learned and popular culture led to a sharp polarization between those opposites that the baroque sensibility of the educated would, on the contrary, have striven to efface. In other words, the gap between those whom we may label as the literate and the non-literate in the context of seventeenth-century Judeo-Italian society hardly allowed a quantitative gain in knowledge to be converted into a qualitative one. To put it very boldly: the literate thought and spoke one thing, the average audience heard and understood another. This was of course a side effect of the printing revolution and of the "sudden" expansion of reading horizons beyond the limitations of the Middle Ages.

Not only did the various nuances of his message not reach popular audiences, the message itself would thus eventually be transformed. The preacher might be tempted to exploit this situation deliberately in order to present more than one level of meaning. I would suggest that in Del

Bene's time, besides being an immanent trend in preaching, such a dou-
bling of meaning was a compelling necessity. Metaphor might easily slip
from the literary field into the social and political one. Change in major
areas of traditional thinking was hesitantly taking root in the minds of
the educated, including the preacher and the learned among his audi-
tors. Yet such change could not at this stage be expressed overtly to a
large audience, and especially not from the preacher's pulpit. Perhaps
the preacher himself might experience some difficulty in formulating
his thoughts in a clear-cut manner. What would then *prima facie* appear to
be the inability of the uneducated audience to understand the educated
preacher might on further consideration emerge as, at least partly, the
deliberate aim of the preacher. In other words, he might choose to be
obscure before the uneducated in order to present metaphorically his
complex, indeed ambivalent thoughts. In such a way the preacher might
appear to advocate continuity when in fact he was hinting at rupture.

In presenting the snake as a symbol of prudence and judgment, Del
Bene was therefore using current Christian symbolism. His message was
thus homologous to the one included in *Kissot le-Veit David*. In one of the
essays included in that book, Del Bene commented upon the success
of Christianity as an integral part of the providential design to defeat
paganism and hasten the redemption.[18] In his view propounded there,
Christianity was an agent of civilization and progress, as indicated by the
Christian acceptance of the Hebrew Bible. It is not surprising that, without of course explicitly mentioning Christianity from the synagogue pulpit, he assumed some kind of conceptual affinity between Judaism and
Christianity. If so, in a very sophisticated way, perhaps in part even
unconsciously, Del Bene was contributing from the pulpit to bringing
Judaism and Christianity under the same conceptual roof. As I have
argued elsewhere, he was by no means alone in pursuing that path.[19]

If we knew the sources of Del Bene's ideas in general, we might be in
a better position to understand this particular example of his exegesis.
Unfortunately, at this stage of our knowledge, we cannot decide if it
was only unconsciously that he linked the ophidian mantic with judicial
discernment, or if he was actually adapting the biblical etymologies to
some notion acquired by his reading of one of the books in which the
educated of his age delighted. What we do know quite well however, is
that, in Christian symbolism and iconography, while usually conveying
the image of the demon, the snake may occasionally have had positive
meanings, such as representing the Christ himself.[16] In pictures and
emblems of Del Bene's period, the snake also signified the virtue of
prudence.[17]

The example of the snake imagery may perhaps be somewhat mislead-
ing. If Del Bene could have foreseen how some years later Shabbetai

Zevi would exploit the symbol he was using, he would probably have refrained from using it in the manner he did! Yet this example may also be highly paradigmatic of the revolutionary potential of apparently conventional texts. In fact, both Del Bene and Shabbetai Zevi borrowed their messianic imagery from the relevant Zoharic text. Shabbetai Zevi's story may, at least in retrospect, be an indirect confirmation that Del Bene's conventional imagery might have carried some hidden revolutionary spark. But how can we be sure that this is not a farfetched construction superimposed upon a symbol which lends itself easily to every kind of contrasting idea, and that Del Bene delivered other problematic messages in the same way? My second example will, I hope, be more transparent.

But before proceeding, it may be useful to digress a bit to show how such examples of hidden meaning may be uncovered in the apparently endless repetition of well-known stereotypical messages. In *Kissot le-Veit David* Del Bene often exerts much effort to stress continuity where, in fact, a deeper analysis uncovers a rupture. Del Bene himself aptly, perhaps subtly, supplies his reader with sufficient means to uncover what we might be entitled to label as the author's hidden intention—no matter how conscious or unconscious it is. Contrary to the medieval literary tradition of citing one's sources very selectively, especially when authoritative support was thought to be necessary for the appropriate exposition of the author's thesis, Del Bene's practice was strikingly different. He was in fact among the first Jewish authors to supply full references to the sources of the ideas discussed in his essays. A careful reading of *Kissot le-Veit David* would apparently provide a rule: rupture is quite clearly detectable wherever the author displays a great effort to make his reader believe that he is in fact confronted with continuity. To this rule, one may add another one, in part, the inverse of the former: wherever the author displays a great effort to make his reader believe that he is confronted with absolute originality, we may expect to discover strong affinities with already existing trends. For instance, this was certainly the case regarding Del Bene's literary approach and theory: when he claimed originality regarding his terribly obscure plays on words, he was in fact using, albeit pushing the device beyond any known limits, a well-tested medieval rhetorical device known at least from the Golden Age of Andalusian Jewry. And when he declared his intention to uncover the existing richness of the Hebrew language, in order to compete with Italian contemporary literary production, he was in fact declaring allegiance to a completely new system of linguistic reference.[20]

That the ultimate product appears to us almost totally unreadable should not lead us to undermine the importance of this fact. It might also be formulated as a rule: digging into the inherited legacy of the past with the intention of uncovering its enormous richness, he was in fact departing from that legacy and discovering a new world. The phenomenon would thus be structurally homologous to all other departures and discoveries of the epoch: the departure from the old geographic system following the discovery of the New World, the departure from Ptolemaic astronomy and the option for the Copernican view of the world, and so on. If the degree of exertion displayed in establishing continuities provides us a means for identifying points of rupture in Del Bene's thought, then we should carefully consider one of his major themes: the traditionally negative view of Judaism towards philosophy. A comparison of his message on this point in his sermons with that emerging from *Kissot le-Veit David* will reveal interesting differences relevant to our understanding of the mediating function of the preacher between elite and popular culture. Accordingly, I turn to my second example.

III.

Quae supra nos, ea nihil ad nos.

One modern scholar squarely stated that Del Bene's thoughts on the subject of negating philosophy "possess neither depth nor originality and are a mere reiteration of earlier statements." On the surface, indeed,

> he opposes both philosophy and the sciences on account of the danger inherent to them to the integrity of faith. They undermine not only the belief in miracles, creation, and the revival of the dead, but also spread skepticism with regard to belief in revelation and the immortality of the soul. Moreover, they are neither truthful nor beneficial in themselves. False and pernicious to faith is, above all, metaphysics. . . . He therefore advises his readers to divert themselves from "speculative, natural, mathematical, or Divine studies" and dedicate themselves only to the Torah.[21]

Indeed, why not come to such conclusions, in view of Del Bene's following statement:

> Study only this Torah and dispense with the multitude of Arabic, Chaldean, or Greek books which are full of assumptions, premises, and syllogisms—the invention of their authors' sophistries.[22]

On more than one occasion he apparently draws straight lines leading, on the one hand, from ancient Greek thought to a contemporary skepticism of religion and a general libertinism and on the other hand from ancient traditional Jewish thought to contemporary fideistic rejection of modern approaches to science, particularly the implications of natural science for metaphysical knowledge. He even supports the latter continuity with the previously mentioned full citation of sources. This is also the clear-cut impression conveyed by Del Bene's sermons as recorded by Ha-Kohen. In one of them, for instance, he is reported to have preached the dismissal of logic and other sciences, such as arithmetic, geometry, astronomy, and natural sciences, on the grounds that all these are unable to lead to the ultimate bliss available only through the study of the Torah.[23] He does not claim that the study of such sciences is pernicious per se. He even adds that "they are permitted to the Gentiles." But as far as the Jews are concerned, it is written (Ps. 147:19), "He reveals His Words to Jacob."[24]

A more thorough investigation of *Kissot le-Veit David* will eventually reveal that even for the Jews the rejection of Greek science is not as absolute as it might first appear from statements like the above. It will also reveal that the continuity with traditional Jewish thought, asserted by Del Bene, should not be taken at face value. In fact, as one might perhaps infer from the definition of "Arabic, Chaldean, or Greek books" as "full of assumptions, premises, and syllogisms—the invention of their authors' sophistries," it was the Aristotelian system of knowledge that Del Bene was specifically attacking. In order to understand this point, let us first remember the entire ensemble of symbolical meanings conveyed in contemporary discussions by the idea of that system. It symbolized primarily the culture of the establishment, of the Church and of the universities. Opposite this stood the Platonic system, as discovered by the Humanists, which only in Del Bene's time appeared finally to have reached wide public circulation.

The way in which people understood the *querelle* between Aristotle and Plato, "his Master," as Del Bene labels him in *Kissot le-Veit David*,[25] illustrates quite well the complexity of the problem faced by contemporary thinkers. The official culture granted to Aristotle the seal of approval associated with learned, illuminated, and sound analytical rationalism in contrast with popular, obscurantist mythological thought associated with Plato. For average churchmen and university professors, Aristotle was then still the symbol of reason leading to progress, as well as of sane authority. Aristotle was representative of elite culture, of philosophical truth, that is of truth formulated in propositions of universal value. He was therefore a symbol of the order and stability that guarantees prosperity and, at least in the Thomistic adaptation to Christian theology, of ultimate bliss. By contrast, Plato represented popular thought obstructed by its irrational longing for myth, no less than by its sound ignorance, a consequence of the foolish rejection of learning. For average churchmen and university professors, Plato therefore symbolized anticonformist, indeed dangerously revolutionary rejection of authority.

For avant-garde anticonformists, the terms of reference should be turned upside down. For them, Aristotle would, of course, represent the tyranny of authority over reason, the repression of sane epistemological doubt as a result of a desire to hold power firmly in hand. Plato would symbolize fertility of imagination, creative stimulus leading to an illuminating free use of reason; without these progress would be unthinkable.[26] The "historical" Plato, however, poorly fits such an anticonformist, almost revolutionary image. Attention was therefore drawn to Plato's teacher, Socrates, whose ideas Plato allegedly adopted when describing them in his dialogues. As one modern author concisely put it, Socrates, viewed as *anima naturaliter christiana*, came to dominate Western philosophical tradition from Montaigne to Descartes, from Rousseau to Hegel, and even beyond.[27] In that epoch of changing attitudes towards knowledge, what Carlo Ginzburg incisively called "the uneasy balance" between daring to know and the traditional warning against intellectual curiosity came to be represented in widely diffused emblem-books by the motto "quae supra nos, ea nihil ad nos," and was ascribed precisely to Socrates.[28]

As far as one can see, at least from the Jewish perspective, Socrates indeed became the hero of some in Del Bene's time. He was a martyr of the struggle for the freedom of reason, a model for expressing epistemological doubt as a foundation upon which to conquer the truth. One may find eloquent words in praise of Socrates in Simone Luzzatto's *Socrate, overo dell 'humano sapere esercitio seriogiocoso* (Venice, 1651). In this work, Luzzatto declares his intention to liberate the human soul from the nooses with which pretentious knowledge keeps it tightly tied.[29] To this purpose, he engages in the intellectual exercise of reconstructing Socrates' trial. He imagines the following plot: Reason is imprisoned and oppressed by human authority, begs to be liberated, and is tentatively released. A special box is installed, however, where people can place secret denunciations of the abuses of Reason and the diffusion of wrong doctrines. Socrates is subsequently accused of attempting to destroy human science and is brought to trial. During his trial, he demonstrates that the cause of his doubt concerning the certainty of human disciplines is rooted in reflection upon the controversies of the learned about the principles of natural things. The judges are uncertain of the verdict to be meted out to him. Plato argues that there should be no sentence. The decision is then finally deferred. Yet Luzzatto's attack on authority is not a hymn to uncontrolled freedom of thought and action. According to him, history develops in the following way: in the far distant golden age, Reason was queen and Authority was her daughter. Authority's task was then to control stupid people. Inebriated by her own power, she conspired against her mother, and with the assistance of Treachery she imprisoned her. In other words, in a world properly conducted, reason should rightly have authority at its service and exercise it against human stupidity. What in fact happened was an abuse of authority, which turned against its source of power. It thus undermined its own legitimacy.[30] We shall not follow Luzzatto in the details of his exposition. For the purposes of our discussion, we should only add that among the few in Luzzatto's text who argued in defense of Authority and against the liberation of Reason was Aristotle, while the main line of Socrates' defence was the basic uncertainty of human knowledge and the inadequacy of the human senses to guide the intellect in its journey towards true knowledge.

Luzzatto's work was printed five years after *Kissot le-Veit David*, where the same kind of elegy of Socrates is to be found, and as we may infer, not by chance. According to Del Bene, Socrates taught that the appropriate method for attaining knowledge in the realm of physics is not applicable to metaphysics. Aristotle's improper use of gnoseology was then a rejection of his master's teaching, for he was a pupil of Plato, who was in turn a pupil of Socrates. The true rebel of reason was Aristotle, while the Socratic teachings were in fact compatible with religion.[31] Therefore any contemporary philosopher who advocated the excellence of empirical sensory knowledge and of natural science in order to draw conclusions in the metaphysical realm was guilty of a simplistic methodological fallacy equal to that responsible for the belief in magic. Such a philosopher was thus identified by Del Bene as a magician.[32] The implication of such an identification in a century crucial for the shaping of European attitudes towards magic may hardly be overestimated. The *sancta simplicitas* of Aristotelian thinkers thus became the true equivalent of heresy and sorcery, not the poor women accused of witchcraft and burned at the stake by virtue of the verdicts of Inquisitors, followers of Thomist theology.

It could not be by mere chance that Del Bene calls the Aristotelian thinker *philosof pashut*, "a simple philosopher."[33] It is important to note here that Simplicius was Aristotle's commentator and the nickname of Galileo's discussant in his *Dialoghi dei massimi sistemi*. Del Bene even goes a step further. According to him, if metaphysical speculation, which is the domain of religion, is not to be thought of as an organic extension of physical knowledge, then natural science, the most praised aim of human knowledge in his time, should in fact be considered as *melakha ve-lo hokhmah*—an art, not wisdom. One may hardly miss the modernity of such a clear-cut statement, which in fact marks a decisive rupture with the medieval holistic epistemological view.[34]

Perhaps we have overestimated the importance of Del Bene's mention of Socrates; perhaps his attitude did not differ essentially from the antirationalistic stance of a typical medieval. Perhaps we should interpret his distinction between Socrates and Aristotle as a mere sophisticated rhetorical device to display awareness of contemporary intellectual trends; per-

haps he, like a modern fundamentalist, exhibited knowledge of fashionable debates simply as a tactic to fight the enemy in his own field. Why
should we not say that in declaring logic, the *quadrivium*, and natural
sciences no longer necessary propaedeutic introductions to metaphysics,
Del Bene, in fact, rejected the foundations of rationalistic thought, simply
declaring allegiance to the anti-Maimonidean irrationalistic party, following the good old medieval tradition? Why should we look for a gap
between the learned exposition of *Kissot le-Veit David* and the popular
sermon recorded by Ha-Kohen? There is no simple answer to this question. But there are many indices pointing to the necessity of dismissing
such simple harmonistic suggestions.

Let us begin by noting that Del Bene took great pains to underline
that he did consider Maimonides' *Guide to the Perplexed* as an integral part
of the chain of Jewish tradition that opposed "Greek wisdom." A quick
look at the references listed at the end of the chapters of *Kissot le-Veit
David* would immediately reveal that the *Guide* is cited more than frequently as one of the main sources of Del Bene's essays. The same is true
for his sermons. His attitude towards Maimonides' works may hardly be
explained by the fact that Maimonides was too much a revered figure for
Del Bene to declare allegiance to his opponents. Even if he did hesitate to
take a clear anti-Maimonidean position, Del Bene might simply have
refrained from referring to Maimonides' philosophical work. Many contemporary thinkers, especially kabbalists, acted that way. We must then
conclude that Del Bene was sincere in referring to the *Guide* as an integral
part of Jewish tradition. Nevertheless, Del Bene could not simply agree
with Maimonides' teachings without first removing from them any element which might be inconsistent with his own *Weltanschauung*. This is
apparently what he did. In preaching to his flock on the intellectual
perfection which will be reached in messianic times, when the cosmic
snake will finally be converted to the service of Good (the same sermon
from which we drew our first example), Del Bene explicitly wanted his
audience to believe that in Messianic times the obstacles encountered on
the way to perfection will decidedly disappear, "as listed by Maimonides
in the *Guide*."[35] (The reference is of course to chapter 34 of Part One.)
Ha-Kohen, however, who apparently took no pains to check the reference, writes here about *four* kinds of such obstacles—not *five*, as stated
in the *Guide*. These obstacles are nonetheless five: (1) insufficiency of
mind, (2) profundity of matter, (3) length of the preliminaries, (4) bad
natural aptitude, and (5) preoccupation with the necessities of the body.
At first glance, one might of course think that this is a mere oversight,
one based on his faulty memory. Yet it was hardly so. He not only states
explicitly that "these *four* causes hinder attainment of wisdom," but in
explaining his text, he leaves no doubt that he did not forget anything:

the fifth Maimonidean cause (that men are occupied with the necessities of the body) is in fact organically inserted within the third (the length of the preliminaries). The result of this apparently insignificant condensation of the Maimonidean text was so far-reaching that Maimonides would undoubtedly have disagreed with what Del Bene, as recorded by Ha-Kohen, encouraged his audience to believe that Maimonides wrote. According to Ha-Kohen Del Bene said that

> The length of preliminaries will no longer exist, because now we need preliminaries and lengthy preparations from books and teachers; the burdens of the necessity of eating will no longer be an impediment to study. In the time of Redemption, God will be the teacher, and there will be no more need of books, as it is written [Jer. 31:33]: "I will write it on their hearts." People also will no longer be concerned by the necessities of their bodies, because everybody will be in possession of a house and a field, and will have enough to supply all his necessities.[36]

In other words, the propaedeutic effort that Maimonides identified with the acquisition of the *trivium* and *quadrivium* was identified in Del Bene's sermon simply as the material difficulty of constant study. It might be useful to recall here that when, some three hundred years before, Yehuda Romano, following Thomas, condensed the five obstacles into three, he wrote:

> Human perfection is impossible, except through [a knowledge of] all the sciences and their systematic study, that is, learning first things first and last things last. That which comes first is the study of logic, which teaches the way of all sciences. And after is the *quadrivium*. . . . And after the *quadrivium* comes natural science, which requires lengthy study, it being acquired through experience. . . . After natural science, practical philosophy which requires lengthy study, it being acquired through experience. . . . And after all the sciences here described must come the divine science which lies beyond the bounds of the senses and imagination and requires a strong and upright soul.[37]

For Del Bene, as Ha-Kohen recorded his sermons, logic and the *quadrivium* could simply be dismissed. But why? Are they totally pernicious for human knowledge? At first glance, again from the wording of the sermon as recorded by Ha-Kohen, it would appear that the answer is yes. However, from *Kissot le-Veit David* we know that Del Bene did appreciate knowledge of logic and the *quadrivium* for other purposes than for the sake of human perfection. In fact he has Socrates stating that "every science has its proper limit, which may be reached but not surpassed . . . therefore, one should leave metaphysical speculation and turn to human research and to useful activities aimed at the edification of the world."[38] There is no *condemnation* of studying logic and *quadrivium*. Del Bene's concern is rather with those who insist in extending the Aristotelian categories of thought and the methods proper to the *quadrivium* to the realm of the divine.[39]

If so, in opposing "Arabic, Chaldean, or Greek books, full of assumptions, premises, and syllogisms," Del Bene was not simply following the medieval antirationalistic stance. Contrary to what might be inferred from an uncritical understanding of the elaborate sentences of *Kissot le-Veit David*, as well as from their popular translation into synagogue sermons, rather than reject "Greek wisdom" in toto, Del Bene was reconsidering its significance in the overall structure of human knowledge. He was beginning to capture the essence of the humanist revolution in a way most humanists did not themselves yet realize: Del Bene was beginning to reject the medieval conception of the opposition between the secular and the religious in terms of mutual exclusion, in order to assign the first a thisworldly function, and the second an otherworldly one. He was also departing squarely from the belief in the harmonic congruence between reason and faith, which was one of the pillars of medieval thought. In showing an awareness of the humanist discovery of the structural opposition between Greek wisdom and religious perception, Del Bene was in fact proposing a way to overcome the impasse.[40] Rather than reject Greek culture, he was releasing it from the tight embrace with religion and theology that was imposed upon it by the medieval mentality. Rather than reject Greek culture, Del Bene was rejecting the idea of the essential unity of the physical and metaphysical worlds. Indeed he felt that such an assumption, after having served medieval men in transforming everything into something religious, was now serving contemporary freethinkers, *still prisoners of the medieval mentality*, in their efforts to transform everything into the secular. If we are right in such an understanding, Del Bene's views may well be considered as genuinely modern.

To be sure, departure from the Maimonidean system of thought, following the necessity of departing from the medieval *Weltanschauung*, had to be performed smoothly, indeed almost imperceptibly. If Ha-Kohen, who was an educated man, did not perceive anything unusual in recording Maimonides' teaching as he did, we must say that in his effort to stress the orthodox continuity of his *Weltanschauung*, Del Bene was successful in stressing continuity when in fact he was contributing to a major rupture. As he was mediating between elite culture and popular culture, our preacher was also demonstrating his ability to mediate between the Middle Ages and the modern era. As we have said, it would perhaps stand to reason that he was not fully conscious of what he was formulating. And, if he was, he wrapped up his message in a cloak of obfuscation, typical of the baroque period. In any case, the deep change that was hesitantly going on in the minds of few, remained imperceptible to average people. Listening to Del Bene's sermons, one might very well miss the point. Haziness and even obscurity were indeed necessary for the inception of the process.[41]

Del Bene's aesthetic literary ideal fits very well into its general framework. Besides his declared effort to demonstrate that Hebrew can effectively compete with Italian in richness and fluidity of expression, he displays in *Kissot le-Veit David* a clear consciousness of innovation. In fact he declares himself proud of the rhetorical and stylistical expressions he is the first to use. Consciousness of originality and novelty went hand in hand with the aesthetic ideal of obscurity. Such a writer could hardly be expected to overtly formulate a clear-cut system of thought. Yet he might be expected to formulate a hesitant beginning of real novelty in an obscure, almost metaphorical way. If double sense and obscurity in literary style may be considered characteristic elements of the *Geist* of Del Bene's context, we should expect him to turn to them whenever he performs any significant literary activity. If so, it would certainly be wrong to give a univocal interpretation precisely to those statements which were of major importance for him. I would argue that this is also an argument in favor of our previous understanding of Del Bene's views vis-à-vis secular studies.[42]

We may then understand why many of the themes hinting at novelty and change in *Kissot le-Veit David* were apparently absent from the sermons Ha-Kohen recorded. It is not necessary to assume that Del Bene never mentioned them at all. For our limited purpose, it suffices to note that Ha-Kohen did not record them. One of these themes is the convergence of Judaism with Christianity. It emerges quite evidently from *Kissot le-Veit David*, and was in fact recently illuminated in scholarly research.[43] It may be considered as the natural consequence of separating human secular activity and knowledge from the realm of faith. Should we be prepared to understand modern ecumenism as free of hidden missionary intentions, that is, as the cooperation of men of faith beyond diversity of religion who share a common desire to oppose the expansion of secularism, Del Bene's message might, without exaggeration, be labeled as ecumenism *ante litteram*. Here too, proceeding outward from the center of the rabbinic establishment, a modern Jewish outlook was taking shape. Yet it was a very strange and ambivalent alliance, indeed, as were most baroque alliances between disparate contrasting elements. After having declared overt hostility to the Aristotelian official philosophy of the Church, this rabbi found himself now allied with churchmen in fighting the application of naturalistic methods to theology and in identifying them with sheer libertinism. In other words, this rabbi found himself allied with Counter-Reformation Catholic attitudes and fears. By the same token, he found himself allied with Counter-Reformation Catholic attitudes in many other fields; for instance, in favoring Inquisitorial censorship of books or in reacting to the apparently obsessive contemporary interest in sexuality. Yet, contrary to the theme of the convergence of Judaism with Christianity, the theme of sexuality is feebly present in *Kissot le-Veit David*, while it is heavily treated in the sermons. In other words, if we may be allowed to generalize from these two specific cases, the list of the themes usually dealt with in sermons may be expected to differ radically from that of the themes treated in learned books. If so, we might formulate some kind of rule and state that a comparison of sermons actually delivered with the literary production of the elite culture may provide a method for measuring the degree of diffusion of cultural change already noted in elite literary production.

We may now apply that rule to the different ways the two types of sources mention a departure from the medieval system of thought. After centuries of critique of Maimonidean thought, the dismissal of the propaedeutic necessity of logic and the *quadrivium* for the formation of a traditional religious outlook might be considered perfectly acceptable. This dismissal would consequently be offered without qualification to popular audiences, as if all secular studies were to be considered as harmful as the much despised Aristotelian philosophy. Yet in the learned essays of *Kissot le-Veit David* qualification was introduced, through the crucial distinction between the Aristotelian and the Socratic legacies, which constituted a real novelty in that epoch. This is why the rejection of logic and the *quadrivium* in the sermons appears differently from their rejection in *Kissot le-Veit David*. A more thorough analysis of Del Bene's sermons as recorded by Ha-Kohen may provide more support for this conclusion.

One more point should be stressed. The inception of changing attitudes towards the relationship between the sacred and the profane, the religious and the secular, was taking place in the mind of a rabbi, a representative of the established Jewish culture, and was organically linked to contemporary trends of thought. To put it boldly, revolution proceeded from the center of the Jewish establishment to the periphery. At least on the surface, Del Bene's opposition to undisciplined learning also determined some kind of virtual alliance between the rabbi and the Catholic establishment. In a sense, rabbis such as Del Bene accomplished a function within Jewish society similar to that accomplished by Jesuits among Christians. They strove to cope with the inception of modernity and secularism without causing any damage to religious faith. They even acted as vehicles of modernity and secularism within Jewish society.

Comparative study of Del Bene's works is only at its initial stage, yet it appears highly promising. It must be carried on in the near future, by me as well as by others. Should the emergence of other comparative studies of elite literary production and of sermons delivered to large audiences be added to the one hesitantly presented here, we will have taken a considerable step forward in understanding the mechanism of aligning popular culture with the achievements of elite culture. For this is ultimately the root of real cultural and social change.

NOTES

1. Isaac E. Barzilay, *Between Reason and Faith. Anti-Rationalism in Italian Jewish Thought, 1250–1650* (The Hague, Paris, 1967), pp. 210–217.

2. Giuseppe Sermoneta, "Aspetti del pensiero moderno nell'ebraismo italiano tra Rinascimento e età barocca" (Rome, 1986), pp. 17–35. Cf. Robert Bonfil, "Change in the Cultural Patterns of a Jewish Society in Crisis: Italian Jewry at the Close of the Sixteenth Century," *Jewish History* 3 (1988): 11–30.

3. As far as I know, this particular aspect of preaching has not so far received much scholarly attention. See Robert Bonfil, *Rabbis and Jewish Communities in Renaissance Italy* (Oxford, 1990), pp. 298–316. For Jewish preaching in general, see, of course, Marc Saperstein, *Jewish Preaching, 1200–1800: An Anthology* (New Haven, London, 1989), where the pertinent literature is exhaustively listed. See also Saperstein's introductory essay in this volume.

4. Ms. Budapest-Kaufmann A 455. I was given the opportunity to use the microfilm in possession of the Institute of Microfilms of Hebrew Manuscripts in Jerusalem. Israel ben Abraham Ha-Kohen is listed in the files of the Institute of Microfilms as having copied Ms. Rab 1508 of The Jewish Theological Seminary, New York, and H 178 A/1 of the Alliance Israelite Universelle, Paris.

5. For instance: Volontaria follia, piacevol male, stanco riposo, utilità nocente, desperato sperar, morir vitale, temerario timor, riso dolente; un vetro duro, un adamente frale, un'arsura gelata, un gelo ardente, di discordie concordi, abisso eterno, paradiso infernal, celeste inferno (G. B. Marino, *Adone*, 6, 174). See also David B. Ruderman, *A Valley of Vision: The Heavenly Journey of Abraham ben Hananiah Yagel* (Philadelphia, 1990), p. 71, n. 1.

6. Especially worthy of mention here is the one delivered for the *parashah* of *Mikkeẓ* and *Hanukka* (on the theme of Judith and Holophernes): pp. 128–134. On the very interesting figure of David Del Bene, very little has so far been written. See David Kaufmann, "The Dispute about the Sermons of David Del Bene of Mantua," *Jewish Quarterly Review* o.s. 8 (1896): 513–524. See also the essay by Moshe Idel in this volume.

7. One for the *parashah* of *Vayehi*, which falls frequently near *Hanukka* (pp. 153–163); one for the *parashah* of *Mishpatim*, which falls frequently near *Purim* (pp. 237–244); five for different days of Passover (pp. 340–341; 352–353; 361–369; 384–385; 395); one for Shabbat ha-Gadol, the Saturday preceding Passover (p. 437); and the remainder for different Saturdays falling in the period immediately preceding or following Passover: two for the *parashah* of *Shemini* (pp. 397–401; 411–420); one for the *parashah* of *Taẓria-Meẓora* (pp. 411–420);

one for *Kedoshim* (pp. 411–420); one for *Emor* (pp. 411–420); and one for *Behar-Behukkotai* (pp. 411–420).

8. To my mind, there is no doubt that sermons were actually delivered in the vernacular, interspersed with Judeo-vernacular idioms. A sample of such a text, written down by a preacher who lived in the same cultural context as Del Bene, although a little earlier, may be seen in Robert Bonfil, "Aḥat mi-derashotav shel R. Mordecai Dato," *Italia* 1 (1976): i–xxxii. But cf. with Saperstein's discussion, *Jewish Preaching, 1200–1800*, pp. 39–44, and see the essays of Saperstein and Idel in this volume.

9. *Yessodato be-harerei Kodesh*, Introduction, p. 13: "The reader should not accuse me of inventing verbs and nouns in several places which are not found in the Hebrew language, since the density of the subject and the language's limitation obliged me to do it."

10. I have briefly discussed this model in my *Rabbis and Jewish Communities in Renaissance Italy*, loc. cit. Joanna Weinberg has recently argued that Del Bene's age may have witnessed some departure from the medieval model and that evidence of this is apparently to be detected in Leone Modena's preaching practice. See her essay in the present volume. Such a development would in principle certainly not be impossible. Having outlined Elijah de Veali's eighteenth-century traditional model of Italian Jewish preaching, I remain skeptical. For de Veali's model, see Robert Bonfil, "Shteim-Esrei Iggeroth Me-et R. Eliyahu b. Shlomo Raphael Ha-Levi De Veali" (Twelve Letters by R. Elijah b. Solomon Raphael Ha-Levi De Veali), *Sinai* 71 (1972): 163–190.

11. *Kissot le-Veit David*, 2, 9.

12. For what follows, I am indebted to Dr. Ariel Rathaus, who is preparing a thorough study of Del Bene's literary theory.

13. See, for instance, Wilbur Samuel Howell, "Baroque Rhetoric: A Concept At Odds With Its Setting," *Philosophy and Rhetoric* 15 (1982): 1–23.

14. *Yessodato be-harerei Kodesh*, pp. 153–163.

15. *Kissot le-Veit David*, 2, 9. See Robert Bonfil, "Halakhah, Kabbalah and Society; Some Insights Into Rabbi Menahem Azariah da Fano's Inner World," *Jewish Thought in the Seventeenth Century*, ed. Isadore Twersky and Bernard Septimus (Cambridge, Mass., 1987), p. 61; idem, "Change in the Cultural Patterns" (*supra* n. 2), p. 19.

16. This point was suggested to me by Professor Walter Cahn of Yale University, whom I thank here very much.

17. See, for example, Louis Reau, *Iconographie de l'Art Chrétien* (Paris, 1955), vol. 1, pp. 98–99; *Lexikon der Christlichen Ikonographie*, ed. von Engelbert Kirschbaum (Rome, Freiburg, Basel, Vienna, 1972), vol. 1, s.v. Schlange, colls. 75–82, and Tugunden, colls. 364–380, and esp. 378.

18. This point was strongly made by Sermoneta, art. cit. See also Bonfil, "Change in Cultural Patterns," pp. 20–21.

19. Bonfil, "Change in Cultural Patterns," loc. cit.

20. I am indebted for this paragraph to Dr. Ariel Rathaus's findings, which he was kind enough to share with me before their publication.

21. Barzilay, *Between Reason and Faith*, p. 211.

22. *Kissot le-Veit David*, 1, 3. Quoted by Barzilay, p. 21.

23. Sermon for the section of *Mishpatim, Yessodato be-harerei Kodesh*, pp. 237–244.

24. *Yessodato be-harerei Kodesh*, p. 240.

25. *Kissot le-Veit David*, 1, 4

26. On the main cultural trends of the period, see Paul Renucci, *La cultura*, in *Storia d'Italia* 2** (Turin, 1974), vol. 6: Il Seicento—Dalla selva barocca alla scuola del classicismo, pp. 1360–1445; Alberto Asor Rosa, *La cultura della controriforma* (Bari, 1979). For an example of the formulation of most of the ideas here mentioned, one may read Sforza Pallavicino's typical characterization of Plato vs. Aristotle:

"Platone in filosofare fu sempre vago di proposizioni meravigliose, e però lontane dalla credenza popolare. Pertanto fu anche in maggior venerazione del popolo, il quale tanto reputa i letterati superiori a sè nell'intendere, quanto li vede a sè differenti nel credere, e più riverisce per sapienti coloro da cui egli è più strapazzato per ignorante. Anche i poeti, come quelli che hanno per livrea de' loro componimenti il mirabile intessuto col verisimile, si fornirono al fondaco non d'Aristotele, ma di Platone, unico nello spacciar maraviglie non derise, ma venerate, e però credute. Aristotele s'inviò per contrario sentiero. Tanto fu alieno dal tracciar lo stupore del volgo, che si elesse per maestro il volgo medesimo, e su' primi e più rozzi ed universali concetti della maraviglia appoggiò le colonne della sua filosofia: la quale, quanto per tal modo fu più sincera, tanto riuscì finalmente più fortunatadella platonica. E videsi tra lor quella differenza che suol essere tra le poesie e l'istorie: quelle, come audaci in mentire, così più meravigliose e però più gustose; queste, come riverenti del vero, così più autorevoli e però più pregiate e più fruttuose. Tal giudizio ha dato di questi due gran maestri il testimonio non errante del tempo."

See *Trattatisti e narratori del seicento*, a cura di Ezio Raimondi, in *La letteratura italiana* (Milano-Napoli, 1960), p. 226. In reading these lines, one should bear in mind that Sforza Pallavicino (1607–1667) was a cardinal, and therefore a genuine representative of the Catholic establishment. He was also author of a *Trattato dello stile*, which deals especially with the issue of the rhetorical use of wonder, focusing on themes similar to those dealt with by Fenelon in his *Dialogues on Eloquence*; see W. S. Howell, "Baroque Rhetoric," cit.

27. Jacques Brunschwig, "Socrate et Ecoles Socratiques," *Encyclopaedia Universalis*, corpus 16, col. 1098.

28. Carlo Ginzburg, "High and Low; The Theme of Forbidden Knowledge in the Sixteenth and Seventeenth Centuries," *Past and Present* 73 (1976): 29–41, and particularly p. 33 and n. 22. See David B. Ruderman, *Kabbalah, Magic, and Science: The Cultural Universe of a Sixteenth-Century Jewish Physician* (Cambridge, Mass., and London, 1988), pp. 103, 205, n. 5.

29. "Attendere la libertà dell'animo humano inviluppato da lacci, con quali l'ardito e troppo pretendente sapere lo tiene legato & stretto."

30. Note here also that "uneasy balance" between authoritative warning against improper use of reason and the necessity of freedom of thought, perfectly coherent with the attitudes toward the theme of forbidden knowledge, already quoted above, n. 28.

31. *Kissot le-Veit David*, 1, 4 (f. 11 [= 16]a); 1, 8 (f. 19 [= 23]b).

32. *Kissot le-Veit David*, 1, 9 (f. 13b). As Prof. Joanna Weinberg very perti-

nently noted, there was a medieval tradition (for instance, in the *Secretum Secretorum*) which considered Aristotle to be a magician. It stands to reason that such a tradition was known to Del Bene as well as to part of his audience. It is therefore possible that we have here one more example of Del Bene's assigning new meanings to well-known medieval concepts.

33. For instance, *Kissot le-Veit David*, loc. cit.

34. For a similar conclusion on the separation of naturalistic learning from Aristotelian metaphysics, and its subsequent linkage with traditional Jewish, even kabbalistic thought, in this period, see David B. Ruderman, "The Language of Science as the Language of Faith: An Aspect of Italian Jewish Thought in the Seventeenth and Eighteenth Centuries," *Anniversary Volume in Honor of Shlomo Simonsohn*, forthcoming. See also the essay of David Ruderman in this volume.

35. *Yessodato be-harerei Kodesh*, p. 160.

36. *Yessodato be-harerei Kodesh*, loc. cit.

37. See Giuseppe Sermoneta, "Prophecy in the Writings of R. Yehuda Romano," *Studies in Medieval Jewish History and Literature*, vol. 2., ed. Isadore Twersky (Cambridge, Mass., 1984), pp. 361–362.

38. *Kissot le-Veit David*, f. 11 [= 16]a.

39. *Kissot le-Veit David*, f. 17a.

40. This theme is dealt with in *Kissot le-Veit David*, 1, 8.

41. See Bonfil, "Change in the Cultural Patterns," pp. 13–14.

42. See above, n. 12

43. *Kissot le-Veit David*, 1, 8; Sermoneta, "Aspetti del pensiero moderno nell'ebraismo italiano"; Bonfil, "Change in the Cultural Patterns."

FIVE

Jewish Preaching and the Language of Science: The Sermons of Azariah Figo

David B. Ruderman

The age in which the preachers of the Italian ghettos delivered their sermons was also the great age of scientific discovery in Europe. Far removed both geographically and culturally from the cramped but ornate synagogues of Venice, Ferrara, or Mantua, Galileo peered through his famous telescope, Vesalius performed his revolutionary anatomical experiments, and Bacon and Descartes reflected deeply on the new methods of fathoming the natural world from their own distinctive perspectives. Beyond the walls ostensibly separating Jews from the social and cultural life of their Christian contemporaries, a revolution was taking place in astronomy, in physics, and in the life sciences. This revolution was accompanied by a thorough diffusion of scientific knowledge accelerated through printed books; by a dramatic re-evaluation of what constitutes knowledge and the authority it commands in European culture, and by a radical transformation in the ways human beings view the cosmos and their place within it.

Did the ghetto barriers successfully filter out that cultural ambiance of the Christian majority? Did they engender a Jewish disengagement, a retrenchment, and a growing estrangement from European cultural developments in general and from scientific developments in particular? I would argue that the Jewish inhabitants of the ghettos were not only aware of scientific advances in their era, their internal cultural world was deeply stimulated by it. Italian Jews read the same books as other educated people; they produced their own medical and scientific literature in Hebrew and other languages; they had personal contact with a highly educated and secularized *converso* emigré population recently settled in or near their already crowded neighborhoods; and most importantly,

Title page from Azariah Figo's *Binah le-Ittim* (Venice, 1653). Courtesy of the Library of The Jewish Theological Seminary of America.

they sent their most gifted sons to study at the famous medical schools of Padua and other Italian cities, and enthusiastically welcomed them on their return. Indeed, the interaction of medicine and science with Jewish culture was an important ingredient in defining the new cultural land-scape of Jews living in Italy as well as in other areas of early modern Europe.[1]

No doubt the most intense interaction between Judaism and the new sciences was felt primarily by Jewish intellectuals, particularly rabbis and physicians. This situation fundamentally mirrored that of the Christian community, where science was nurtured essentially by political and Church leaders. To what extent, however, were scientific matters the concern of the many within the Jewish community rather than the few? The challenge of the cultural historian to measure a wider impact of ideas beyond the elite circles described by the extant sources is surely daunting. Our search through expository texts, scientific handbooks, bib-lical commentaries, and philosophical and kabbalistic writings suggests beyond a doubt a restricted reading public both sufficiently motivated and capable of reading and digesting such esoteric and complex materi-als. How many Hebrew readers could comprehend the long excurses on mathematics and astronomy in Joseph Delmedigo's *Elim*, or even the more simplified explanations of the heavens and the earth in David Gans's *Nehmad ve-Naim*? Even Tobias Cohen's or Jacob Zahalon's hand-books of contemporary medical practice, despite the intentions of the authors, could hardly be called "popular" compendia accessible to the "masses" in the same way that Dr. Spock's volumes on baby care are found in many households today. There is no evidence to suggest that such Hebrew textbooks were to be found readily in the libraries of many Jewish households.[2]

The voluminous literature of Jewish sermons preached in this era in every community might offer us the possibility of identifying a wider audience interested in scientific accomplishment. As Marc Saperstein has argued, "For scholars concerned with the development of Jewish thought, sermons containing philosophical or kabbalistic teachings re-moved from their technical sources and addressed to ordinary congrega-tions provide a crucial means for measuring the impact of ideas not merely on a small circle of original minds but also on a whole commu-nity."[3] The central place assigned questions of scientific import in the sermons of Christian preachers, especially in England, is well known and has allowed historians to draw distinct connections between the practi-tioners of science and both religious radicals and religious establish-ments.[4] No such undertaking has ever been attempted with respect to Jewish sermons, a source still relatively untapped in general, as Sap-erstein's discussion makes abundantly clear.

No doubt, sermons still tell us less than we would like to know. The printed sermon is never identical with its initial oral form. We have little sense of who heard the sermon, how the congregation responded to it, and whether the preacher actually succeeded in communicating his message.[5] Many printed sermons appear so convoluted and dense that one wonders how they could have been delivered in the first place, let alone understood by a laity, even a highly educated one.[6] And in the case of scientific subjects, what preacher would be moved even to introduce such topics when he was exclusively preoccupied with religious and spiritual matters?

I propose to examine the sermons of one Italian Jewish preacher hardly known for his scientific interests or accomplishments. At first glance, he appears to be the most unlikely candidate to teach "science" in the course of his religious homilies. But precisely because he appears to be so unlikely, his sermons are intriguing. And if I can make a case for the penetration of scientific attitudes into the domain of his seemingly traditional and even "antirational" teachings, the likelihood of finding other candidates with similarly shared attitudes seems promising.

My candidate is Azariah Figo, or Picho, the rabbi of Pisa and later Venice who lived from 1579 to 1647, during the height of the era of the Italian ghetto. Figo is primarily known through his two major printed works: his commentary *Giddulei Terumah* (Venice, 1643), an extensive commentary on the *Sefer ha-Terumot* of Samuel Sardi (1185/90–1255/56), the first comprehensive code of Jewish law devoted exclusively to civil and commercial law; and his collection of sermons entitled *Binah le-Ittim*, printed in Venice in 1648, a year after his death, and subsequently republished some fifty times.[7]

In recent years, Figo's claim to fame as a preacher (at least, the academic kind) is due, to a large extent, to the sympathetic portrait Israel Bettan painted of him in his classic work on Jewish preachers.[8] Bettan's choice of Figo among the hundreds of other preachers he might have chosen placed him immediately in the illustrious company of such luminaries as Isaac Arama, Jonathan Eybeshitz, and Figo's contemporary, Judah Moscato. But even without Bettan's stamp of approval, Figo undoubtedly commanded the attention of many readers of sermons, especially the Jews of Eastern Europe, where his volume was published on numerous occasions. Figo's sermons still evoke interest among traditional Jews, as evidenced by the attractive new edition published in Jerusalem as recently as 1989.[9]

Figo's image as a traditionalist preacher, antirationalist, and renouncer of "gentile wisdom" is certainly reinforced by Bettan's assessment of him as a man who "violently wrenched himself away from the intellectual pursuits of an earlier day and calmly retreated within the four ells of the law."[10] Bettan's portrait is virtually the same as the earlier descriptions by Abba Apfelbaum and Israel Zinberg.[11] The latter even labeled Figo a typical preacher of the old Franco-German type who wished to know nothing of secular matters. Harry Rabinowicz offered a similar conclusion regarding the fundamentalist image of Figo: "[He] leaned toward a strict interpretation of Jewish law. He opposed the establishment of a theater in the ghetto of Venice and criticized the members of his community for usury, flaunting their wealth, internecine wrangling, laxity in ritual observances, and sexual irregularities."[12] And finally, Isaac Barzilay devotes an entire chapter to Figo in his book on antirationalism in Jewish thought, underscoring Figo's critique of rationalism as a danger to Jewish uniqueness and his consciousness of exile and longing for national redemption.[13]

One important piece of information that appears to challenge this standard assessment of Figo's intellectual leanings is his close relationship with Leon Modena, the celebrated rabbi of Venice, the formidable critic of Kabbalah, the close colleague of the scientifically minded Simone Luzzatto and Joseph Delmedigo, and the rational expositor of Judaism among Christian intellectuals.[14] Figo composed a sonnet to adorn Modena's Hebrew collection of sermons published in 1602 and Modena actually listed him among his students.[15] Modena again enlisted him in 1624 to flatter his disciple Joseph Hamiz through poetry in celebration of Hamiz's graduation from the medical school of the University of Padua.[16] Figo's participation in this event not only suggests his ongoing relationship with the older Modena but also points to his own identification with Modena's strongly felt commitment to the study of medicine and the sciences among Italian Jews. The fact that Figo never refers to the kabbalah in any of his sermons (unlike those of his contemporary Judah Moscato)[17] also might suggest his tacit agreement with Modena's emphatic criticism of the place of mysticism in Jewish culture.[18] Figo's aversion to the kabbalah also stands in sharp contrast to Joseph Hamiz's later passionate embrace of it, Modena's disapproval notwithstanding.

The scholarly characterizations of Figo's spiritual proclivities mentioned above are based on a reading of his sermons and especially on his introduction to *Giddulei Terumah*, where he wrote:

> I went . . . after the vanity of a love of "the children of strangers," secular studies of various kinds. But immediately upon reaching the beginning of the harvests of the time of my adolescence [*ha-baharut*], the Redeemer had compassion on me . . . for the eyes of my ignorance were opened. . . so I beheld and recognized the shame of my youth whereby I had made the principal thing unimportant and the unimportant the principal thing. I was exceedingly ashamed that my hands were weakened from the essential words of the Torah, the study of the Gemarah and all related to it.[19]

By Figo's own account then, he had once involved himself in secular pursuits but soon realized their vanity and turned to the exclusive study of rabbinic sources. All of the historians mentioned above plainly accepted Figo's declaration at face value. They apparently never considered that such an acknowledgment may have constituted no more than a literary device in the sixteenth century and that such a standardized opening made good "political" sense in winning the favor of readers of an original commentary on a relatively unstudied legal text.[20] That traces of his earlier pursuits of the "children of strangers" were to be found in his later sermons was reluctantly acknowledged by both Bettan and Barzilay, particularly Figo's preoccupation with the problem of the essence and method of philosophy vis-à-vis Judaism, and his frequent use of medical analogies. Bettan even admitted that Figo's "grand renunciation" of his secular interests was made either too late or was not quite complete enough to affect the essential character of his preaching.[21] Commenting on Bettan's description, Yosef Yerushalmi considered this inner contradiction an "oscillation between attraction and resistance to gentile wisdom" typical of other thinkers of his day.[22]

Yet acknowledging the paradoxical co-existence of attraction and resistance to secular pursuits in the thought of a Jewish preacher is not the same thing as explaining it. To what degree Figo renounced his intellectual past and retreated into Talmudic studies remains an open question and invites a fresh reading of his sermons. Moreover, it behooves us to ask the questions of what actually constituted for him legitimate intellectual pursuits and what did not, what so offended him about certain rational involvements while he apparently approved of others, and how it is possible to understand Figo as a thoroughly stable and consistent religious thinker (as opposed to an oscillating one) with a clear pedagogic agenda for the Jewish constituency he served. In answering these queries about Figo's thinking, we are also offered the rare opportunity to characterize more broadly through his sermons the mental universe he shared with members of the Sephardic congregation of Venice who listened and may even have been moved to concur with the message of his skillfully presented homilies.

Let us begin our examination of Figo's sermons with one delivered in Venice on a Rosh ha-Shanah that happened to fall on the Sabbath. After quoting a midrashic passage about God's raising his voice on the New Year, he opens with the following remark:

> The human being was given intelligence by [God] . . . who bestowed him with great strength . . . until He filled his heart on numerous occasions with the capacity to make artificial inventions analogous to the actions of nature. Because of the weakness of matter or the deficiency in its prepara-

tion . . . man tries to correct and replace it by some discovery or invention drawn from his intelligence to the point where he will not appreciate what is lacking in nature. We have indeed noticed weak-eyed persons who, out of a deficiency of the matter of their eyes, were unable to see at a distance or [even] close up and were thus very nearsighted. Yet human intelligence was capable of creating eyeglasses placed on the bridge of the nose which aid in magnifying the strength of vision for each person, depending on what he lacks, either a little or a lot. This was similarly the case for the eyeglass with the hollow reed [i.e. the telescope] of Rabban Gamaliel [where it is stated] in chapter 4 of Eruvin: "Whereby as soon as I looked, it was as if we were in the midst of the [Sabbath] boundary.[23]

One wonders what a congregation of worshipers might have thought of so bizarre an opening for a sermon on the first day of the high holy days. But Figo apparently must have known and appreciated the mental universe of his audience, so he chose to begin with something familiar to them. He would introduce his lesson on Jewish religious values by espousing an ideal both he and his congregants apparently shared: that of the human mandate to replicate, to intervene, and to improve upon nature. The products of nature often appear deficient or unfinished; they invite human craftsmen and inventors to correct and improve God's handiwork. The examples of eyeglasses and the telescope (which Figo explicitly claims as an originally Jewish invention that long preceded the invention of Galileo) unambiguously place the rabbi's remarks in their seventeenth-century context of scientific invention and discovery, especially in the fields of optics and astronomy. By beginning in such an unconventional manner, Figo undoubtedly assumed that he would gain the attention of his audience more readily than by plunging into a more typical rabbinic discourse.

Figo pauses to illustrate his point about correcting inadequate vision with two illustrative biblical phrases.[24] But then he proceeds to enlarge upon his original insight: "One can draw analogies to other deficiencies like lameness and broken legs. Not only such cases but even that which is lacking from one's intelligence can be repaired as in the case of enhancing one's memory. One can make an effort to remember things as is well known from the invention of spatial memory [i.e. memory systems]."[25] He illustrates this invention by reference to Joseph's request to the cupbearer to remember him to Pharoah (Genesis 40:14). According to Figo, Joseph asked him "to engrave the impression in his imagination . . . so that he will conceive and relate the thought of Joseph to that of some well-known object that often occurs to him. By visualizing the object, he will remember Joseph." Of course, the cupbearer "did not employ [the technique] of spatial memory on his behalf. Accordingly he forgot to mention him to Pharoah."[26]

Where Figo is leading his curious listeners with this unusual slant on the familiar biblical story is now made clear:

> It follows that if by natural means related to material things, a person can try to correct his deficiencies by substitutions, by exchanging one thing for another, what might one do regarding spiritual things and with matters related to the perfection of one's soul dependent on the fulfillment of the divine commandments? With the latter example, a person is obliged, in any respect, to make signs and inventions in order not to forget them, as in the case of *ẓiẓit*, about which it is stated: "And you shall see them and remember."[27]

If the fringes on the prayer shawl can be perceived as a technique of enhancing memory, the need to create an artificial sign to remember the sound of the shofar on a Sabbath day when it cannot be sounded might logically follow: "God gave our hearts something to replace the sounds of the shofar on this holy day of Shabbat and Rosh Ha-Shanah . . . but the commandment was not completely abolished since the memory evoked by the biblical verses that speak about the shofar . . . are sufficient to cause an impression of replacement exemplifying the commandment of the sounding itself."[28]

Such a strategy of stimulating his listeners to conjure up the memory of the sound of the shofar on a day when they needed to hear it but could not, might be dismissed as nothing more than a clever rhetorical device if not for the fact that this preacher was taking for granted what we should not take for granted. What was familiar to and what appealed to his congregation was the notion of human beings gaining mastery over the natural world. The process of illustrating this notion by reference to the manufacture of eyeglasses and telescopes, to the creation of artificial limbs and memory systems, and finally to *ẓiẓit* and the biblical passages that recall the sound of the shofar might appear to us a long and convoluted manner of making his point, but to the mind of Figo, he was teaching his Jewish message by appealing directly to the immediate cultural context of his listeners. He was not teaching contemporary science to his coreligionists; he rather assumed that this knowledge was a commonplace in their experience with the world around them. As any wise preacher would do, Figo appropriated that experience to make his point about the religious message of the Jewish holy day. To us, his assumptions about what his congregants knew and liked offer some sense of the impact "scientific" modes of thinking were having on rabbi and congregation alike.

Both Bettan and Barzilay have already noticed Figo's frequent employment of medical analogies to convey his spiritual message. Barzilay concluded that such references do not warrant the inference of an intimate acquaintance with either science or philosophy; it should rather be attributed to "the impact of the spirit of the time."[29] Of course, as I already have argued, Figo's sermons do reveal a particular spirit or mentality, a scientific one, characteristic of the age in which he lived. But Figo's preoccupation with the functioning of the body and human illness in the light of his connection with Modena, Ḥamiẓ, and Padua might even suggest more: an informal or even formal contact with medical education. Be that as it may, it is apparent that he proudly displayed his medical knowledge and was fond of utilizing it when preaching.

A good example of Figo's use of medical analogies in preaching is offered in a sermon delivered on Shabbat Teshuvah. Figo opens by referring to the line in Jeremiah (3:14, 3:22): "Turn back O rebellious children, I will heal your afflictions."[30] The connection between repentance and healing in the verse and in a rabbinic elaboration on the verse offers Figo the appropriate opportunity to discant on the treatment of a sick patient. Following conventional Galenic therapy, Figo suggests two approaches to healing a person overtaken by the "the evil humour which sickens the body and brings a person to the danger of death": either by natural means "whereby he will fortify himself to fight with his illness and defeat it"; or by artificial means, that is, "evacuations and bloodletting and the like." Echoing his point in the sermon described above, he adds: "Thus a person will try by human industry to help nature and to gain what it lacks."[31]

The connection between healing the body and healing the soul is now made explicit: "This evacuation is none other than the essence of repentance that discharges and removes all sin and guilt and crime and restores a person to be healed." Just as there are two avenues of healing the body, there are likewise two avenues of repentance: "repentance from love whereby the strength of one's intelligence will grow by itself . . . or repentance out of fear which is truly an external healing."[32]

Although artifical healing is licit, it is inferior to natural healing in at least three ways. In the first place, artifical remedies are uncertain, since the physician can only estimate the proper dosage to be offered the patient. It often occurs that he misdiagnoses his patient, evacuating insufficiently or excessively and subsequently causing more harm than good. Secondly, artificial remedies such as bloodletting weaken the body and diminish the patient's strength, for good humours are eliminated along with the evil one. Finally, artificial remedies are usually administered under coercion, often causing pain or other discomfort. In contrast, natural evacuation transpires pleasantly without undo agitation. All three advantages of natural healing correlate with the realm of the spirit. A repentance out of love is always superior to one gained through the fear of chastisements. Like the doctor who misdiagnoses his patient and causes him harm, a person might repent solely out of fear of his punishment while ignoring the sin which is the principal cause of his moral deficiency. Just as evacuation might cause the elimination of good humours along with the bad, so too the removal of a bad quality by external means might also encourage a person to distance himself from a good one. Finally, repentance out of love is never accompanied by the stress and inner turmoil accompaning repentance out of fear.[33]

Figo adds a fourth advantage of natural over artificial healing to complete his analogy, an advantage more significant than all the others. Healing dependent upon external drugs is usually not totally effective; the bad humour is not completely removed and the illness eventually returns. This is not the case for natural healing where the body is cured conclusively. The distinction between voluntary repentance and that effectuated under duress can also be correlated in this respect.[34]

In other sermons, Figo similarly favors such comparisons between moral and medical therapy. In one place, he differentiates between an immoral person who can still repent with one whose condition is hopeless by drawing the analogy of the patient who still feels pain, even excruciating pain, and the one whose limb is dead, feels nothing, and whose condition is hopeless.[35] In another place, he enumerates four steps in maintaining a good regimen of health and demonstrates how the prevention of moral sin can virtually be described by the same prescriptions.[36] Once he compares the gradual increase of dosage to a sick patient to the gradual educational process of teaching Torah.[37] He even expresses his uncertainty about whether to make a funeral oration long or short by reference to an analogy of a doctor who finds contradictory symptoms in his patient, making his diagnosis extremely difficult.[38] None of these analogies exhibits highly specialized knowledge of medicine or the biological sciences. They are simple and easy to comprehend, as they should be for the forum in which they were meant to be presented. They do reveal, however, an intimate sense of the actual practice of medicine, the authentic dilemmas the doctor daily faces, the uncertainty of his cures, the dangers and inadequacies of standard medical treatment. They suggest in their entirety the perspective of a person very close to the medical profession, one who fully appreciates the meaningful connection between the medical and rabbinic professions, indeed a physician who also happens to be a doctor, a most common coincidence within the Italian Jewish community Azariah Figo served.[39]

Isaac Barzilay has correctly pointed out Figo's constant emphasis on the dangers of rationalism and its corrosive character in undermining the Jewish community's faith in its unique revelation.[40] In a fully conventional way, Figo seeks to demonstrate the inadequacy of human reason in contrast to revealed truth on two counts: it is inaccessible to the majority of people and it lacks moral concern. In the first place, since only the few have the capacity to acquire natural knowledge, a belief in miracles and divine intervention in the natural order is necessary since miraculous occurences impress the uninitiated more than does the mere uniformity and regularity of nature.[41] And in the second place, the Gentile astronomer who searches the heavens does so merely to fulfill the needs of his intellectual appetite, not his moral or spiritual one.[42] For the Jew who masters astronomy, his knowledge leads him to perform divine commandments and to serve his Creator. Such arguments suggest for Barzilay a fundamental antirationalism, what he perceives as part of a newly emerging mentality of a kind of "Jewish nationalism" in the late sixteenth century.[43]

There is no doubt that Figo's utterances reflect an antagonism to philosophical speculation and a deep conviction in the superiority of the revealed wisdom of the Jewish sages (though not necessarily kabbalistic ones). But Barzilay's analysis remains deficient in ignoring the language and conceptual underpinnings of Figo's defense of Jewish revelation and in failing to appreciate the actual scientific context informing his criticisms of philosophy.

Figo's sermon on the second day of Shavuot offers a most convincing illustration of the preacher's underlying assumptions.[44] His theme is precisely the difference between the knowledge of the philosophers and the revelatory experience of Sinai. "It is well known," he writes, "that the sciences based on foundations of learning and built on rational assumptions are dangerous and unreliable since human intelligence is limited, small, and weak." It is liable to error and omission and lacks the assurance of complete truth. In contrast, "those things to which the senses and experience testify are truthful; no doubt will arise regarding them or fear of error or false knowledge. . . . Regarding the latter, the sage in Ecclesiastes [7:23] stated: 'All this I tested with wisdom: I thought I could fathom it but it eludes me.' " Figo interprets the line to mean that all that was acquired "through experience which I gained through the experiential faculty of knowledge" can be known truthfully. But "theoretical knowledge denuded of sensual knowledge is certainly far from me."[45] To a student of seventeenth-century culture, the distinction is a commonplace: that of the Scholastic philosopher versus that of the natural philosopher and the empiricist. One can only know the heavens and the earth by observation and experiment, not by theoretically constructing their apparent reality in the mind's imagination.

For Figo the epistemological basis of the new empiricism is equivalent to that of the Torah: "The Divine Wisdom [God] understood that the holy Torah would not be accepted by the Israelite nation on the basis of knowledge stemming from investigation and research . . . but rather with things felt and familiar through seeing and hearing. . . . No man can acquire an idea except by way of the senses . . . the Torah gives strength and vitality to what the senses acquire."[46]

Figo's argument regarding the superiority of the experiential knowledge of the Torah versus the theoretical and inevitably finite knowledge of the philosophers patently echoes Judah Halevi's medieval critique of Spanish Jewish philosophy and that of even earlier thinkers.[47] Equally unoriginal is his accompanying argument that while knowledge of the Torah is complete and stands on its own, that of the secular sciences requires mutual dependencies:

> Someone cannot be an astronomer without prior knowledge of mechanics and mathematics, nor a doctor without prior knowledge of natural philosophy. Nor can a person acquire any knowledge unless he is accustomed to logic. . . . It happens that one [field] justifies and prepares for the other, for without the prior one, the latter would have no reality. But our Torah does not require any other wisdom nor any external knowledge for everything is in her; she guides and informs herself with her own conclusions, principles, and ideas.[48]

I have quoted at length in order to propose that Figo was more than a mere borrower of Halevi's classical anti-philosophical arguments. His description of the interrelatedness of all sciences betrays an unmistakable familiarity with them. He leaves the distinct impression that he knows what it takes to be an astronomer or a physician and that he had studied the fields he enumerates. More importantly, while he argues for the insufficiency of the sciences, he clearly does not dismiss their validity altogether. What he finds reprehensible is a knowledge lacking all empirical foundations, based solely on intellectual constructs, and arrogantly claiming to perceive of reality and of the truth. It is no mere coincidence that the language of "hearing and seeing" of the Torah and the rabbis was also the hallmark of his own era, the rallying cry of a Galileo or a Bacon or of other virtuosi. I would contend that he was fully aware of its seventeenth-century associations when he evoked it, and, more importantly, the convergence of its traditional and modern meanings resonated unmistakably in the ears of his listeners. By couching his advocacy of Torah learning in the contemporary language of experience and empiricism, he was clinching his argument for the relevance of Judaism in a way Halevi could never have achieved. In Halevi's time, such language was surely perceived as anti-intellectual, fundamentalist, and conservative. To an audience fully attuned to seeing and hearing rather than cogitating, his defence of Judaism surely must have sounded modern and up-to-date.

A succinct description of Azariah Figo's intellectual style based on a correct reading of his sermons would thus emphasize a clear and consistent understanding of the relationship between Judaism and the larger cultural space he inhabited. Figo did not oscillate whimsically between rationalism and irrationalism, between Talmud study and that of the secular sciences. His sermons, written after his apparent renunciation of the sciences in the introduction to his halakhic commentary, betray a man supremely cognizant and confident of his knowledge of medicine and the sciences. They are unmistakably part of his universe of discourse and that of his congregants, and he boldly appropriates their conceptual framework in teaching Judaism. Figo surely deplored the useless speculations of philosophers of the old Scholastic style and particularly their pretensions to understand the world better than those who place their trust in divine revelation. But such criticism was not synonymous with antirationalism. For him and for those he addressed, the value of empiricism, a firm reliance on the senses, along with the human mandate to create and improve upon nature were to be taken for granted.

And Figo's position, a kind of "mitigated or constructive scepticism,"[49] was becoming extremely fashionable among Jews and Christians alike by the middle of the seventeenth century. In the new discourse of pious science as articulated by such luminaries as Mersenne and Gassendi,[50] science was no more than a hypothetical system based solely on experience and verified only through experience. It never claimed possession of absolute truth, only a mere description of the appearance of things, and subsequently it never competed with the sacred indubitable verities of divine revelation. By separating physics from Scholastic metaphysics, and by establishing a legitimate "division of labor" between the natural sciences and Judaism, Figo had located a formidable argument through which to defend intellectually the legitimacy of Jewish revelation in his day. By incorporating it skillfully into the rhetorical style of his public sermons, he had apparently discovered an effective strategy to project the compelling image of "a wise and discerning people"[51] in the minds and hearts of his discriminating congregation.

NOTES

1. On this subject, see David B. Ruderman, "The Impact of Science on Jewish Culture and Society in Venice (With Special Reference to Graduates of Padua's Medical School)," *Gli ebrei e Venezia secoli XIV–XVIII*, ed. G. Cozzi (Milan, 1987), pp. 417–448, reprinted in David B. Ruderman, ed., *Essential Papers on Jewish Culture in Renaissance and Baroque Italy* (New York, 1992); idem, *Science, Medicine, and Jewish Culture in Early Modern Europe*, Spiegel Lecture in European Jewish History (Tel Aviv, 1987); idem, *Kabbalah, Magic, and Science: The Cultural Universe of a Sixteenth-Century Jewish Physician* (Cambridge, Mass., 1988); idem, "The Lan-

guage of Science as the Language of Faith: An Aspect of Italian Jewish Thought in the Seventeenth and Eighteenth Centuries," *Festschrift in Honor of Shlomo Simonsohn*, forthcoming. I am presently preparing a book-length study on the place of medicine and the sciences in early modern Jewish culture. For a recent overview of the cultural setting of science in the Christian community, with up-to-date bibligraphical references, see Margaret C. Jacob, *The Cultural Meaning of the Scientific Revolution* (Philadelphia, 1988).

2. All of these Hebrew works are discussed in Ruderman, *Science, Medicine, and Jewish Culture*, and idem, "The Impact of Science."

3. Marc Saperstein, *Jewish Preaching 1200–1800: An Anthology* (New Haven, London, 1989), p. 1, and see his essay in this volume.

4. See, for example, Richard S. Westfall, *Science and Religion in Seventeenth-Century England* (New Haven, 1958); Margaret C. Jacob, *The Newtonians and the English Revolution* (Ithaca, N.Y., 1976); Charles Webster, *The Great Instauration: Science, Medicine, and Reform* (London, 1975).

5. These issues are discussed by Saperstein in the introduction to his anthology (note 3), as well as throughout the essays in this volume.

6. This is especially the case for Figo's contemporary, Judah Moscato. See Moshe Idel's judgment on his corpus in his essay in this volume.

7. A number of Figo's sermons were published in Samuel Aboab's *Devar Shemuel* (Venice, 1702).

8. Israel Bettan, *Studies in Jewish Preaching* (Cincinnati, 1939), pp. 227–272.

9. *Sefer Binah le-Ittim* (Jerusalem, 1989), 2 vols. My citations below are from this volume. It is worth noting that among all the preachers in this volume, Figo was surely the most popular. While the more colorful and prolific Leon Modena published a single volume of sermons that was never reprinted after his death, Figo's own collection went through some fifty editions, as we have indicated. Such extraordinary popularity as a preacher, particularly among Eastern European Jews, surely requires a historical explanation. Part of the answer is obviously related to the elegant simplicity of Figo's style, the relevance of his ethical messages, and his effective affirmation of traditional Jewish concerns. Part of his effectiveness and popularity might also be due to the language of science he adduces in conveying his message. Surely, the message could have resonated among Eastern European congregations of the nineteenth century as well as among Italian ones in the seventeenth century.

10. Bettan, p. 228.

11. Abba Apfelbaum, *Rabbi Azariah Ficcio [Fichio]* (Drohobycz, 1907); Israel Zinberg, *A History of Jewish Literature* (Cincinnati, New York, 1974), vol. 4, pp. 175–177.

12. Harry Rabinowicz, "Figo, Azariah," *Encyclopaedia Judaica*, vol. 6, p. 1274. See also his *Portraits of Jewish Preachers* [Hebrew] (Jerusalem, 1967), pp. 150–158.

13. Isaac Barzilay, *Between Reason and Faith: Anti-Rationalism in Italian Jewish Thought 1250–1650* (The Hague, Paris, 1967), pp. 192–209.

14. On Modena, see most recently, Mark Cohen, ed. and trans., *The Autobiography of a Seventeenth-Century Venetian Rabbi: Leon Modena's Life of Judah* (Princeton, 1988).

15. See Apfelbaum, pp. 87–91.
16. See Nehemiah S. Leibowitz, *Seridim Mikitvei ha-Philosof ha-Rofe ve-ha-Mekubbal R. Yosef Ḥamiẓ* (Jerusalem, 1937), pp. 50–51.
17. On the use of kabbalah among other contemporaries, see Elliott Horowitz's essay in this volume.
18. On Modena's attitude to the kabbalah, see Moshe Idel, "Differing Conceptions of Kabbalah in the Early 17th Century," *Jewish Thought in the Seventeenth Century*, ed. Isadore Twersky and Bernard Septimus (Cambridge, Mass., 1987), pp. 137–200. On the place of kabbalah in Moscato's sermons, see Idel's chapter in this volume.
19. Azariah Figo, *Sefer Giddulei Terumah* (Zolkiev, 1809), p. 3b.
20. Compare, for example, the introduction to Abraham Portaleone's *Shilte Gibburim* (Mantua, 1612), where he similarly acknowledges and renounces his youthful sins in studying the secular sciences. Yet any reader of his book will readily notice that this renunciation was hardly complete!
21. Bettan, p. 230.
22. Yosef Hayyim Yerushalmi, *From Spanish Court to Italian Ghetto* (New York, 1971), pp. 373–374.
23. *Binah le-Ittim*, vol. 1, pp. 72–73. On the "telescope" of Rabban Gamaliel and Galileo, see Ruderman, *Kabbalah, Magic, and Science*, p. 98. Figo refers to Babylonian Talmud Eruvin, 43b.
24. *Binah le-Ittim*, p. 73
25. Ibid. On memory systems in the sixteenth century, see Jonathan Spense, *The Memory Palace of Matteo Ricchi* (New York, 1987).
26. *Binah le-Ittim*, p. 73.
27. Ibid., pp. 73–74.
28. Ibid., p. 75.
29. Barzilay, p. 193.
30. *Binah le-Ittim*, p. 81.
31. Ibid., pp. 81–82.
32. Ibid., p. 82.
33. Ibid., pp. 84–87.
34. Ibid., p. 87.
35. Ibid., I, pp. 90–105.
36. Ibid., I, pp. 105–124.
37. Ibid., II, pp. 16–23.
38. Ibid., II, pp. 388–397.
39. On this, see the references in note 1.
40. Barzilay, especially pp. 195–202.
41. See especially *Binah le-Ittim*, vol. 1, pp. 267–275.
42. Ibid., vol. 2, pp. 110–127, especially 110–114.
43. Barzilay, p. 197.
44. Ibid., vol. 2, pp. 85–94.
45. Ibid., p. 85.
46. Ibid., pp. 85, 88.
47. See, for example, Judah Halevi, *Sefer Ha-Kuzari*, bk. 2, pp. 56, 63–66; bk. 3, p. 53, bk. 4, pp. 24–25.

48. Ibid., p. 88.

49. The term is Richard Popkin's as discussed in his *The History of Scepticism from Erasmus to Spinoza* (Berkeley, Los Angeles, London, 1979), chap. 7.

50. Besides Popkin's work cited above, see most recently Peter Dear, *Mersenne and the Learning of the Schools* (Ithaca, London, 1988), and Lynn Sumida Joy, *Gassendi the Atomist: Advocate of History in an Age of Science* (Cambridge, 1987). See Robert Bonfil's similar conclusions regarding Judah Del Bene in his essay in this volume.

51. See Deuteronomy 4:6.

SIX

Preaching in the Venetian Ghetto: The Sermons of Leon Modena

Joanna Weinberg

I.

The personality of the Venetian Rabbi Leon (Judah Aryeh) Modena (1571–1648) has intrigued scholars both past and present.[1] Widely divergent evaluations have been proffered of the man and his work. His *Weltanschauung* has been variously described as medieval, Renaissance, and baroque;[2] he has been called a hypocrite and a precursor of the reformers,[3] while in the most recent assessment, an impassioned plea has been made to appreciate Modena as a genuine defender of rabbinic tradition and an accomplished scholar in a wide range of subjects including the Christian Scriptures and Italian literature.[4]

That scholars of repute have reached diametrically opposed conclusions as to the historical period reflected in Modena's writings seems to indicate that these categories are too vague to be useful and do not enhance the reader's understanding of the subject. The purpose of this chapter is to discuss and analyze Modena's mode of preaching. Rather than apply such designations as medieval or baroque to his sermons, I shall demonstrate how a Jew living in the ghetto in Counter-Reformation Italy was able to structure his sermons according to Christian specifications while their content remained predominantly Jewish in theme and source.

Modena's sermons won him paeans of praise from Jews and Christians. He himself, in his own inimitable fashion, unabashedly acknowledged that he was deserving of such a reputation. As he writes in his Autobiography, "And even though for more than twenty years I have . . . preached in three or four places each Sabbath, this holy community

חלק ראשון

מספר
מדבר יהודה
מדרשות
יהודה אריה
בכהר יצחק ממודינא זל

ונם מס הן דרשות׳ מס תהיינה
דרושות ׳ מולי תהיינה כדרמות ו
נדפס בויניציאה ע׳ דניאל
זאנוטי וככיקי סוף ספת
הי׳חודה אריה מודיגא

לפק

עמ׳ עש׳ו

Con licentia de i Superiori

Title page from Leon Modena's *Midbar Yehudah* (Venice, 1602). Courtesy of the Library of The Jewish Theological Seminary of America.

has not grown tired of me, nor had its fill of my sermons. . . ."[5] Modena may have perfected the art of pulpit oratory; the task of the scholar, however, is to evaluate the sermons in their literary form. This task has been undertaken by a variety of scholars. That same diversity of approach which marks scholarly treatment of Modena's entire literary legacy to which I alluded above is also conspicuous in the different studies of his homiletical productions. In 1950, Ellis Rivkin wrote an article briefly describing the subject of Modena's sermons, pointing to their specifically Jewish resonances and the stimulating approach of the author to familiar theological issues.[6] According to Rivkin, Modena attached central importance to the form of the sermon which was "an end in itself." In other words, Modena was a "Jewish preacher of the Baroque." A more detailed investigation was provided in 1972 by Israel Rosenzweig in his book entitled *A Jewish Thinker at the End of the Renaissance.*[7] Rosenzweig attempted to analyze Modena's sermons in their historical context. He argued that Modena was grappling with the reality of his time while seemingly addressing himself to traditional theological themes such as exile, covenant, repentance, and redemption. Rosenzweig found allusions to Christian (and particularly Protestant) doctrine[8] and detected in Modena's treatment of penitents reference to *conversos* who had reverted to Judaism.[9] The oft-mooted view of Modena's hypocrisy and his criticism of rabbinic Judaism is perhaps reflected in Rosenzweig's opinion that Modena often veiled his true opinion by means of ambiguous imagery and phraseology. Modena raised intractable problems regarding the death of the righteous or the prolongation of the exile, but by means of consummate homiletical skills he erased the sting from these distressing subjects.

Among his various discussions of Jewish sermons, Joseph Dan also touched on the subject of Modena's rhetorical work.[10] Dan suggested that some of Modena's sermons were written with other preachers in mind. In other words, those sermons in which Modena appeared not to be expressing his own view on the subject under discussion and which were composed with a clear schematic structure were intended as model sermons that could be used by other preachers for specific festivals or occasions.

As may be seen from these brief summaries, interpretation of Modena's sermons, whether in regard to their structure or historical significance, is still at a preliminary stage. The documentation and analysis that is provided in the ensuing pages should facilitate a more precise reading of Modena's sermons.

"For of the three elements in speech-making—speaker, subject, and person addressed—it is the last one, the hearer, that determines the speech's end and object."[11] This recommendation of Aristotle was one which Modena certainly endorsed. On several occasions, he stressed the importance of adapting the sermon to the intellectual capabilities of the audience. At the same time, he was conscious of the difficulties attendant upon satisfying all his listeners.[12] The greater part of Modena's preaching career was spent in Venice, where Ashkenazi, Italian, Sephardi (both Levantine and Ponentine) Jews lived in close proximity to each other, while maintaining their separate rites and praying in separate synagogues.[13] Over the course of the years, Modena addressed all sectors of the Venetian community and was the main preacher in the Great Ashkenazi syngagoue and in the academy of Kalonymus Belgrado.[14] Such was his reputation that "many esteemed friars, priests and noblemen" also came to listen to his sermons.[15] Modena's powers of communication and sensitivity to his audience are perhaps best illustrated by his introduction to the sermon which he delivered in the Sephardi synagogue on the Sabbath preceding the wedding day of his friend Abraham Lombroso.[16] Modena prefaces his sermon with the statement that every action must match the subject, time, and place. Implicit in these words is the message that as an outsider, an Italian Jew, he was to deliver a sermon which would suit the Sephardi context into which he had entered. The Scriptural pericope for that Sabbath was the story of Noah. Having described the Jewish people in exile in Noachian terms—they are enclosed in the ark of the exile and are tossed over the waters until the final exodus—Modena states: "for various reasons, your holy community bears more affinity to Noah than any other sector of the Jewish people." Modena does not go on to enlarge on the "various reasons." What he seems to be insinuating is that the Sephardim, who had suffered from the inquisition and had been exiled from place to place, are like Noah, righteous survivors, on whose merit the world depends. By means of such an introduction, Modena simultaneously communicated his sympathy for the community he was addressing and engaged their attention.

Modena bequeathed only a small sample of his sermons to posterity. Of the four hundred sermons he claimed to have delivered, only twenty-one were brought to print.[17] On the basis of Hebrew outline notes, Modena reconstructed some of the sermons he had delivered in Italian in the first ten years of his preaching career (1593–1602), and working under pressure, submitted them in a Hebrew version to the printer over the course of six weeks. The work was published in Venice in 1602.[18] He entitled the collection *Midbar Yehudah* (*The Wilderness of Judah*) or *Mi-Debar Yehudah* (*From the Words of Judah*) "because these are the words which I spoke in the congregations and because I am living today scorched in the wilderness, bereft of all goodness, waiting for God to bestow His favour on me, and also because I know that most of it is dry and waste like a wilderness. . . ."[19] In fact, the introduction to the collection reveals that apart from financial considerations, a neurotic obsession with his posterity, and jealousy of other preachers, combined with an assurance about his own skills as a preacher, prompted Modena to the publication of the *Midbar Yehudah*.[20]

To the great benefit of the scholar, Modena has left fairly full descriptions of his method and aims in composing sermons and of his own conception of the role of the preacher. This invaluable information may be extracted from his introduction to the *Midbar Yehudah*, from the first sermon in the collection, and from various letters and autobiographical remarks dispersed among his other works. In the light of this evidence, and following the classical rhetorical triad of *ordo* (arrangement), *facundia* (style) and *res* (subject-matter), we shall analyze Modena's sermons in regard to structure, style, and subject-matter (including sources) and then, using one sermon as a test-case, examine how the theoretical principles become transposed into the final product.

The clearest statement regarding the structure of the sermons is to be found in a letter which Modena wrote to his teacher Samuel Archivolti.[21] He claims:

> The sermons blaze a truly new path, for I have made them a blending of the Christian sermon and the traditional Jewish homily. After the verse from the Torah [*nose*] and the rabbinic statement [*ma'amar*] comes a brief introduction which they [i.e. the Christians] call *prologhino*. Then comes the first part of the sermon and then the second part, followed by an explanation of the *nose* and *ma'amar*. At the end there is a recapitulation of the entire sermon called *epilogo*[22] and finally, a petitionary prayer in the accustomed manner. This is the structure of every sermon. There is no section without some biblical verse or rabbinic statement and the sermon is developed by means of suitable connections based on the rules of oratory and *retorica*.

In this letter, Modena describes himself as an innovator and claims that his originality consists in his blending of Christian and Jewish modes of composition. As has been demonstrated by Marc Saperstein in his recent book on preaching, certain norms and conventions governing the structure of Jewish sermons were introduced from the second half of the fifteenth century onwards.[23] In particular, the use of the Scriptural verse (*nose*) and the rabbinic text (*ma'amar*) at the beginning of the sermon became a standard way of beginning a sermon. An introduction to the sermon which contained justification of the sermon was sometimes employed. As regards the development of the sermon, Saperstein points to two different forms: the homiletical model, which usually lacked structural unity; and the *derush*, where the sermon was constructed around one specific conceptual problem and which would also contain exegesis of various Scriptural and rabbinic passages. It does seem, however, that there were no set conventions for the actual development of the theme. At first glance, Modena's sermons would seem to belong to the second category of *derush*. Nevertheless, his reference to the structure of Christian sermons, which is made explicit by his use of the terms *prologhino* and *epilogo*, clearly indicates that apart from the use of the *nose* and *ma'amar*, the main structure of his sermons followed a convention used by Christian preachers. Modena laid great importance on the art of communication, and a clear structure facilitated communication. In the absence of specific Jewish guidelines, he chose to compose his sermons on Christian models. Fortunately, it is possible to identify the specific model he followed and, as will be shown, it constitutes a significant source for understanding not only the structure of Modena's sermons, but also his role as preacher at the end of the sixteenth and beginning of the seventeenth century.

An inventory of the goods and Hebrew and vernacular books of which Modena was in possession was drawn up after his death in 1648.[24] The name Panigarola and a work *Modo di compor prediche* (*How to Compose Sermons*) figure under the list of vernacular books.[25] Francesco Panigarola (1548–1594) was the Bishop of Asti, and a prolific writer, poet, and popular preacher. Panigarola was a respected member of the Catholic establishment and a staunch defender of Tridentine doctrine. While there were numerous Christian preachers and theorists of preaching in Modena's time, Francesco Panigarola was reputed to be a "Demosthenes Christianus," one of the most distinguished and popular preachers of the sixteenth century, whose style has been characterized as anticipating baroque mannerism.[26] It may be more than coincidental that similar stories are told about Panigarola and Modena in regard to early manifestations of preaching talent. It is told that the young Panigarola was able to repeat by heart a sermon he had heard with such grace and facility that his teacher Cornelio Musso predicted that he would become a famous preacher.[27] Similarly, Modena narrates in his Autobiography that when he was nine years old his teacher Hezekiah Finzi predicted that "this boy will become a preacher to the Jews for from his manner it is clear that he will be fruitful in preaching."[28] Panigarola's sermons were translated from Italian into Latin and French and were reprinted several times.[29] He published an annotated edition of the classical rhetorical work *On style*, attributed to Demetrius of Phalerum, in which he incorporated a discourse on ecclesiastical preaching and its relation to classical oratory.[30] This subject had become a crucial issue once the Council of Trent had set down official guidelines on preaching. Preachers like Panigarola trained in both the "secular" and "sacred" were concerned to construct a theory of preaching which did justice to both camps.[31] Panigarola's small work on preaching that was in Modena's library also contained a

short tract on the art of memory.[32] (It is interesting to note that Modena
was also to write a tract on memory, the *Leb ha-Aryeh*, in 1611.) That
Modena read the books in his library, and Panigarola's works in particular, is confirmed by a close examination of Panigarola's tract on how to
compose a sermon. In fact, Modena's use of one word, *prologhino*, lends
even more support to such a claim, for according to Battaglia, Panigarola's works constitute the first attestation of this word.[33]

Panigarola's tract was intended for use by Franciscan novices. Nevertheless, its general guidelines could certainly be adapted to religious sermons of any description. Modena, as will be shown, almost invariably
constructed his sermons along the lines set down by Panigarola. The
amalgamation of Jewish and Christian forms provided Modena with a
perfect medium for composing sermons that, despite their rhetorical
ornamentation and exegetical meanderings, preserved a clear structural
and conceptual unity.

The stylistic features of Modena's sermons were conceived in relation
to his perception of the role of the preacher. In the *prologhino* to the first
sermon in the *Midbar Yehudah*, Modena describes the unenviable task of
the preacher who must cater to the differing intellectual expectations of
his audience.[34] He writes:

> If he [the preacher] soars like an eagle and speaks of the great and pro-
> found mysteries of wisdom, his proud speech will not sit well with the
> badgers who are weak in the deeper meaning of the Torah . . . for they
> will not know what he is talking about. But if he should speak at a low level,
> simply and plainly, the learned will turn their backs on him and say, "What
> does he think he is teaching us?" If he speaks softly and fails to reach the
> very pinnacle of rhetoric and eloquence, they grow tired of hearing him.
> . . . Thus whoever preaches in public is looking for trouble, kindling con-
> tention.[35]

Modena therefore sought to find a compromise between the highly
polished and mannered style of the Mantuan Rabbi Judah Moscato,
which he claims was very unpopular, and the simpler language of the
majority of Levantine and Ashkenazi Rabbis.[36] Modena thus describes
three "genera dicendi" that in classical terms would correspond to the
genus sublime, the *genus mediocre* and the *genus humile*.[37] Modena's invective
against current modes of preaching reaches rhetorical extremes in his
highly mannered introduction to the *Midbar Yehudah*.[38] He pours scorn
on overly ambitious preachers who are insensitive to the niceties of Talmudic discussion, but use "Aristotle and company" as a means to gain
a reputation. They propagate useless ideas which encourage others to
entertain misguided views about rabbinic tradition. Preachers of this
kind, he alleges, have caused the current widespread disaffection with

sermons and preachers. The effective preacher must possess two skills: the ability to conceptualize (*hokhmat ha-iyyun*) and the homiletical art (*hokhmat ha-derush*).[39] (By *hokhmat ha-iyyun*, Modena appears to refer to lucid interpretation of any kind.)[40] Preachers should emulate the example of the rabbis of the Mishnah and Talmud (and also some of the more recent preachers) who had a fine grasp of complex issues, but were models of clarity when they expounded in public.

Modena may have been encouraging emulation of the rabbis when he selected the art of wisdom and the art of eloquence as the two-fold banner of the effective preacher. But he was also consciously or not expressing the humanist ideal which set the highest store by the combination of wisdom and eloquence. His formulation may also reflect a trend in Jewish preaching of the late sixteenth-century in Italy detected by Bonfil, in which the overtly philosophical sermon was replaced by a more eclectic sermon in which allegorical and kabbalistic interpretation of the aggadot untrammelled by technical vocabulary was employed in order to deepen the religious consciousness of the public.[41]

Modena stressed that the purpose of his sermons was to instill in his listeners the fear of God, instruct them in ethics and beliefs, and offer explanations of the precepts of the Torah. He suggested that "valuable, useful, and pleasurable" (*tob, mo'il, areb*) would be appropriate designations of some of his sermons. The selection of these three adjectives is significant. In his tract on preaching, Panigarola discusses the three classical genres of oratory—the deliberative, judicial, and demonstrative (epideictic)—and adds a fourth genre, the didactic. He argues that depending on the nature of the sermon, any one or a mixture of these categories may be implemented. Recently O'Malley has argued that during the Renaissance, the epideictic genre was adopted by orators at the Papal court.[42] The medieval thematic sermon had emphasized teaching; now the demonstrative oration sought to inspire love and fear of God and to move and delight the listener. O'Malley also discussed Melanchthon's treatise on preaching which influenced both Catholic and Protestant theorists of preaching.[43] Melanchthon introduced the didactic genre (*genus didascalicum*) used in dialectic and applied it to rhetoric. Melancthon formulated three other genres of rhetoric: the *didascalicum*, which teaches true doctrine, the *epitrepticum*, which exhorts to faith, and the *paraneticum*, which exhorts to good morals. While it is difficult to classify Modena's sermons dogmatically into any one of the genres described above, it does seem that his use of the three adjectives, "valuable, useful, and entertaining," and his express aim to teach fear of God and ethical qualities and to explain the reasons for the precepts of the Torah, combines some of the features of the epideictic genre with that of Melanchthon's categories. Moreover, Modena expressly states that his purpose is neither to castigate

nor to set himself apart from his audience. While such a statement is
clearly a tactical ploy to win the confidence of his audience, it also suggests the purpose of epideictic oratory, which seeks to impress ideas on
the audience without explicit intention to teach or to spur to action.

From classical times, theorists of rhetoric compared oratory to the
visual arts, and saw a relation between epideictic oratory and painting
and sculpture.[44] It was commonplace for Renaissance orators to compare
themselves to painters. This commonplace appears in the first sermon
of the *Midbar Yehudah*, albeit with an original twist. Modena quotes a
famous passage from tractate Berakhot (10a) in the Babylonian Talmud:

> Come and see how different is the capacity of human beings from that of
> the Holy One Blessed be He. A human being has the capacity to draw a
> figure on a wall, but he is unable to invest it with breath and spirit, bowels
> and intestines. But the Holy One Blessed be He shapes one form within
> another and invests it with breath and spirit, bowels and intestines. That is
> what Hannah meant when she said, "There is none as holy as the Lord,
> neither is there a rock [zur] like our God" [1 Sam. 2:2]. There is no painter
> [zayar] like our God.

Modena's interpretation of this aggadah follows the pattern he uses
throughout his sermons. Its logical consistency is examined and questioned. Superficial problems are raised and then rejected on the basis of
a more probing examination of the underlying message of the text. Modena wonders why the author of the aggadah used the strange analogy
of the wall-artist. He suggests that the choice was dictated by the author's
wish to convey both the art of the painter and that of the sculptor. In
particular, he questions the validity of the final statement in which, by
means of a play on the words "rock" and "painter," God is described
as the ideal painter.[45] At first glance, the aggadah would appear to be
referring to God's unique powers as creator. He argues that the comparison between God and human beings only becomes valid if the analogy is
indeed being drawn between the artistic faculties of God and those of
humans. He thus argues that the intention of the aggadah is to stress the
fallible qualities of human artists who are not even able to imitate nature,
in this case, the human body, with any degree of verisimilitude. Having
interpreted the aggadah as an illustration of God's mastery of the plastic
arts, Modena then draws an analogy between the painter and the writer,
and the sculptor and the preacher. The painter and the writer can erase
any defect in their painting or writing. The sculptor, on the other hand,
cannot undo any blemish which appears once the stone has been chiseled.
Similarly, the speaker cannot bite back the words once he has uttered
them. Only God has perfect control over the stone and the pen. With
the rabbinic text as his basic proof text, Modena appears to have adopted

the Renaissance idea of the preacher as artist, and given it a novel application. The work of the preacher consists in *imitatio dei*. By means of a disingenuous method of preempting any criticism of his shortcomings as preacher, Modena expresses the vulnerability of the preacher who takes on the awesome task of *imitatio dei*, but can never ensure the perfection of his art.

Modena contrasted his style with that of one of the most distinguished preachers of his generation, Judah Moscato. One of the notable features of Moscato's sermons is his extensive citation of non-Jewish sources; the paucity of references to non-Jewish authors is one of the most distinctive features of Modena's sermons. The difference between the two preachers in this regard is particularly noteworthy given that Modena published his sermons only fourteen years after Moscato's sermons appeared in print. It was not for lack of familiarity with secular sources that Modena eschewed non-Jewish references in his sermons. His other works bear evidence of his wide knowledge of Christian texts. On the few occasions that he does cite a non-Jewish author or a story he has read in a secular source, he usually does not give the name of the author, even when it is clearly a well-known writer such as Aristotle or Livy. It would seem that Modena's highly developed sensitivity to the preacher's task dictated his use of sources. One of the techniques of humanist rhetoricians was to avoid citations of classical sources *in extenso*. This was regarded as one of the characteristics of a refined and polished style. Naturally, the non-Jewish references did not have the same value for Modena as did the classical sources for the humanists. Nevertheless, a similar concern for the elegance of the sermon prompted Modena to avoid explicit allusions to extraneous works. The main body of his sermons was concerned with interpretation of the rabbinic aggadot and midrashim. Modena ensured that the references to non-Jewish texts should not interrupt the flow of the argument and intrude on the audience's attention. The interpretation offered here does not necessarily discount the validity of the idea expressed by Moshe Idel that by Modena's time, "Renaissance Jewish syncretism had ended its full turn: in lieu of numerous citations from alien sources in support of the Torah, there is a return to the Bible itself . . . a fideistic attitude becomes more and more evident."[46] It would seem to me, however, that it was the particular context of the pulpit which determined the manifestation of a "fideistic approach," if indeed that is the appropriate way to designate Modena's sermons. It cannot be overlooked that two years before his publication of the *Midbar Yehudah*, Modena printed his Hebrew translation and adaptation (*Zemah Zaddik*) of the Italian medieval moralistic treatise *Fiore di virtù*. This alien text was replete with references to pagan sages and Christian saints. Although he modified, truncated, and replaced the Christian sayings with rabbinic stories, Modena apparently regarded the work as suitable material with which to edify the Hebrew-reading public. Indeed, some of the anonymous stories with which Modena entertains his readers in his sermons are taken from the *Fiore di virtù*.[47]

As I have said, Modena's sermons are built on interpretations of midrashim and aggadot of the Talmud.[48] He never cites legal texts, although, as I will demonstrate, a halakhic dimension is sometimes implicit in his discussion. By the end of the sixteenth century, the major classical midrashim were available in print. Modena tended to comment on the most famous talmudic aggadot and midrashim from the collections of the *Midrash Rabba* and *Yalkut Shimoni*. He also gave extensive interpretations of Scriptural passages, particularly of the Psalms and Proverbs, following the order of the verses. This was a mnemonic device widely used by both Jews and Christians. It is interesting to note that Panigarola recommends that the preacher should have in his possession a good biblical concordance and make thorough use of the indices when preparing his sermon. Modena often interspersed his sermons with lexical comments on biblical words and expressions and some passages are patently constructed on the basis of consultation of concordances. He also occasionally ended his sermons in a symbolic manner on the basis of the notes in the *Masorah Magna*, which gives detailed information as to the occurrence of words and letters in biblical texts.

Modena is economical in his citation of post-Talmudic sources. It is thus striking that the few medieval Jewish sources that he does quote are mostly derived from kabbalistic sources and in particular, the *Zohar*. In later life, Modena was to acquire a reputation as a virulent anti-kabbalist and in a famous responsum (circa 1625) to the question whether it is permitted to teach kabbalah in public, Modena attempted to disclaim real knowledge of this esoteric body of literature.[49] He implied that his kabbalistic allusions were simply concessions to the expectations of some of his listeners.[50] In a pioneering article focusing on the *Ari Nohem*, Modena's critique of kabbalah, Moshe Idel has traced the cultural context in which Modena developed his antikabbalistic bias and also the specific elements in kabbalah which Modena challenged.[51] Idel demonstrated that Modena's views were partly fashioned by his awareness that Christian theologians used the kabbalah to strengthen their own doctrine. In addition, they were influenced by his involvement in the current debates regarding the validity of rabbinic tradition and thus he drew a distinct line between rabbinic tradition, that is, the Oral Law, and any other phenomenon including kabbalah. What emerges from Idel's discussion is that Modena was not averse to kabbalah per se, but rather to its misappropriation by others. It thus becomes clear that the citation of kabbalistic texts in his youthful *Midbar Yehudah* in contrast to his attack on kabbalah in his maturity is not an indication that Modena radically changed his view on the subject, nor that he was posing as a partisan of kabbalah. Rather, and this is substantiated by an examination of the mode in which he cites the kabbalistic texts, Modena used kabbalistic interpretation where it fitted into his own scheme of thinking. The kabbalistic allusions had no more or less authority than his other references to medieval texts even if he added the epithet "holy" when he referred to Simeon bar Yoḥai, the ascribed author of the *Zohar*.

The twenty-one sermons of the *Midbar Yehudah*, written for different occasions and different audiences, were uniform in style and structure, but varied in subject matter. Nevertheless, as Rosenzweig demonstrated in his book on Modena, certain themes recur in various forms throughout the sermons. Prominence is given to questions of exile and redemption,[52] the covenant between God and Israel, repentance and the immortality of the soul. Adam's sin is a pet subject and one to which he returned in many of his subsequent publications.[53] Since a comprehensive treatment of the sermons is beyond the scope of this chapter, I have selected one sermon for detailed analysis.

II.

The tenth sermon in the *Midbar Yehudah* was given in 1597 on the Sabbath preceding the fast day of Tishah b'Ab, which commemorates the destruction of the Temple. For Modena, the day acquired greater poignancy because it marked the end of his thirty-day mourning period for the death of his mother. The concurrence of personal bereavement and communal mourning provided Modena with the theme of his "prologhino." The Scriptural verse (*nose*) with which he begins his sermon was carefully chosen to enable him to connect his personal situation with that of the community. Modena cites the verse, "How can I alone bear your trouble, your burden and your strife?" (Deut. 1:12), but following a rhetorical ploy which became widespread from the end of the fifteenth century, he fragments the verse, playing with the word "I bear" (*esah*) which in other contexts can have the meaning of "raising the voice." He thus reads the verse "How can only I raise my voice in lamentation? How can I alone bear your trouble, your burden and strife?" He then gives the rabbinic text (*ma'amar*) which was to be analyzed in the last part of the sermon.

One of the characteristic modes of beginning a sermon was for the preacher to justify his call to the pulpit. In this case, Modena claims that he is the best candidate for the task of mourning the loss of the Temple because he is in a state of bereavement for the death of his mother, the worst disaster that can befall a man. Using kabbalistic imagery, Modena associates the loss of his mother with the loss of the Temple, for "our mother has wandered far away from us, that is the *Shekhinah* of God, truly, the holy mother." After a somewhat facetious account of the reasons for lamenting the death of a mother more than that of a father, Modena proceeds to introduce the theme of the sermon, which is in the form of a question.[54] Should one feel more pain for the grief of the individual or for that of the community? He then ends the introduction with a rhetorical flourish aimed at winning the sympathies of the audience, or perhaps, suggesting to the reader the situation of the lachrymose Modena in the pulpit: "My sorrow has got the better of me. Look away from me that I might take a little comfort. Though I speak, my grief will not be assuaged."

In the first part of the sermon, Modena examines the arguments for each side of the question introduced in the *prologhino*. He first puts the individual's case, opening his discourse with an idiosyncratic, but revealing, use of the legal expression "A man never incriminates himself," which in this context must be translated "A man values his own person."[55] Since this proposition is true, Modena argues, one might infer that the individual sets the highest store by his own happiness and conversely, that his own suffering is the hardest to bear. An aggadah in the Babylonian Talmud (Berakhot 7a) in which Moses asks God to grant him three requests supplies him with the proof of such a contention. Analyzing and questioning the aggadah in the manner demonstrated above in respect to the "artist" analogy, Modena comes to the conclusion that the three requests correspond to three specific and distinctive characteristics of Israel: (1) Moses asked that the *Shekhinah* should rest on Israel when he said, "Is it not that you go with us?" (Ex. 33:16). This, according to Modena, alludes to the physical existence of a specific people, Abraham's descendants; (2) Moses requested that the *Shekhinah* should not rest on the wicked of the world when he said, "So that we are distinguished, I and your people" (ibid.). This alludes to the people's distinctive spirituality that stems from their observance of the precepts; and (3) Moses asked God to show him His ways (ibid., v. 13). This is an allusion to the righteous, who are the *crème de la crème*. By means of an allegorical interpretation of Isaiah's song of the vineyard (chap. 5) and an allusion to its interpretation in the *Zohar*,[56] Modena argues that the purpose of Moses' request was to ensure Israel's attachment (*devekut*) to the *Shekhina* in their lifetime.[57] He extends the idea of the specific when he points to the strange formulation in one of Moses' requests. His statement, "So that we are distinguished, I and your people," according to Modena, specifies the specific. Moses, whose prophetic powers were unique, who stood out as an individual among individuals, wanted to be the recipient of God's favor. Thus, the good is enhanced the more specific and individualized it becomes. The same is true of personal disaster. The more specific the disaster, the greater the suffering. Modena discusses this with reference to the midrash in Ekhah Rabbati (1:9) in which it is stated that the demise of the righteous is more grievous to God than the ninety-eight curses in Deuteronomy and the destruction of the Temple.

Constructing a bridge to the other side of the argument, Modena quotes the popular saying, "The affliction of the many is semi-solace."[58] Among the illustrations of this saying, Modena alludes to a story in the *Fiore di virtù*. Alexander of Macedon's last instructions to his mother were to make a party after his death and to invite only those who had never suffered in their life. Nobody appeared at the feast. His mother was to take solace by the fact that she was in the same position as everybody else.[59] Modena reverts to the discussion between God and Moses when taking up the other side of the argument. Moses' statement "that we are distinguished, I and your people" indicates that he did have altruistic sentiments. He included the people in his request in the knowledge that his good would be enhanced by the general good. The importance of giving priority to the good of the many is illustrated by the aggadah in tractate Ta'anit in the Babylonian Talmud, in which Rabbi Ḥaninah ben Dosa comes to the realization that his well-being exists at the cost of the discomfort of the rest of the world.[60] This leads to the idea that "dulce et decorum est pro patria mori." Modena cites examples from the "gentiles who killed themselves for the sake of their countries." Without naming his source, he quotes a story from book six of Livy which describes how a cavalryman was prepared to follow an oracle's advice and throw himself into the earth's chasm in order to avert the destruction of the entire population of Rome. He cites a similar case of self-sacrifice told in the Bible. Mesha, King of Moab, killed his first-born son in a desperate attempt to save his people from Israel (2 Kings 3:27). Modena seeks to understand these actions, which from a personal perspective he finds incomprehensible. Two alternatives faced the individuals in question: either to participate in the universally bad situation, or to eradicate the suffering of the many. Modena thus concludes that the more universal the disaster, the more momentous it is. This conclusion serves as a transition into the final part of section one. Modena returns to the theme of the day, the destruction of the Temple, the most universal of all disasters which affects Israel, all peoples of the world, and even God. And he ends with a reference to the *nose*. "How can I bear it by myself. It is the duty of every person to raise his voice in lamentation."

In the first part of the second section of the sermon, Modena produces evidence from various aggadot that demonstrate that the destruction of the Temple was the most universal of all calamities. His opening text is a striking aggadah that describes the unique qualities of Mount Zion, "the joy of the whole world."[61] Various texts are cited which demonstrate that Jerusalem was the focal point of the world. "Had the nations of the world realized what a boon the Temple was for them, they would have built fortifications around it in order to protect it."[62] The famous *aggadah* describing God weeping over the ruined Temple brings the first part of this section to a dramatic climax.[63]

At this juncture, Modena raises the question of the relevance of the destruction of the Temple for his contemporaries. The mourning for the destruction of the Temple, he explains, has not become obsolete. In fact, one should mourn with even greater intensity because God's decrees may be reversed at any moment. An interpretation of the first verses of chapter one of Lamentations then follows. Like the *nose* verse, the chapter begins with the word *Ekhah* (How): "How does a city sit solitary?" The significance of this word is further elaborated by means of a *midrash* which states that three prophets, Moses, Isaiah, and Jeremiah, all predicted the fall of Jerusalem using the expression *ekhah.*[64]

Having ended the second section by focusing on the meaning of the word *ekhah*, Modena then proceeds to examine the rabbinic text that he recited at the beginning of the sermon in the light of his foregoing comments.

> Rabbi Abahu began his discourse with the verse "For they like man [Adam] have transgressed the covenant" (Hosea 6:7). The Blessed One said: "I put Adam in the Garden of Eden and gave him a commandment which he transgressed. I punished him by expulsion and by sending him forth and I lamented over him *Ekhah* [this is a play on the word *ayekha*, "Where are you?" (Gen. 3:8)]. So, too, I put his descendants into the land and lamented over them, 'How does a city sit solitary?'" (Lam. 1:1)[65]

Modena's analysis of this aggadah skillfully brings together some of the central points in his sermon. Adam was an individual, but his sin had universal repercussions.[66] Similarly, Israel's sin, which resulted in banishment from their land and destruction of the Temple, had universal implications. The expressions "banishment" and "sending away" signify the different stages in God's meting out of punishment. Initially, His intention was to punish Adam with eternal punishment, but then He simply sent him away in the hope that he would repent. When God realized that he had not repented, when He said to Adam in the Garden, "Where are you?" (*ayekha*), he was not merely inquiring where he was, but was crying out in pain, "How can it be that you do not repent?"[67]

Modena refers to the poignancy of the ending of the aggadah: "Who is there who on hearing this does not shed tears for our calamity?" He proceeds to comfort the people with the assurance that the reversal of the decree of banishment can be reversed by means of repentance. Using the *Masorah Magna*, Modena refers to the three passages in the Bible in which one verse ends and the following verse begins with the word "the earth": "In the beginning God created the heavens and the earth. And the earth . . ." (Gen. 1:1); "The earth faints and fades away . . . the earth also is defiled under its inhabitants" (Isaiah 24:4,5); "And it shall respond to the earth and the earth shall respond." (Hosea 2:23–24). This lexical information that has been culled from the *Masorah Magna* is then overcast with kabbalistic imagery. Modena states: "The creation of the world from chaos was an act of undiluted mercy. . . . The people have contaminated the earth, but the earth will respond. Thus, if Israel repents, they will be answered and the earth will return to its former strength when our Messiah comes to build the Temple speedily in our days. May it be Your will."

Towards the end of the sermon, after speaking of the tears which should be shed for "our calamity," Modena states that he has fulfilled the aim of the sermon. He has assembled the arguments as to whether the good or evil of the individual is of greater moment than that of the general community. He does not offer any response to the question. Nevertheless, his interpretation of the *ma'amar* does implicitly answer his proposed question. The individual is inextricably linked with the universal. The actions of the individual Adam and likewise those of the individual people Israel had universal consequences.

Modena based his arguments on his own interpretation of various aggadot which were not explicitly concerned with the question he poses. And yet, there are various other aggadot and midrashim that deal with the question he raises in terminology strikingly similar to his own. In tractate Moed Katan in the Babylonian Talmud (14b) two views are given as to the meaning of the phrase "baẓar lakh" ("in your distress") in the verse "when you are in distress . . . He will not fail you" (Deut. 4:30–31): "Any distress that is confined to the individual is real distress, but any distress that in not confined to an individual is not real distress." The other opinion states: "Any distress shared by Israel and the nations is real distress, but any confined to Israel is not."[68] These two contradictory opinions sum up Modena's quandary. There is yet another rabbinic text which seems to underlie more than one aspect of the sermon. In tractate Yebamot (43b) of the Babylonian Talmud a practical legal problem is raised as to whether public mourning for the destruction of the Temple takes precedence over personal bereavement. Rav Ashi uses the same terminology as Modena when he refers to the mourning for the destruction of the Temple as "old bereavement" and the opinion is put forward that an individual who is in mourning for a personal loss is subject to more stringent regulations than those governing public mourning for the Temple. The implications of the halakhic question raised in the Tal-

mud are exploited to the full by Modena.[69] He explains to his congregation that they should not entertain the idea that the past has no relevance
for the present. Mourning for the loss of the Temple is not outdated,
but has direct bearing on each individual and on the entire community.
Even he, Modena, who had recently suffered the loss of his mother,
participated in his community's suffering and prayed for the rehabilita-
tion of the people in their own land.

Modena's sermon is constructed on the basis of rabbinic texts which
he fashioned and transformed into a question of crucial relevance for
his community. His adaptation of rabbinic materials demonstrates both
his interpretative and preaching skills, while the structure of the sermon
is clearly modeled on Panigarola's guidelines. Panigarola gives detailed
instructions for the construction of the sections, each of which should
constitute a sermon in miniature (*predichetta*).[70] The *prologhino* should be
like the opening of a madrigal, free-moving, leading up to the main body
of the sermon but independent of it.[71] It should not be longer than half
a page. The introduction to the first section should contain a proposition
which is then developed by a series of arguments that are marshaled in
such a way that the audience is not conscious of the formal logical principles underlying the discussion. The transitions between the various sections should be artfully constructed, like concealed hinges, to enable the
listener to progress almost unaware from one point to the other.[72] The
rigors of the first part should be alleviated in the opening of the second
section by recapitulating or by producing proofs that contain entertaining or pleasurable narratives.[73] The end of the second part should sum
up the whole sermon, and the epilogue should give expression to devout
sentiments and sometimes, according to the occasion, exhort or castigate.[74]

In Modena's sermon, the short *prologhino* functions as a prelude. The
first part begins with the arguments for giving priority to the individual's
case. The introduction of the popular saying, "The affliction of the many
is semi-solace," which as it were presents an intermediate stage in the
argument, serves as a transition into the second half of the first section.
The ending of the first section anticipates the subject of the second part.
The second section opens with a striking passage that, after the complexities of the first section, is less taxing on the listener's attention. The
interpretation of the *ma'amar* ties together the different elements in the
discussion and brings the main point of the sermon, the reason for
mourning for the Temple, into relief. The peroration exhorts the people
to repentance.

This sermon is representative of the majority of the sermons in the
Midbar Yehudah. Modena adapts some of the most characteristic elements
of Jewish preaching to the recommendations of an Italian bishop. By the

end of the sixteenth century there was a glut of Christian works on the art of preaching. Modena chose to model himself on Francesco Panigarola, who was one of the most famous preachers of the time and whose sermons became a model of style for both religious and secular *litterati*.[75] The Christian preacher had official status in post-tridentine Italy and the sermon was used as a vehicle for expressing the views of the establishment. For the Jewish preacher, there were no official rules and regulations. From Modena's statements, it would appear that it was the demands of the audience that partly dictated the kind of sermon that was to be delivered. And yet, the role which Modena consciously assumes as preacher does bear affinity to that of his Christian counterpart. Modena prides himself on his sermons, which are composed with a fine eye to structure and style.[76] If Panigarola composed sermons to combat the heresy of the Reformers, Modena interspersed his interpretations of rabbinic literature with discussions that were aimed at challenging Christian views or simply posing fundamental questions that were intended to underline the meaning of Jewish tradition in contemporary society. His consciousness of the responsibility of the preacher to his congregation was derived in no small measure from what he had learned from his Christian neighbors.

NOTES

1. An overview of Modena's life and work with full bibliography is given in Howard E. Adelman's *Success and Failure in the Seventeenth-Century Ghetto of Venice, The Life and Thought of Leon Modena 1571–1648*, Ph.D. diss. Brandeis University, 1985. Mark Cohen's translation and edition of Modena's autobiography, *The Autobiography of a Seventeenth-Century Venetian Rabbi: Leon Modena's Life of Judah* (Princeton, 1988), with introductory essays by Mark R. Cohen, Theodore K. Rabb, Howard E. Adelman, and Natalie Zemon Davis and historical notes by Howard E. Adelman and Benjamin Ravid, is also a mine of useful information. All references to the Autobiography will be to Cohen's translation.

2. See, for example, Cecil Roth, *The Jews in the Renaissance* (Philadelphia, 1959), who makes constant reference to Modena throughout the book as a typical Jewish representative of the Renaissance. See also Giuseppe Sermoneta's analysis of Modena's tract on memory, the *Leb ha-Aryeh* (*The Heart of the Lion*) (Venice, 1612), *Italia Judaica* (Rome, 1986), vol. 2, pp. 17–26, which stresses the essentially medieval orientation of the work and its author. In contrast, see Robert Bonfil, "Change in the Cultural Patterns of a Jewish Society in Crisis: Italian Jewry at the Close of the Sixteenth Century," *Jewish History* 3, no. 2 (1988): 19–20, who argues that Modena's use of magic and alchemy together with classical knowledge had a mediating function in its Jewish context. He further claimed that Modena's translation of foreign works including the medieval moralistic tract *Fiore di virtù* was not indicative of medieval sensibilities, but rather indicative of a modern thrust in Jewish society to narrow the gap between Judaism and Christianity.

3. See Howard E. Adelman, "Towards a New Assessment of Leon Modena," *The Autobiography*, pp. 38–39. For a detailed account of Modena's attitude to and defense of rabbinic tradition, see Ellis Rivkin, *Leon Modena and the Kol Sakhal* (Cincinnati, 1952), pp. 40–79.

4. See Howard E. Adelman's essay, "Towards a New Assessment of Leon Modena," *The Autobiography*, pp. 38–49.

5. *The Autobiography*, p. 95 (11a).

6. Ellis Rivkin, "The Sermons of Leo da Modena," *Hebrew Union College Annual* 23, no. 2 (1950–51): 295–317.

7. Israel Rosenzweig, *Hogeh Yehudi mi-Kez ha-Renesans: Yehudah Aryeh Modena ve-Sifro Midbar Yehudah* (Tel Aviv, 1972).

8. In chap. 7, in particular, Rosenzweig analyzes Modena's concept of covenant in the background of Modena's debates with Christians. The substantial evidence of Modena's meeting with English Protestants postdates the publication of his collection of sermons. See C. Roth, "Leon da Modena and England," *Transactions of the Jewish Historical Society of England* 11 (1924–1927): 206–207. However, it is certainly true that on occasion, Modena offers interpretations of Scriptural passages which are intended as refutations of well-known Christian views. See, for example, his interpretation of Is. 52: 13–14, "Indeed, My servant shall prosper, be exalted and raised to great heights. Just as the many were appalled at him . . ." (*Midbar Yehudah*, p. 34a), in which he stresses that although the expression "My servant" is in the singular, it refers to the people of Israel (and therefore not to Jesus) and he cites other passages which indicate that the use of the singular form in designating Israel is a convention of biblical language.

9. Rosenzweig treats the subject in an appendix to his book (pp. 132–138). He cites, for example, Modena's interpretation of the passage in the Babylonian Talmud (Menaḥot 53b) in which Abraham bemoans the fate of "my children" with God (*Midbar Yehudah*, p. 13a). In the course of his defense of the people, Abraham entreats God to remember the covenant of the circumcision to which God replies with a quotation from Jeremiah 11:15, "The hallowed flesh has passed from you." Modena focuses on this reply and infers that the loss of the land of Israel is the result of the failure of the people as a whole to fulfill the commandment of circumcision. Rosenzweig suggests not implausibly that Modena pinpoints this element in the passage in order to make a veiled reference to those *conversos* who had chosen not to revert to Judaism.

10. Joseph Dan, *Hebrew Ethical and Homiletical Literature (The Middle Ages and Early Modern Period)* [Hebrew] (Jerusalem, 1975), pp. 199–200. Dan analyzes one of Modena's sermons for a Bar Mitzvah (*Midbar Yehudah*, pp. 94b–96a). He expresses the same view, but gives it a more general application in "The Aesthetic Elements in Hebrew Homiletical Literature" [Hebrew], *Ha-Sifrut* 111 (1971–72): 566. In his opening note to the sermon, Modena states that he is going to keep the sermon short "because the child is just a child." As far as I can see, Dan's thesis can only be applied to the two sermons in the collection which Modena wrote on behalf of the boys who were becoming Bar Mitzvah.

11. Aristotle, *Rhetoric*, 1358^a, 36–38.

12. One might assume that he also adapted his sermon, which he would give in Italian, to the needs of the non-Jewish members of his audience.

13. See Modena's statement in his *Zikne Yehudah*, responsum 26, ed. Shlomo Simonsohn (Jerusalem, 1957), p. 43, "Here in Venice, although the main community consists of individual communities, when they come together, they follow the majority decision"; cf. Bonfil's discussion of the pluralistic society of the Venetian ghetto in "Cultura e mistica a Venezia," in *Gli ebrei a Venezia secoli XIV–XVIII*, ed. Gaetano Cozzi (Milan, 1987), pp. 469–506.

14. For details of the chronology of Modena's preaching activities, see *The Autobiography*, pp. 203–204.

15. See *The Autobiography*, p. 96 and n. g, p. 204.

16. *Midbar Yehudah* (Venice, 1602), p. 81a.

17. In his Autobiography (p. 102) for the entry June–July 1602, he writes that after putting together the *Midbar Yehudah*, he still had four hundred sermons in his possession.

18. See *Midbar Yehudah*, p. 4b; *The Autobiography*, pp. 101–102; and the letter to his teacher Samuel Archivolti in *Iggerot R. Yehudah Aryeh Modena*, ed. Yakob Boksenboim (Tel Aviv, 1984), letter 40, pp. 83–84, which is translated by Marc Saperstein in *Jewish Preaching 1200–1800: An Anthology* (New Haven, 1989), pp. 411–412.

19. *Midbar Yehudah*, p. 7b.

20. The opening lines of Modena's introduction are difficult to translate, owing to the gushing stream of rhetoric which perhaps intentionally obfuscates the meaning. The gist of the first two paragraphs is that Modena's need to publish stems from his anxiety that his name will be forgotten. Modena's concern for posterity, which is given such exaggerated expression in his introduction, seems to me to be uncharacteristic of Jewish writers. According to Ephraim Shmueli, *Between Faith and Heresy: An Essay on Leon da Modena and Uriel da Costa* [Hebrew] (Tel Aviv, 1963), p. 13, Modena's desire for posterity is due to his doubts about the afterlife.

21. See n. 15. I have followed Saperstein's translation, but made some changes where necessary.

22. The reading here is unclear. Modena may be using the word *epiloghino*.

23. See Saperstein, *Jewish Preaching*, pp. 63–79.

24. The inventory is published by Clemente Ancona, "L'Inventario dei beni appartenenti a Leon da Modena," *Bollettino dell'istituto di storia della società e dello stato veneziano* 4 (1962): 249–267.

25. This is unquestionably a reference to Panigarola's *Modo di comporre una predica*. Scholars have tended to disregard this reference to Panigarola, while usually noting that the inventory lists the sermons of Savonarola. One cannot detect any influence of Savonarola on Modena.

26. A detailed discussion of the life and work of Panigarola with particular attention to his position as the major representative of sacred oratory in the Counter-Reformation is given by Frederico Barbieri, "La riforma dell'eloquenza sacra in Lombardia operata da S. C. Borromeo," *Archivio storico lombardo* 15, no. 38 (1911): pp. 231–262. See also, Roberto Rusconi, *Predicazione e vita religiosa nella società italiana* (Turin, 1981). For a short analysis of Panigarola's style, see Giovanni Pozzi, "Intorno alla predicazione del Panigarola," *Italia sacra: Problemi*

di vita religiosa in Italia nel Cinquecento. Atti del convegno di storia della chiesa in Italia, Bologna 1958 (Padua, 1960), pp. 315–322.

27. See *Biographie Universelle* (Paris, Leipzig, 1932), s.v. Panigarola, vol. 32, pp. 70 col. a–71 col. a.

28. *The Autobiography*, p. 86.

29. There is no complete list of the many editions of his works.

30. *Il Predicatore overo parafrase commento e discorsi intorno al libro dell'elocutione di Demetrio Falereo* (Venice, 1602).

31. See Peter Bayley, *French Pulpit Oratory 1598–1650* (Cambridge, 1980), p. 39.

32. *Modo di comporre una predica del Rev. Panigarola Vescovo di Asti con l'aggiunta di un trattato della memoria locale* (Padua, 1599). The work was dedicated to Marco Cornaro, the bishop of Padua. I consulted this edition of the work. The first edition was printed in 1584 and there were several subsequent editions including translations into Latin and French.

33. See Salvatore Battaglia, *Grande dizionario della lingua italiana* (Turin, 1988), s.v. *prologhino*, vol. 14, p. 580.

34. *Midbar Yehudah*, pp. 5a–8a. This was the first sermon he preached in the Great Ashkenazi synagogue (see *The Autobiography*, p. 95). It was delivered in 1593. The entire introduction deals with the problems of effective preaching. Modena explains that he made the introduction longer that the other introductions in the collection because it was the first sermon. Modena seems to have conceived it as an excursus on the nature of preaching and the difficulties of the preaching profession, presumably to justify any shortcomings his critics might discover in his sermons.

35. *Midbar Yehudah*, pp. 6b–7a. I have used Saperstein's translation, *Jewish Preaching*, pp. 409–410.

36. Modena makes these claims in his letter to Samuel Archivolti, p. 412.

37. These Ciceronian *genera dicendi* were adapted by Augustine. In his *De Doctrina Christiana*, IV, 17, he recommends the moderate style, the *genus temperatum*, which is neither unornamented nor ornamented in an unbecoming way. Its object is to entertain the listeners while leading them to obedience.

38. *Midbar Yehudah*, p. 3b. I have presented a synopsis of his main ideas.

39. Modena was not the first Jewish preacher to stress the importance of the homiletical art for preaching. In the earliest known tract on Jewish preaching, the *En ha-Kore*, the fifteenth-century Spanish philosopher Joseph ibn Shem Tob states: "Thus the best of the arts for preaching is the art of rhetoric. The more the preacher masters this art, and the more at home he is in the techniques of speech and argumentation that will persuade the listeners to accept what he says, the greater will be his stature in the category of rhetoric." Cited from Saperstein, *Jewish Preaching*, p. 300.

40. Modena sometimes used allegorical and kabbalistic interpretation of the *aggadot* and *midrashim* in his sermons. In the introduction to his Responsa, the *Zikne Yehudah*, which is dated Venice 1630 (ed. Shlomo Simonsohn, Jerusalem, 1957), he first states that he was the best preacher that ever was "as is well known," and then states that he had a fine grasp of legal matters and did not spurn "iyyun," that is, he did not adopt casuistic interpretations.

41. See Robert Bonfil, *Rabbis and Jewish Communities in Renaissance Italy* (Oxford, 1990 [translation from the Hebrew, Jerusalem, 1979]), pp. 298–316.

42. John W. O'Malley, *Praise and Blame in Renaissance Rome, Rhetoric and Reform in the Sacred Orators of the Papal Court c. 1450–1521* (Los Angeles, Berkeley, 1979).

43. John W. O'Malley, "Sixteenth-Century Treatises on Preaching," in *Renaissance Eloquence* (Los Angeles, Berkeley, 1983), pp. 238–252.

44. See John M. McNanamon, *Funeral Oratory and the Cultural Ideals of Italian Humanists* (Chapel Hill, N.C., 1989), p. 31.

45. Modena suggests another play on words for the conclusion of the passage. "There is no creator [yoẓer] like our God."

46. Moshe Idel, "Differing Conceptions of Kabbalah in the Early 17th Century," *Jewish Thought in the Seventeenth Century*, ed. Isadore Twersky and Bernard Septimus (Cambridge, Mass., 1987), p. 174.

47. See, for example, the story about the reaction of the philosophers to Alexander's death recounted in the section entitled "Del vizio della tristizia e della morte di Alessandro" (*Ẓemaḥ Ẓaddik*, chap. 9), which Modena applies in his eulogy of Samuel Judah Katzenellenbogen (*Midbar Yehudah*, p. 69a).

48. Of the twenty-one *ma'amarim* with which he begins his sermons, ten are taken from aggadot of the Talmud and eleven from midrashim.

49. The Responsum is n. 55 of his collection of his Responsa entitled *Zikne Yehudah* (pp. 76–78). A partial translation of the letter is given in Saperstein, *Jewish Preaching*, pp. 406–408. Modena writes (Saperstein's translation): "To my distress, the truth is that I do not know a single book from that discipline which today they call "Kabbalah" and "true wisdom." Nevertheless, I was able to appear publicly in my sermons as if I too knew a little of it. This was like those preachers who need to preach about the talmudic tractate Erubin in order to placate the confused minds of their listerners."

50. Robert Bonfil, "Cultura e mistica," pp. 492–493, states that Modena's response should not be taken at face value. Modena had been conscious of the growing appeal of kabbalah and realized that he should be discrete in revealing his true opinions about kabbalah.

51. See Idel, "Differing Conceptions."

52. In treating this theme, he often is implicitly referring to the realities of ghetto life. See his first sermon (*Midbar Yehudah*, p. 10a–b) where he discusses the three conditions which determine the greatness of a nation: numbers, the qualities of virtue and wisdom, and a good geographical position. With regard to the question of numbers, he asserts that when the Jews lived in the land of Israel they were numerous but appeared few in number, but now being in exile, "we are few, but appear many such that five Jews together make a greater impression than ten people of any other nation."

53. Modena often attacks the Christian notion of original sin, stressing that Adam bequeathed physical, but not spiritual sin to subsequent generations. This subject, which had been treated in previous centuries, acquired more urgent solution in light of the dogmatic rulings given at the Council of Trent. In his anti-Christian tract *Magen ve-Ḥereb*, ed. Shlomo Simonsohn (Jerusalem, 1960), p.

20, he even refers to Paolo Sarpi's *Istoria del Concilio Tridentino*, lib. 2, chap. 4, ed. Renzo Pecchioli (Florence, 1965), vol. 1, p. 213. Sarpi lists the propositions discussed at the sessions of the Council, the second of which seemed to imply that Adam's sin was not transmitted, but simply imitated by his descendants: "Che il peccatto d'Adamo si chiama originale perchè da lui deriva nella posterità, non per trasmissione, ma per imitazione." The Council unanimously rejected the proposition as heretical.

54. In chap. 2 of *Modo di comporre una predica*, Panigarola states that it does not matter whether the subject is put in the form of a proposition or a question since ultimately the question gets reduced to either a positive or negative proposition.

55. The expression occurs in Babylonian Talmud Sanhedrin 10a: "Every man is considered a relation to himself and none can incriminate himself." The choice of this opening phrase is revealing since there is a halakhic dimension to this sermon.

56. *Zohar*, 1, 96b, ed. Reuben Margaliot (Jerusalem, 1940–1944).

57. Nahmanides articulated the idea that "devekut" is an attainable ideal in the life of the individual. See Gershom Scholem, *Major Trends in Jewish Mysticism* (New York, 1961, 3d ed.), p. 233. See also, Maimonides, *Guide of the Perplexed*, bk. 3, chap. 51, where he states that the patriarchs attained this ideal in their lifetime.

58. This saying occurs in many languages. It is found in Hebrew (e.g., in the *Josippon*); various versions are quoted in Erasmus' *Adagia*; an Italian version of the proverb is "Mal commune mezzo gaudio." Plantavit de la Pause, with whom Modena was in correspondence in later life, gives a Latin rendering in his *Florilegium rabbinicum* (Lodève, 1645), p. 322: "Afflictio multorum dimidiam consolationis."

59. See n. 51. For the purposes of the sermon, Modena does not adhere to his own Hebrew translation of the story in which he employed biblical phraseology and terminology.

60. Ta'anit 24b: "R. Ḥanina ben Dosa was going on a journey . . . and it began to rain. He said: 'Master of the Universe, the whole world is at ease, but R. Ḥanina is in distress.' The rain stopped. When he reached home, he exclaimed: 'Master of the Universe, the whole world is in distress and Ḥanina is at ease.' The rain fell."

61. Shir Ha-Shirim Rabba 36:1.

62. Bamidbar Rabba 1:3 (ad Num. 1:1).

63. Ekhah Rabbati, proem XXIV.

64. Ibid., ad Lam. 1:1.

65. Ibid., proem IV.

66. See n. 59.

67. On the question of repentance, see Bereshit Rabba 22:16, ed. Theodor and Albeck (Jerusalem, 1965), in which Adam is confronted by Cain, who claims to have repented and to have had his punishment revoked, and cries out in amazement, "Such is the power of repentance and I did not know it."

68. In a parallel version in the *Yalkut Shimoni*, par. 827 (ad Deut. 4:30), the

second opinion is reversed: "Any distress shared by Israel and the nations of the world is not real distress, but any distress confined to Israel is."

69. I am grateful to Rabbi James Ponet, who suggested to me the possibility of a halakhic dimension to Modena's question.

70. The *predichetta* should have "un poco d'introduttioncella in una sol clausula o due, la narratione dello stesso capo della prova e doppo lui, tutte quelle cose che lo amplificano e finalmente un picciolo epiloghetto al quale possa poi applicarsi l'introduttioncella dell'altra prova che seguita" (p. 56r).

71. "Si come la ricercata non è parte del madrigale ma è solamente un preludio" (p. 43v). Panigarola recommends the use of analogies for the *prologhino*. On many occasions, Modena begins his sermons with analogies or images.

72. "Questi Epiloghetti con le introduttioni seguenti vengano quasi ad essere gangheri sopra quali si volta l'oratione . . . che si faccia passare l'animo dell'ascoltante da una prova all'altra per ponto cosi coperto ch'egli non si avvegga pure d'haverlo passato" (p. 58r–v).

73. Pp. 40v–41r.

74. P. 41r.

75. See Giovanni Pozzi, "Intorno alla predicazione," p. 322.

76. Modena's style is not as ornate or as "baroque" as that of Panigarola, who is noted for his radical transformation of syntax and exaggerated use of synonyms.

SEVEN

Speaking of the Dead: The Emergence of the Eulogy among Italian Jewry of the Sixteenth Century

Elliott Horowitz

The question is raised in the Talmud as to whether the eulogy is intended chiefly to honor the dead or the living,[1] and indeed the historian (who must, if he be honest, ask the same question of his own rhetorical discipline[2]) may find himself wondering, while wading through the thickets of dense erudition and luxuriant eloquence sprinkled throughout most of the funerary sermons preached by rabbis of early modern times, what their real subject is. Is it the deceased himself and the shape of his life, or is it the meaning of his death or, indeed, of Death in general? Is death itself, as event and experience, looked by the preacher squarely in the eye, or does he prefer to cleverly gloss some remotely related rabbinic dicta, or to move on, by the by, to academic discussions of the immortality of the soul? Is it knowledge with which the author of the sermon most wants to leave his audience, or sentiment, or perhaps some combination thereof? What, in turn, does his audience seem to expect from him, and who, in fact, does he really address? Does he strive primarily for dramatic effect before a live audience, and is his written sermon essentially a script? Or does he seek rather to construct an elaborate and timeless text, the live presentation of which is a mere formality, which will preserve his own memory no less than that of his purported subject, and serve, moreover, as a lasting monument to their relationship?

The historian, if he perseveres, will find in these sermons some information about the living and some about the dead, some about preachers and some about their audiences. He may, in fact, learn something about the relationship between the living and the dead on the one hand, and

עלינו

רבינו

נחלה

Manuscript page from a collection of funeral sermons of Abraham of Sant'Angelo. Courtesy of the Library of The Jewish Theological Seminary of America. Mic. 5470–1599:20, folio 176a[10].

preachers and their audiences on the other. It will be harder for him to learn much of value, however, about attitudes toward or conceptions of death, which, when discussed in formal eulogies, generally reflect the somewhat stilted traditions favored by the learned (e.g. of the righteous enjoying everlasting life after their deaths, or of their deaths resulting from the sins of their generation) rather than the more dynamic earthiness of popular views. Although some rabbis may have felt themselves obliged to engage in intellectual slumming from time to time, the opposite seems more often to have been the case: they strained, sometimes rather eclectically, for the upper reaches of the reigning intellectual culture in order to lend an especially dignified tone to the funerary occasion and lofty honor to the memory of the deceased. These sermons may, however, teach us more about the organization of death than about its (perceived) meaning, more about changing conceptions of how a man's (or less frequently, a woman's) departure from the world might be made into an elaborately orchestrated event, experienced—from beginning to end—in the public domain, than about attitudes associated with the transition from this world to the next. The two, admittedly, cannot be completely sundered, for the formal aspects of funerary convention undoubtedly convey something of a culture's underlying notions—and especially its anxieties—concerning the fate of the individual after his death.

This chapter, which will concern itself primarily with the culture of Italian Jewry and with the emergence in its midst of formalized funerary preaching during the sixteenth century, will not strive to deal conclusively with even a small number of the questions raised above, nor will it deal comprehensively with all the eulogies, in print and manuscript, surviving from that period. It will, however, try to uncover and, somewhat more tentatively, to explain the beginnings of the phenomenon, while paying special attention to the funeral sermon's ties to two of the dominant themes in Italian Jewish life of the sixteenth century: the tension between the traditions of Ashkenazic Jewry and those of Mediterranean Jewries (Sephardic as well as native Italian), and the debate over the proper role of kabbalah in Jewish society. Some attention will also be given to the possible impact of late Renaissance culture upon Jewish funerary preaching in Italy.

In 1393 the humanist Pier Paolo Vergerio (the elder) composed a funeral oration in memory of Francesco il Vecchio da Carrara, lord of Padua, who died in a Visconti prison. Vergerio's is the earliest funeral oration yet found by Renaissance scholars which follows classical (as opposed to medieval) norms for oratory. As opposed to the thematic sermons of a more general nature preached by others on the same occasion,

Vergerio's classicizing panegyric focused on Francesco himself, reviewing his virtuous actions in both the private and public realms in a manner which, it has been claimed, "slavishly imitated ancient rhetorical canons."[3] In the following decades this classicizing form of eulogy became increasingly influential. In 1428, as Hans Baron has shown, the Florentine chancellor and noted humanist Leonardo Bruni modeled his oration on the death of Nanni degli Strozzi, a prominent general in the anti-Viscontean coalition, on the funeral speech of Pericles as reported by Thucydides.[4] A recent study has found, in fact, that of the three oratorical genres inherited from classical antiquity, epideictic (as opposed to judicial and deliberative) oratory, the performative form of rhetorical discourse to which the eulogy belonged, "constituted the leading genre throughout the Italian Renaissance." More significantly for our purposes, it has been found that Renaissance orators "practiced funeral oratory more extensively than their ancient predecessors ever did."[5]

These developments evidently had some impact, albeit belated, upon Jewish society in Italy. When, on Lag ba-Omer of 1572, R. Moses Isserles, perhaps the leading Polish rabbinical authority of his time and one who, in his short life, had achieved international recognition, died in Krakow, he was eulogized in the ghetto of Venice by his relative, colleague, and frequent correspondent, R. Samuel Judah Katzenellenbogen. The latter's was probably not the only eulogy for Isserles that was delivered, but it is evidently the only one whose text was deemed worthy of preservation. This was not because his Polish contemporaries were niggardly in their praise for their great rabbi. R. Solomon Luria, his twin tower in the rabbinic world of sixteenth-century Poland, had written to Isserles during his lifetime that "from Moses [Maimonides] to Moses [Isserles] there has been none like Moses," and this encomium, never used lightly, was inscribed with even greater permanence upon his tombstone.[6]

Rather, it must be recognized that the funeral sermon was a far less developed literary genre in the culture of sixteenth-century Ashkenazic Jewry than it was among their Italian brethren, among whose Christian neighbors, as noted above, funeral oratory had been especially cultivated since the early Renaissance.[7] What is striking, however, in the case of Rabbi Katzenellenbogen of Venice, is that he too, as he would have been proud to admit (and as his name could scarcely conceal) was an Ashkenazi, but one born and bred in northern Italy.[8] He was thus possessed of a rather different cultural orientation, of which his sermon on the death of Isserles is but a small indication, from those of his ilk beyond the Alps. Despite his clear Ashkenazic affiliations as a member of the Minz rabbinic dynasty,[9] Katzenellenbogen was capable of delivering, very possibly in Italian, funeral sermons of considerable polish and sophistication, if not as dazzling in their rhetorical flourish as those of his Mantuan colleague,

R. Judah Moscato.[10] And yet, one might argue that it was precisely on account of those same Ashkenazic affiliations that he was prompted to launch his career as an eloquent public eulogist in Venice with the death in distant Krakow of R. Moses Isserles.

R. Samuel Judah was then just past his fiftieth birthday, and had succeeded his father R. Meir Katzenellenbogen (known also as "Maharam Padovah" and regarded by scholars as the greatest Italian rabbi of the period) to the position of senior member of the Venetian rabbinate, possibly even before the latter's death in 1565.[11] Of the six eulogies which he later published in *Shneim-Asar Derashot*, his 1594 collection of selected sermons,[12] five can be assigned at least approximate dates, and of these the earliest is that delivered upon the death of Isserles in 1572.[13] None of the published Jewish funerary sermons from Italy were delivered before that date, although, as we shall see, some delivered as early as fifteen years previously survive in manuscript, and earlier ones may, of course, yet be discovered. It nonetheless appears that the humanistic revolution in funerary oratory inaugurated in Italy by Pier Paolo Vergerio in 1393 had no more than a limited, and certainly delayed, impact on Jewish society.

Internal developments stemming originally from outside of Italy, however, may be of greater significance. If Vergerio's eulogy in memory of Francesco da Carrara is the earliest surviving Renaissance funeral oration to have followed classical norms for oratory, the sermon composed in the same year by the recently (and perhaps forcibly) baptized Profiat Duran, residing then in Perpignan, may be the earliest surviving text of a medieval Hebrew funeral oration. Funerary poetry in the elegiac mode, known as the "*kinah*," may be found among Spanish Jewry in relative abundance from the eleventh century through the late thirteenth,[14] but funerary sermons emerge as a written genre only considerably later. Duran sent his to Gerona, upon the death there in 1393 of R. Abraham Tamakh. He explained in an accompanying missive to the latter's son Joseph, in whose voice the eulogy was written, that he had composed it on account of his love for both the deceased and his son, but more importantly, because he had heard that R. Abraham had not been eulogized properly by those who, he felt, should have done so. On account of his formal apostasy, Duran, who signed the letter off as "your brother the Levite whose song has been spoiled," was obviously in no position to deliver his Hebrew sermon in person. He therefore composed a text that could be read publicly by Joseph Tamakh as a eulogy for his late father.[15]

Except for such unusual circumstances, it would appear unlikely that a fourteenth-century Jewish funerary sermon (whether in Spain, Provence, or elsewhere in Europe) would be committed to writing and preserved. Of the twelve sermons of Tamakh's townsman R. Nissim Gerondi (d. c. 1375) which were preserved as a unit and later published, not a single one is a funerary eulogy. By contrast, when some two centuries later R. Samuel Judah Katzenellenbogen of Venice published twelve of his sermons in a collection that was based, as was there acknowledged, upon Gerondi's model,[16] fully half were eulogies. Something had clearly changed in the matter of Jewish speaking (or writing) of the dead in Western Europe.

Earlier in the sixteenth century (in 1506), R. Samuel Judah's great-grandfather, R. Judah Minz, died in Padua where, as befitting his position as the leading rabbi of the region and the leader of Ashkenazic Jewry in Italy, he was brought to burial amid great (and to the minds of some, excessive) pomp. According to the eyewitness account of his funeral composed by R. Elijah Capsali, at least three sermons were delivered in honor of the deceased rabbi.[17] Yet none of these has been preserved, and it would appear that they were never formally committed to writing. The eulogy seems still to have been regarded among the Ashkenazic Jews of Padua, even when carried out on a relatively grand scale, more as an "event" to be experienced and remembered than as a "text" to be transcribed and reread—or reused by resourceful preachers.

Among the Iberian exiles who had settled in the Ottoman Empire, however, texts of funerary sermons, transcribed sometimes in advance of their delivery (which did not always actually take place), may be found during the same period in relative abundance. R. Joseph Garçon, a Portuguese exile of Castilian origin, composed no less than twenty such sermons during the first decades of the sixteenth century, most for notable rabbis, while residing in Salonika and then in Damascus.[18] Like Duran a bit more than a century earlier, he would sometimes utilize the ventriloquistic method of addressing the deceased through the voice of a close relative, such as a son or a wife. To a greater degree than Duran's single sermon, however, those of Garçon would seem to signal a shift from the poetic *kinah* to the sermonic *hesped* as the favored form of formal discourse concerning the dead among late medieval Spanish Jewry—a shift which may ultimately have been rooted in the transition from Muslim to Christian influence in its cultural values.[19] The poetic genre did not, of course, disappear—witness the many *kinot* written upon the death of R. Joseph Caro in 1575[20]—but the audience capable of comprehending (and appreciating) such creations seems to have been shrinking steadily.

In the cultural orbit of the Spanish exiles there is even evidence of sons publicly eulogizing their recently deceased fathers. In 1559 R. Samuel Ashkenazi Jaffe (of Constantinople) composed a highly stylized sermon upon the death of his father, R. Isaac (of Bursa).[21] This is to be contrasted with the Ashkenazic Katzenellenbogen family in Venice, where it would appear that upon the death of the great Maharam in 1565, his son and successor, R. Samuel Judah, either never eulogized him publicly, or delivered on that occasion a sermon less worthy of preservation than the sort later anthologized in his *Shneim-Asar Derashot*. It may have been less sophisticated in its structure and content as well as in its language (possibly Yiddish),[22] and may never have been committed to writing, just as those delivered in Padua early in the century upon the death of R. Judah Minz seem never to have been written down.

If we have no written eulogy of R. Meir Katzenellenbogen by his son and successor, we do have one by the noted scribe and itinerant teacher R. Abraham of Sant'Angelo, which was delivered in Bologna, where he then resided, before a local Jewish confraternity known as "Ḥevrat Nizharim."[23] Two other eulogies by the same R. Abraham have survived, both delivered during his stay in Bologna, where the presence of a sizable group of Iberian Jews may have helped to create a demand for formal funerary sermons.[24]

Earlier than these, however, is the text of a eulogy copied by R. Abraham which had been delivered by his father-in-law, R. Isaac de Lattes, in nearby Pesaro during the winter of 1557–58, shortly after he had been invited to head a yeshiva there. This would appear to be the earliest known text of a Jewish funeral sermon preached in Italy, predating that of R. Samuel Judah Katzenellenbogen on the death of R. Moses Isserles by some fifteen years, and bringing the beginnings of the *hesped* as a literary genre in that country closer to where we might expect them—among the Jews of Mediterranean origin (Spanish, Provençal, or native Italian) rather than among the Ashkenazim of the Veneto. R. Isaac de Lattes had come to Italy from southern France in the late 1530s and had spent a decade in Rome, where there were no less than three congregations of Spanish Jews, before moving north.[25] It is therefore likely that he had encountered along the way, if not actually practiced himself, the more formal and textually based style of funerary preaching favored among his contemporaries in the Sephardic diaspora, which rendered the sermon, parallel to the epitaph, as a lasting verbal monument to the memory of the deceased. The importance of being eulogized well in public may have been perceived, moreover, as part of the general importance of dying well in public, which was receiving increasing emphasis among Italian Jewry of the mid-sixteenth century.[26]

R. Abraham Sant'Angelo's eulogizing style sometimes drew heavily, as we shall see, upon that of his father-in-law, although his sermon on the death of R. Elhanan Yael (Angelo) Fano, the first we shall discuss, exhibits little such influence. Fano had been a banker in Florence early in

the sixteenth century but eventually moved to Bologna, where he quickly
became one of the Jewish community's leaders. During the 1530s he was
referred to by such figures as R. Azriel Diena of Viadana as "a prince of
God" (cf. Gen. 23:6), and Gedalia ibn Yaḥya was later to pair him with
Don Samuel Abravanel as one of the two wealthiest Jews in Italy.²⁷ As
befitted his status, R. Elhanan Yael was eulogized in Bologna upon his
death not only by R. Abraham of Sant'Angelo, but by three other local
rabbis.²⁸ His funeral, of which we unfortunately have no account, was
probably quite a spectacle and undoubtedly included many torches,
whose processional use was not yet prohibited for the Jews in the Papal
States.²⁹

Of the four sermons delivered in Fano's home, only R. Abraham's has
been preserved, though not in its entirety. Thus his comparison of R.
Elhanan Yael with the patriarch Abraham, both of whom received, according to the preacher, four major gifts from God, remains incomplete.
We are told of the wealth they both shared, and the children (the second
gift) as well as the grandchildren (the third) they lived to see, but the
fourth gift which they held in common is revealed on a leaf which has
been lost, and can only be conjectured.³⁰ R. Abraham had elsewhere in
his eulogy compared the late R. Elhanan Yael to the patriarch Abraham,
seeing the former's death as having left the community of Bologna without its leader and helmsman.³¹ One wonders whether the association
between the two was not prompted in some way by the prominent references to the deceased during his lifetime as "a prince of God,"³² the
title acquired by the biblical Abraham, as the preacher R. Abraham's
contemporaries would have known, as part of his real estate deal with
the Hittites. The eulogist may also have been struck by R. Elhanan's near
uniqueness in his generation, declaring that "there is hardly one like him
in the land, from the rising of the sun to its setting," making him thus
similar to Abraham who, in the words of the prophet Ezekiel "was one,"
and was regarded in later Jewish tradition as having been unparalleled
in his time.³³ Thus, although there was no obvious connection between
the name of the deceased and the biblical patriarch, various textual associations may have been responsible for Rabbi Abraham's decision to use
the figure of Abraham (his own namesake!) as a frame for the former's
eulogy.

The eulogy for R. Mordecai Canaruto, whose death is described as
having been both sudden and untimely and who evidently left behind
him neither sons nor grandsons,³⁴ was apparently delivered sometime
after 1560,³⁵ and is as different from that for Fano as were the lives of
the two men themselves. It addresses not the community of Bologna as
a whole, but the members of its Nizharim confraternity in whose study
hall it was delivered. Among them it singles out especially the sons of the

"royal princess" (see Ps. 45:14) Fiammetta and the late R. Abraham Pisa, whose teacher and apparently constant companion R. Mordecai had been for more than seven consecutive years.[36] R. Abraham mentions explicitly (though not, perhaps, without some rhetorical exaggeration) that he had been not merely invited but forcefully pressured by the members of the Pisa family ("those glorious ones, my masters and patrons") and by the Nizharim confraternity to eulogize the deceased, and that he was doing so as an act of obedience. Consequently, he asserted, if his words were to prove unequal to the occasion only they were to blame. In order to be sure that these somewhat delicate phrases came out in actual delivery in precisely the way they were intended, R. Abraham made sure to insert in the margins of his Hebrew text some of the Italian words (in transliteration) that he planned to use: *provocato, obbedienza, incolparsi.*[37] These were not the only Italian words he inserted in the margins. No less than a dozen such instances occur in the eulogy for Canaruto, although none, curiously, is to be found in the Hebrew text of R. Abraham's eulogy for R. Elhanan Yael Fano. It would appear then that the latter was transcribed *after* its delivery, which apparently took place, with little notice, on the day of Fano's death,[38] whereas the former was written *in advance*, perhaps for the regular weekly lesson of the Nizharim confraternity which, according to its inaugural statutes, all members were required to attend.[39] Italian would appear, then, to have been the language of actual delivery on both occasions, to which the written text bore a different relation in each instance.

Another readily observable difference in the texts of the two sermons is that the one for Canaruto contains not only references to the teachings of the kabbalists but extensive quotations from the *Zohar* itself.[40] Both R. Abraham and his father-in-law, R. Isaac de Lattes, had been instrumental in the controversial publication of the Mantua edition of the *Zohar* (1558–1560) a short time earlier, so his familiarity with the work is hardly surprising. What might surprise us more, however, is the act of launching texts regarded as esoteric into the realm of public preaching. Prior to the publication of the *Zohar*, as Robert Bonfil has noted, even rabbis of avowedly kabbalistic orientation, such as R. Isaac de Lattes, avoided explicit references to its teachings in their sermons.[41] After its publication, however, the work gradually lost much of its esotericism, and even such intellectually conservative preachers as the Ashkenazic R. Samuel Judah Katzenellenbogen, were, before the century's end, to make liberal use of the *Zohar* in their public (and published) sermons.[42]

This would help to explain why he refrained from overt Zoharic references at the more public and official occasion of his eulogy on the death of R. Elhanan Yael Fano, where, as we recall, three other Bolognese rabbis were prominently present, presumably in the company of the local communal establishment. In the more intimate surroundings of the Nizharim confraternity's study hall, where, moreover, he seems to have taken over the late Canaruto's position, R. Abraham may have felt freer to break the obsolescent taboo by quoting from the newly published work. Nonetheless, if the eulogy for Canaruto constituted his inaugural lecture before the members of the confraternity, the act required not only a certain amount of daring (unless Canaruto had begun quoting from the *Zohar* in the sermons he delivered prior to his death) but also some commitment, though not necessarily messianic, to the spread of kabbalah as a form of exoteric wisdom, a commitment for which there is ample evidence from other quarters.[43] His sermon before Ḥevrat Nizharim was, among other things, an act of self-presentation, and in quoting amply from the *Zohar* R. Abraham was, in effect, saying to its members, "this is what you can now expect from the likes of me."

It is striking, therefore, that in his third and last surviving eulogy (as well as his longest), also delivered before the members of Bologna's Nizharim confraternity[44] on the death in 1565 of R. Meir Katzenellenbogen, R. Abraham abstained from quoting the *Zohar* or any other kabbalistic work. This was probably intended as a diplomatic gesture in the direction, however, not of his audience, which had presumably already become accustomed to hearing him use such sources, but of the deceased, who had been one of the most prominent opponents in Italy of the *Zohar*'s publication.[45] Yet it is curious that in his eulogy R. Abraham made a point of stating, among the praises of Maharam (whom he knew personally), that the latter had achieved perfection in opinions and in the highest forms of wisdom "ascending to the highest level," and that through religious study "the secrets and hidden meanings of the Torah were revealed to him."[46] This would seem to suggest that Italy's great Ashkenazic rabbi, "Maharam Padovah," was more kabbalistically inclined, though not necessarily in the direction of Zoharic kabbalah, than some scholars have been willing to acknowledge, and to lend support to the previously disputed testimony that he had compiled a work on practical kabbalah during his lifetime.

The testimony is that of R. Elazar Altschuler of Prague, who early in the seventeenth century claimed to have copied such a work. He asserted that it bore the name of Maharam and contained more than five hundred entries, including medical remedies and discussions of the seventy-two-letter divine name. The work, he claimed, was composed "mostly of practical kabbalah from the delightful book *Berit Menuḥah*, which is known to the kabbalistic elect" and which, as described more recently by Scholem, combined ecstatic with theosophical mysticism.[47] Yet one modern scholar has seen the attribution of such a work to R. Meir as "nothing other than the invention of a practical kabbalist seeking to lend credence to his craft" and another has been equally skeptical, citing in this connection R. Samuel Judah Katzenellenbogen's description of himself (in a responsum to Isserles) as "neither a kabbalist nor the son of a kabbalist."[48] The latter statement, however, which clearly drew upon Amos (7:14, "I am no prophet, nor the son of a prophet"), was obviously intended with some irony, since its immediate continuation ("but I have [in my possession] a kabbalistic commentary on the Song of Unity") considerably undermines its beginning. It needs qualification, moreover, in light, not only of the familiarity with sephirotic symbolism evinced by its author later in the same passage, but of the no less than thirteen references to the *Zohar* in R. Samuel Judah's twelve published sermons. The statement's truth regarding the father may be roughly equal, therefore, to its degree of veracity regarding the son—and to the truth of its biblical antecedent as well.[49] It would appear, as we shall see further, that historians would do better to accept at face value Altschuler's straightforward testimony concerning Maharam's compilation of an essentially derivitive work on practical kabbalah than to treat naively R. Samuel Judah's clearly ironic statement about his own and his father's kabbalistic proclivities.[50]

Evidence for such a tendency on the part of Maharam may also be seen in a recently published letter to him by one the sons of Ishmael Rieti, written evidently in 1564, a year before Maharam's death. The letter, which refers to its recipient in royal terms and speaks also of the great respect which the late Ishmael (a difficult man to impress) harbored for Maharam (and graphically demonstrated to the members of his household) mentions among his many merits that "those who know the [divine] names put their trust in you." Although the words contain a clear allusion to Psalm 9:11, it seems neither necessary nor appropriate to emend the phrase to read "those who know Your name," as in the biblical original.[51] Rather, there would appear to be here a reference to Maharam's expertise in the various versions and vocalizations of the divine name and the uses to which it could be put, described in such works as the *Berit Menuḥah*, as well, perhaps, as an allusion to his being an actual "master of the name" (*ba'al shem*).[52] As to how the members of the Rieti family might know about this generally concealed aspect of Maharam, it should be noted that their household tutor during the mid-1550s was R. Isaac de Lattes, who in late 1557 became the father-in-law of their relative (and our preacher) Rabbi Abraham Sant'Angelo.[53]

The aforementioned eulogy written by R. Abraham provides further evidence of Maharam's "practical" kabbalistic tendency, which, according to his account, seems to have possessed a strong messianic streak as well. After mentioning the great rabbi's access to the "secrets and hidden meanings of the Torah," the eulogist goes on to report an incident which occurred while Maharam was on his deathbed. An hour or so before "the expiration of his pure soul" after seventy-eight years,[54] he summoned one of his students named Joseph and instructed him to take a wife who would soon, he claimed, give birth to a male child. The boy was to be named Judah, "and he shall be the Messiah son of Joseph."[55] R. Abraham seems to have taken this story quite seriously, noting that "a man does not jest in his dying hour" (*Baba Batra* 175a) and expressing the hope that Maharam's prophecy would prove correct. What R. Samuel Judah Katzenellenbogen, Maharam's son and successor who was presumably present at his father's deathbed, made of this story is less clear, for he, as noted above, either never eulogized his father or, if he did, never saw fit to include his eulogy among the others later published in *Shneim-Asar Derashot*. One might surmise, if the former was the case, that besides finding the formal eulogy still (in 1565) a bit too richly Italianate for his taste, R. Samuel Judah may have found his father's dramatic death scene a difficult act to follow.

R. Abraham Sant'Angelo, in tactfully avoiding overt references to, or quotations from, the *Zohar* in his eulogy for Maharam, may have intended thereby to show respect for a person he regarded not as an anti-kabbalistic opponent of the *Zohar's* publication, but as a figure whose opposition, like that of R. Moses Basola and even R. Jacob Israel Finzi, derived from a position essentially sympathetic to the kabbalah.[56] The motives of Maharam and Basola in their respective oppositional stances during the late 1550s controversy have been discussed in the scholarly literature, with the former generally being regarded as the stauncher and more principled opponent of the *Zohar's* publication than the latter, a prominent kabbalist whose reservations seem to have been related primarily to the matter of timing. Yet, as has been noted, Maharam was surprisingly timid in his public stance, clearly waiting for Basola to take the initative in the matter of the proposed ban on the publication or purchase of kabbalistic works.[57]

Although the possibility has been raised that Maharam saw no possibility, on pragmatic grounds, of instituting a *ḥerem* to halt the publication and sale of kabbalistic works without the support of Basola (who had previously supported their dissemination), it now seems equally possible that the Ashkenazi rabbi's respect for the great kabbalist was genuine rather than merely tactical, and that he felt it best to defer to his judgment in matters of kabbalah, especially the Zoharic variety.[58] Whatever Maharam's true motives were, R. Abraham Sant'Angelo, in his 1565 eulogy, could certainly regard him as having been (like Finzi, as well as his own teacher Basola) a "sympathetic" rather than "hostile" opponent of the *Zohar's* dissemination, whose position, even after it had been rendered obsolete, was not to be slighted on the occasion of his eulogy.

Although the condition of the manuscript does not allow us to determine with certainty where R. Abraham's eulogy for Maharam ends, it seems to have concluded with a verse-by-verse gloss, most likely extemporaneous, of the alphabetical section, "Eshet Ḥayyil," at the end of the final chapter of the book of Proverbs. Read "creatively," it was a paean not to the biblical "good wife," but to the soul of the late great rabbi.[59] Although only the presentation of the plan, rather than its actual execution, has been preserved in the written text of the eulogy (which, like that delivered on the death of Canaruto, contains some transliterated Italian words in its margins in order to facilitate smooth delivery), it is likely that R. Abraham, who may not have finished writing his sermon on time (or may not have really tried), managed to carry it off reasonably well. This is because he had already followed the same formula in the conclusion of his earlier sermon on the death of R. Mordecai Canaruto.[60] There, too, however, the written version breaks off before the end, suggesting that the preacher felt that a partial text would suit his needs, but not before he managed to demonstrate the style of "biographical exegesis" to be followed, and to provide some useful information concerning the deceased.

We learn, for example, of the generous sum of fifty gold scudi which, as a devoted son, the late R. Mordecai had sent his parents before the previous Rosh ha-Shana (linked to the words "and he will have no lack of gain" [Prov. 31:11]), and of his regular custom of rising at midnight for Torah study (linked to "She rises while it is yet night" [31:15]).[61] The earlier phrase "and works with willing hands" (31:13) is glossed by R. Abraham as a reference to the novellae and sermons which his predecessor had delivered "in this honorable place of Ḥevrat Nizharim." The beginning of that verse, "She seeks wool and flax," seems also to be linked by the eulogist with R. Mordecai's preaching (punning on the word *darshah*), but if so, it is the content rather than the locus of the sermon which is addressed: "the reasons for the commandments and the laws, the hidden explanation of 'sh'atnez,' [the mingling of] wool and flax, the secret of the [divine] attribute of mercy ('sod midat ha-raḥamim') . . . the secret of the [divine] attribute of justice ('sod midat ha-din')."

This would seem to suggest that Canaruto had sought the secret (kabbalistic) reasons for the commandments, and perhaps even preached publicly about them before the members of Nizharim. Yet it would be unwise to accept R. Abraham's sermonic testimony at face value, for the same gloss of the verse in Proverbs may be found in another text upon which he clearly drew—the eulogy delivered some years earlier in Pesaro by his father-in-law R. Isaac de Lattes, which R. Abraham copied and preserved in his own collection of sermons.[62] There the entire "Eshet Ḥayyil" was glossed as the sermon's peroration, which helps to explain why R. Abraham was able to jot down only partial (in Maharam's case very partial) notes concerning the biblical text for those sermons in which he was planning to conclude with it. When in doubt as to what to say about a particular verse, he could always fall back on his father-in-law's version—which he did at least twice in the eulogy for Canaruto.[63] In addition, then, to the actual "good wife" through whom R. Abraham Sant'Angelo and R. Isaac de Lattes were linked familially, their styles of speaking of the dead were textually linked through the Proverbial "eshet ḥayyil," who, for a preacher in need, could be "more precious than jewels."

It should be noted, moreover, that the exegesis of the words "she seeks wool and flax" in Proverbs 31 as alluding to the biblical prohibition of *sh'atnez* is neither original with R. Isaac de Lattes nor taken from Rabbinic literature, but is rooted rather in the *Zohar*,[64] the very work in whose dissemination he and and his son-in-law played a vital role. There the "good wife" is the divine *Shekhina* whose inquiries concerning wool and flax relate to finding out "who it is that joins them together," for the sake of meting out punishment. For "whoever tries to join them together," according to the *Zohar*, "arouses a spirit that is not fit, which then comes over him, for one comes from this side and the other comes from that side. Therefore we are not permitted to join them together."[65]

The eulogies delivered by R. Abraham Sant'Angelo and R. Isaac de Lattes were joined together not only through their mutual references to those substances whose joining together was prohibited by biblical law, but also, if less directly, by that great work whose publication joined the two men together, the *Zohar*. Yet in sixteenth-century Italy, one did not necessarily have to consult the *Zohar* in order to gain access to its interpretations of the commandments. Many of these came to the attention of a wider audience through such commentaries on the Torah as that of R. Menahem Recanati, published in Venice in 1523 and 1545,[66] and especially that of R. Baḥya b. Asher, first published in Naples as early as 1492, and then frequently republished in Italy through the sixteenth century.[67] In the latter work, in fact, the Zoharic explanation for the prohibition of mixing wool and flax in a single garment is presented *in extenso*, without citation of source, as the kabbalistic explanation, and there too, Proverbs 31:13 is linked with the esoteric interpretation of the commandment.[68] In introducing this teaching in a public sermon preached in Pesaro (where R. Baḥya's Torah commentary had been published three times earlier in the century), R. Isaac de Lattes was hardly taking a decisive step in the dissemination of the kabbalah, and may even seem to have been carrying coals to Newcastle. There may, nonetheless, have been a deliberate edge to his remarks, which also included a description of the deceased's soul as returning to the bosom of its "husband" in the garden of Eden.[69]

His sermon was delivered during the winter of 1557–58, just after the publication of the *Tikkunei Zohar* and the Ferrara edition of *Ma'arekhet ha-Elohut* (in which Lattes had played a role) but before the appearance, during the summer of 1558, of the first volume of the *Zohar* together with R. Isaac's responsum supporting its publication.[70] Moreover, Pesaro, where the sermon was delivered, was in 1557–1558 a community sharply divided on the issue of whether the esotericism of kabbalistic texts should be preserved, or whether they should be released into the open. Of the two leading figures in the community responsible for bringing R. Isaac there, R. Judah (Laudadio) de Blanis, his former teacher (and fellow physician), supported the exoteric tendency characteristic of the more philosophically inclined adherents of the kabbalah.[71] R. Menahem of Foligno, however, the other *parnas* of the Jewish community, was against publication of the *Zohar*, and it was he who encouraged R. Jacob Israel Finzi, one of the prime opponents, to take his vigorous stand on the matter.[72]

It is not clear, therefore, if the mystical allusions in R. Isaac's eulogy, the first known to us in Italy, were part of an attempt to bring the kabbalah further into the open, or whether they were merely a slip of the tongue on the part of a (possibly extemporizing) preacher, in whose learned mind rabbinic and Zoharic teachings might, with equal ease, arise and there converge, and who might have gradually dropped his guard as the sermon approached its end.[73] Unlike the eulogies of R. Abraham Sant'Angelo in Bologna, we do not know whether it was delivered before a general, communal audience, or before a more intimate one, such as the members of a yeshiva or confraternity. In the case of the latter, however, some caution would still have been in order, since among the members of the yeshiva/study confraternity which had invited R. Isaac to Pesaro was not only R. Judah de Blanis, who shared his position in favor of exotericism, but also R. Menahem of Foligno, who clearly did not. Politics aside, R. Isaac would not have wanted to jeopardize the extremely generous one hundred scudi a year contract (for three years) which had apparently been his primary motivation for leaving Bologna.[74] By including in his peroration a kabbalistic gloss on "she seeks wool and flax" which originated with the *Zohar* but which had been widely disseminated in the published Torah commentary of R. Baḥya, R. Isaac may have been (or felt himself) able to please the proponents of exotericism without unduly upsetting its opponents. As was evident in the sermons of his son-in-law R. Abraham, who was *present* at a eulogy could affect its content as much as who was being eulogized.

Yet the human subject, as in the case of his sermon on the death of Maharam Padovah, was clearly of importance as well, for on that occasion R. Abraham, in evident deference to the deceased, omitted the overt quotations from the *Zohar* which he had earlier included in the eulogy for R. Mordecai Canaruto, delivered before the very same audience of Ḥevrat Nizharim. The 1565 sermon on the death of Maharam seems, as I have previously mentioned, also to have concluded with an improvised verse-by-verse gloss of the "Eshet Ḥayyil" section at the end of Proverbs, the sort of improvisation at which R. Abraham may well have become quite adept in the seven years since his father-in-law used that formula in Pesaro. We shall never know, however, whether in his peroration he continued to studiously avoid using Zoharic material, or whether upon reaching the verse "she seeks wool and flax" he dropped his guard and spoke of the secret reasons of the commandments and of the dangers of joining those things that should not be joined. Maharam, according to R. Abraham's own testimony earlier in the sermon, had come to know "the secrets and hidden meanings of the Torah," so a kabbalistically tinged gloss of "Eshet Ḥayyil" might have been an appropriate conclusion for his eulogy. But there was always the danger that it might have violated the late great Ashkenazic rabbi's stand in favor of esotericism. Maharam had been so well known, if controversial, a figure among Italian Jewry of his day that R. Abraham may have decided simply in favor of audience participation—letting his confraternal audience, which had heard him go through "Eshet Ḥayyil" at least once before, decide themselves how to gloss each verse in the hope that they would, like the proverbial good wife, open their mouths in wisdom.

R. Samuel Judah Katzenellenbogen, who seems to have sighed silently upon the death of his distinguished father, decided to open his mouth in wisdom before the Jews of Venice some seven years later upon the death (in 1572) of R. Moses Isserles in Krakow. The great Polish rabbi had been not only his relative and correspondent, but also an important ally to the Katzenellenbogen family some twenty years earlier. When the Giustiniani press in Venice released a "no-frills" edition of Maimonides' *Mishneh Torah*, intended to undercut the lavish annotated edition Maharam had published there in 1550 (with the competing Bragadini press), Isserles responded by issuing a ban prohibiting all Jews, under pain of excommunication, from purchasing the cheaper edition of the work, a ban which seems to have been quite effective but which ultimately may have led to the tragic burning, some years later, of the Talmud in Italy.[75]

This may explain why R. Samuel Judah did not bother to mention this particular debt of loyalty in his 1572 eulogy. He also made no mention there of the support he had received from the Polish rabbi in another delicate matter—that of imposing, in Venice, the Ashkenazic custom of having women go by night rather than (as according to "Italiani" practice) by day to prepare themselves for (monthly) ritual immersion, an issue which might have caused some members of his (presumably ethnically mixed) audience to bristle with resentment.[76] R. Samuel Judah chose rather to focus on the remarkably wide readership that Isserles had reached through his halakhic writings and the many students he had acquired thereby, citing in this connection the words of Daniel (12:3) that those "who turn the many to righteousness" shall shine "like the stars for ever and ever."

These writings also had an Ashkenazic agenda, however, in that they gave the opinions of medieval Franco-German authorities greater prominence than they had recently been given by R. Joseph Caro in his influential code, the *Shulkhan Arukh*. Katzenellenbogen, though, chose rather diplomatically to remain silent about this crucial aspect of Isserles' oeuvre in the eulogy for him which he delivered in Venice—the city whose publishers (in marked contrast to those in Krakow) were effectively to boycott Isserles' glosses to the *Shulkhan Arukh* in their editions of that work until as late as sixty years after his death.[77] A preacher who had been at the helm little more than seven years could not afford to alienate even a small segment of his audience. On the other hand, Katzenellenbogen was evidently keenly aware of the fact that the late Polish rabbi was not likely to receive in Krakow the sort of stylized public sermon commemorating his death that he might be given in the Italian ghetto of Venice. His decision to eulogize him there publicly may thus be compared to Profiat Duran's decision, some two centuries earlier, to compose a sermon on the death of R. Abraham Tamakh, whom, he feared, had not been eulogized in the grand manner he deserved. It appears then, somewhat paradoxically, that the sermon delivered in Venice upon the death of Isserles, the sermon in which Katzenellenbogen first emerged there as a public eulogist, had much to do with the Ashkenazic bonds between the two rabbis (although these were never mentioned explicitly), but was related also to the Italian standards acquired by Katzenellenbogen. When his father, the great Maharam, died in 1565, R. Samuel Judah knew that he could count on someone else in Italy (even someone, such as R. Abraham Sant'Angelo, who had not always agreed with his father's views) to eulogize him properly. Upon the death of Isserles in 1572 this was considerably less clear.

Katzenellenbogen chose on that occasion to begin his sermon with a discussion of the famous but enigmatic verses at the end of Daniel (12:2–3): "And many of those who sleep in the dust of the earth shall awake. . . . And those who are wise shall shine like the brightness [*zohar*] of the firmament; and those who turn many to righteousness, like the stars for ever and ever." He offered one explanation which saw an era of abundant and shining wisdom as arriving with the advent of the messianic age and the resurrection of the dead, and another which understood the verse as claiming that the purified bodies of the wise and righteous would shine brightly upon their resurrection. Katzenellenbogen's stated preference was for the second interpretation, which he saw as the plain meaning (*peshuto*) and which, he noted, agreed with the opinion of "Naḥmanides and all the kabbalists" (as opposed to that of Maimonides) that resurrection was indeed to be corporeal. In his view, those who had acquired wisdom would shine at that time like the firmament, but those who, like the departed, had also imparted their learning to others ("those who turn many to righteousness") would shine upon their resurrection with the *greater* brightness of the stars.

One interpretation of the verse in Daniel that Katzenellenbogen pointedly ignored, however, was the one which R. Isaac de Lattes had quoted some years earlier in his controversial responsum concerning publication of the *Zohar*, a responsum which had been prominently featured in the famous first edition of Mantua, 1558. Lattes there cited the *Zohar*'s own view of the verse, especially in the opening sections of the *Tikkunei Zohar*, as referring quite literally to itself and as justifying, to some degree, an exoteric tendency in kabbalistic matters. He quoted, among others, the following passage: " 'And those who are wise'—these are Rabbi Simeon [b. Yoḥai] and his companions, 'shall shine like the brightness [*zohar*] of the firmament' . . . when they created this work there was agreement from above, and it was called *Sefer ha-Zohar*."[78]

Katzenellenbogen, though he evinced in his eulogy for Isserles a marked sympathy for the views of the kabbalists, also shows signs of having been struggling there with the question of exotericism. Throughout the bulk of the sermon he seems to have avoided any overt mention of, or quotation from, the *Zohar*, though these were to figure prominently in some of his later eulogies (e.g. on R. Isaac Foa). At the very end, however, after mentioning another recent death—that, in Safed, of R. Joseph Sagis—there is a sudden turnaround and Katzenellenbogen quotes rather extensively from the same kabbalistic work he had previously excluded in the same sermon. In attempting to explain the deaths of the two rabbis he cites the view of the *Zohar* that the illness or misfortune with which the righteous are sometimes afflicted can atone for the entire world. "How do we learn this? From the organs of the body. When all the organs are afflicted with a grievous disease, one limb has to suffer in order that all the others may be healed. Which one is it? The arm. The arm is punished and blood is taken from it [by bloodletting], and then all the parts of the body are healed."[79] Katzenellenbogen goes on to cite from the *Zohar* the view that under conditions of severe disease, even two arms must suffer. What he skips over between the two passages, however, is the Zoharic proof text: "What proof have we? From the verse

'He was wounded because of our transgressions, he was crushed because of our iniquities . . . and with his stripes we are healed' [Isaiah 53:5]. 'With his stripes'—this refers to bloodletting . . . 'we are healed'—healing comes to us, to all parts of the body."[80]

This last passage seems to have been deleted by Katzenellenbogen in his public sermon not because of its (less than considerable) kabbalistic content, but because of its unavoidable Christological associations for an Italian Jewish audience. It drew upon "the remarkable [biblical] chapter which," as Driver and Neubauer noted over a century ago, "has for ages formed one of the principal battle-fields between Christians and their Jewish opponents."[81] Why the *Zohar*'s author would intentionally use such a verse is a question which need not concern us here.[82] But it was clearly easier for a conservatively inclined rabbi such as Katzenellenbogen to quote liberally from that work in a public sermon than to cite some Christian-sounding passages based on Isaiah 53. Despite Katzenellenbogen's own conservatism, however, he was careful to pepper his sermon on the death of Isserles with an eclectic range of references which, beyond the *Zohar*, included the medieval exegetes Ibn Ezra and David Kimḥi, as well as, for the philosophically inclined, Plato (on knowledge) and Maimonides (on resurrection). These learned and somewhat random references seem to have been intended to satisfy as wide an audience as possible,[83] but even in a cosmopolitan Venetian synagogue it is unclear how many of those present would have been pleased to hear that the late R. Moses Isserles had been, like an earlier member (some believed) of his race, "wounded because of our transgressions" or "crushed because of our iniquities." Although the words were from Isaiah, they had come to be associated in the minds of Italian Jews more with Christian preaching than with Jewish.

In 1597, however, a somewhat spunkier and certainly sprightlier rabbi of native Italian origin, Leon Modena (who was not yet thirty years old), was considerably less careful about avoiding such Christological motifs in the sermon which he delivered in Venice upon the death there of Katzenellenbogen. He was willing to go as far as to assert that the weakness which had begun to afflict the late rabbi since ascending to his position of leadership "was on account of our iniquities, the trembling that had taken hold of him was because of our transgressions, his illness was caused by our sins, and his death the result of our rebelliousness and contentiousness, for he, in his righteousness, would have continued living much longer."[84] Modena, who was later to compose a learned polemical work against Christianity, undoubtedly knew that he was playing with fire by implicitly comparing Katzenellenbogen with Christ, but perhaps pursued that paradox intentionally as a rhetorical device. He may also have been playfully nodding in the direction of the Christians who, he later claimed, would come to hear his sermons in the ghetto. In the same sermon Modena also compared the late rabbi, less controversially if more explicitly, to Alexander the Great, whose silencing (by death) was said to have paradoxically activated the lips of others.[85]

Modena's range of Jewish references was also quite wide and rather catholic. He did not fail, despite his avowed hostility to the kabbalah, to quote the *Zohar* in that same 1597 sermon (as in others), nor did he neglect, in the companion poetic elegy he composed on Katzenellenbogen's death, to praise the Ashkenazic rabbi for being not only a great judge and able leader, but also beyond possible error in "hidden matters." Modena's playful, if perhaps for some contemporaries maddening, eclecticism, even in matters funereal, went considerably beyond that of his Ashkenazic predecessor in both style and substance. Moreover, his consciousness and cultivation of paradox, whether in the use of Christological motifs to explain the death of a pious rabbi, or in his reliance upon the *Zohar* despite questioning its antiquity, signify a wider shift towards the mannerist sensibility that ushered in the baroque era.[86] There are indications, which I hope to discuss in a future study, that towards the end of his life Katzenellenbogen showed a new openness to the classicizing aesthetic values of the Italian Renaissance. Ironically, however, by that time the baroque, with its emphasis upon conflict rather than harmony, was taking its place in the cultural arena, as can be glimpsed from his younger colleague's more mannered style of speaking of the dead.

NOTES

1. Babylonian Talmud (hereafter B.T.) Sanhedrin, 46b.

2. J. H. Hexter's masterful essay on "The Rhetoric of History" is worth consulting even by those who have little interest in reading about Bobby Thomson's 1951 home run. See D. L. Sills, ed., *The International Encyclopedia of the Social Sciences* (1968), vol. 6, pp. 368–394, reprinted in J. H. Hexter, *Doing History* (Bloomington, 1971), pp. 15–76.

3. See J. M. McManamon, S. J., *Funeral Oratory and the Cultural Ideals of Italian Humanism* (Chapel Hill, N.C., 1989), pp. 10–11. On pre-humanist thematic funeral sermons, which "gravitated towards philosophical lectures on issues suggested by the Scriptural theme and only remotely touched on the life of the person eulogized," see ibid., p. 10. On Vergerio see also idem, "Innovation in Early Humanist Rhetoric: The Oratory of Pier Paolo Vergerio (the Elder), "*Rinascimento* n.s. 22 (1982): 3–32.

4. See Hans Baron, *The Crisis of the Early Italian Renaissance* (revised ed. Princeton, 1966), pp. 412–413. According to Baron "Bruni allowed his eulogy of the dead general to grow into a Florentine counterpart to Pericles' oration." See also McManamon, *Funeral Oratory*, p. 23.

5. McManamon, *Funeral Oratory*, pp. 34–35. For a discussion of epideictic see also W. H. Beale, "Rhetorical Performative Discourse: A New Theory of Epideictic," *Philosophy and Rhetoric* 11 (1978): 221–246.

6. On the date of Isserles' death and the text of his epitaph, see Asher Siev, ed., *She'elot u-Teshuvot ha-Rema* (Jerusalem, 1971), p. 13. For Luria's comment see ibid., no. 67.

7. Note the forty-four-page appendix containing a list of funeral orations delivered in Renaissance Italy ca. 1374–1534 in McManamon, *Funeral Oratory*, pp. 249–292. As he observes, "at least thirty-five funeral orations had appeared in print by 1500" (ibid., 24–25), so that sixteenth-century Italian Jews seeking to familiarize themselves with the written genre could so with relative ease.

8. For biographical information see the entries by Meyer Kayserling in the *Jewish Encyclopedia* (hereafter *JE*) (1901–1906), vol. 7, p. 455, and by Umberto Cassuto in the (German) *Encyclopaedia Judaica* (1928–1934), vol. 9, pp. 1083–1084. The entry by Shlomo Tal devoted to R. Samuel Judah's father, R. Meir Katzenellenbogen, in the new *Encyclopaedia Judaica* (hereafter *EJ*) (1972), vol. 10, pp. 829–830, contains some information on the son, as well as additional bibliography. More recently see Asher Siev, "R. Shmuel Yehudah Katzenellenbogen," *Ha-darom* 34 (1972): 177–201, which is still far from definitive. On the sermons of R. Samuel Judah see the brief but useful study by Gedaliah Nigal, "Derashotav shel R. Shmuel Yehudah Katzenellenbogen," *Sinai* 36 (1971–1972): 79–85, and the illuminating comments of Robert Bonfil, *Rabbis and Jewish Communities in Renaissance Italy*, trans. J. Chipman (New York, 1990), especially pp. 309–311.

9. The famous R. Judah Minz was his great-grandfather, whose granddaughter was married to R. Samuel Judah's father, R. Meir. On the family as a rabbinic dynasty see Cecil Roth, *History of the Jews in Venice* (hereafter *Venice*) (Philadelphia, 1930), p. 280.

10. For the view that Jewish sermons in Italy were delivered in "mellifluous Italian" see Cecil Roth, *The Jews in the Renaissance* (Philadelphia, 1959), p. 36; Moses Shulvass, *The Jews in the World of the Renaissance*, trans. E. I. Kose (Leiden, Chicago, 1973), p. 345; and, more recently (and comprehensively) Bonfil, *Rabbis* 301–302; idem, "Aḥat mi-Derashotav ha-Italkiot shel R. Mordekhai Dato," *Italia* 1 (1976) (Hebrew section), pp. 2–3. On the language of delivery see also the general comments of Marc Saperstein, *Jewish Preaching 1200–1800, An Anthology* (New Haven, London, 1989), pp. 39–44. On Moscato, whose style, as Alexander Altmann noted, "exemplified, and did not merely discourse upon, the humanist concern for *ars rhetorica*," see idem, "*Ars Rhetorica* as Reflected in Some Jewish Figures of the Italian Renaissance," in B. D. Cooperman, ed., *Jewish Thought in the Sixteenth Century* (Cambridge, Mass., 1983), pp. 15–21. Note also the comment of Leon Modena on Moscato's style in Yacob Boksenboim, ed., *Iggerot Rabbi Yehuda Aryeh mi-Modena* (Tel Aviv, 1984), p. 84. Modena, in his eulogy upon R. Samuel Judah's death, praised him as possessing not only Scriptural and rabbinic learning, but also "ẓaḥiot" (or possibly "ẓaḥiut") by which he would seem to mean eloquence or rhetoric. See Leon Modena, *Midbar Yehudah* (Venice, 1602), 68b. On "ẓaḥut" as a term for rhetoric see Jacob Klatzkin, *Thesaurus Philosophicus Linguae Hebraicae* (Berlin, 1933), 3: 240.

11. On Maharam see the entries by Max Seligsohn in *JE*, vol. 7, p. 454, and Umberto Cassuto in the German *EJ*, vol. 9, p. 1079. More recent studies include Simon Schwarzfuchs, "I responsi di Rabbi Meir da Padova come fonte storica," *Scritti in memoria di Leone Carpi* (Milan, Jerusalem, 1967), pp. 112–132; Asher Siev, "Maharam mi-Padovah," *Ha-darom* 28 (1969): 160–195; for Maharam as "the greatest rabbi of the period" see Shulvass, *Jews in the World of the Renaissance*, p. 91, and note the seventeenth-century testimony quoted by Bonfil, *Rabbis*, p. 132, n. 159 and mentioned also in (the new) *EJ*, vol. 10, p. 829. On R. Samuel Judah's rabbinical status in Venice, see Roth, *Venice*, p. 280; Bonfil, *Rabbis*, p. 229, n. 86; and M. A. Shulvass, "Venezia," in J. L. Maimon, ed., *Arim ve-Imahot be-Yisrael* (Jerusalem, 1950), vol. 4, p. 77.

12. *Shneim-Asar Derashot* (Venice, 1594). The date of publication is sometimes given erroneously as 1588. See, for example, M. S. Ghirondi in *Kerem Ḥemed* 3 (1838), p. 95. The number of eulogies in the collection is reported erroneously as five by Joseph Dan, *Sifrut ha-Musar veha-Derush* (Jerusalem, 1975), p. 197.

13. Besides the one for Isserles (no. 6), sermons were delivered upon the deaths of R. Judah Moscato (no. 3), R. Isaac Foa (no. 5), R. Joseph Caro (no. 10), and R. Zalman (Solomon) Katz (Cohen-Rapa) (n. 11). The sixth, which appears as the final sermon in the collection (whose organization, however, is not chronological), was recited upon the untimely death of an unnamed young man.

14. Moses ibn Ezra composed nearly forty of this variety. On his poems, and on the genre in general, see the excellent chapter (no. 8) in Dan Pagis, *Shirat ha-Ḥol ve-Torat ha-Shir le-Moshe ibn Ezra u-Venei Doro* (Jerusalem, 1970), pp. 197–224, and the more limited remarks in idem, *Ḥiddush u-Masoret be-Shirat ha-Ḥol ha-Ivrit* (Jerusalem, 1976), pp. 162–163. See also the book-length study by Israel Levin, *Al Mavet: ha-Kinah al ha-Met be-Shirat ha-Ḥol ha-Ivrit bi-Sefarad al Rek'a ha-Kinah ba-Shira ha-Aravit* (Tel-Aviv, 1973), together with the critical remarks of Pagis, *Ḥiddush u-Masoret*, p. 374. Levin's study ends with the poet Todros Abulafia (d. c. 1300), who composed some thirty *kinot*. For some Spanish examples between the eleventh and thirteenth centuries see also H. Schirmann, ed., *Ha-Shira ha-Ivrit bi-Sefarad uve-Provens*, 2 vols. (Jerusalem, Tel Aviv, 1972), nos. 67–70, 257, 334.

15. Profiat Duran, *Ma'aseh Efod*, eds. J. Friedländer and J. Kohn (Vienna, 1865), pp. 189–197. On Duran see R. W. Emery, "New Light on Profayt Duran 'The Efodi'," *Jewish Quarterly Review* n.s. 58 (1967/68): 328–337 and the sources cited there. For bibliographies of surviving eulogies see Aharon (Adolph) Jellinek, *Kuntres ha-Maspid* (Berlin, 1884), and the more complete work by Duber (Bernhard) Wachstein. *Mafteaḥ ha-Hespedim* (Vienna, 1922–32), which nonetheless needs considerable updating.

16. An edition of Gerondi's twelve sermons had been published in Constantinople earlier in the sixteenth century, and another appeared in Venice in 1596. See M. Steinscheider, *Catalogus Librorum Hebraeorum in Bibliotheca Bodleiana* (2nd ed. Berlin, 1931) (hereafter *CB*), p. 2063.

17. See the account of Elijah Capsali, *Seder Eliyahu Zuta*, ed. Aryeh Shmuelevitz et al. (Jerusalem, 1977), vol. 2, p. 255.

18. See Meir Benayahu, "The Sermons of R. Yosef b. Meir Garson as a Source

for the History of the Expulsion from Spain and [the] Sephardic Diaspora," [Hebrew] *Michael* 7 (1981): 144–198 passim; Joseph Hacker, "On the Intellectual Character and Self-Perception of Spanish Jewry in [the] Late Fifteenth Century" [Hebrew] *Sefunot* (new series) 2, no. 17 (1982): 66–69, 82–95.

19. On Arabic influence upon the medieval Spanish *kinah* see Levin's study mentioned above (n. 14). On the transition in cultural values see Bernard Septimus, *Hispano-Jewish Culture in Transition: The Career and Controversies of Ramah* (Cambridge, Mass., 1982). Note there p. 8 on R. Meir Abulafia's thirteenth-century poem on the death of his sister, in which it is the latter who speaks. On this poetic device see ibid., p. 122, n. 50.

20. See Meir Benayahu, "Kinot Hakhmei Italia al R. Yosef Caro," in *R. Yosef Caro: Iyyunim u-Mehkarim*, ed. Y. Raphael (Jerusalem, 1969), pp. 302–359.

21. For the 1559 sermon of R. Samuel Ashkenazi Jaffe see Meir Benayahu, "Hespedo shel R. Shemuel Ashkenazi," *Kobez al Yad* 8, no. 18 (1976): 438–449, and the latter's introductory comments there, pp. 435–437.

22. On the use of Yiddish in Ashkenazic preaching of the sixteenth century see H. H. Ben-Sasson, *Hagut ve-Hanhaga* (Jerusalem, 1959), p. 39. On Yiddish as the language of preference among Italian Ashkenazim see Shulvass, *The Jews in the World of the Renaissance*, pp. 222–227, and Riccardo Calimani, *The Ghetto of Venice*, trans. K. S. Wolfthal (New York, 1987), p. 141.

23. On R. Abraham of Sant'Angelo, known also as R. Abraham b. Meshullam of Modena, see Isaiah Tishby, "The Controversy about the Zohar in the Sixteenth Century in Italy" [Hebrew], in *P'raqim: Yearbook of the Schocken Institute for Jewish Research* (1967–1968), vol. 1, pp. 131–132 [= idem, *Hikrei Kabbalah u-Sheluhoteha* (Jerusalem, 1982), vol. 1, pp. 79–80]; Ephraim Kupfer, "New Documents concerning the Controversy about the Publication of the Zohar," *Michael* 1 (1973): 304–318 (Hebrew section), and Moshe Idel, "Major Currents in Italian Kabbalah Between 1560–1660," *Italia Judaica* (Rome, 1986), vol. 2, pp. 246–247. See also Ya'akov Boksenboim's biographical sketch in his edition of *Iggerot Melamdim: Italia [5]315–[5]351* (1555–1591) (Tel Aviv, 1985), pp. 44–52. The third collection of correspondence published there (pp. 249–361) is mostly between R. Abraham, his students, and the members of his family (such as his father-in-law R. Isaac de Lattes). On the "Nizharim" confraternity see Bonfil, *Rabbis*, pp. 216–217, and now Bracha Rivlin, "Takkanot Hevrat Nizharim be-Bologna mi-Shenat [5]307," *Asufot* 3 (1989): 357–396.

24. One of the remaining two was delivered before the members of "Nizharim" upon the death of its previous teacher, R. Mordecai Canaruto, and another, the earliest of the three, delivered on 16 November, 1562, in the home of R. Elhanan Yael Fano, who, until his death, had been the leading figure among the Jews of Bologna. All are contained in ms. Jewish Theological Seminary of America mic. 5470 (hereafter ms. JTSA), no. 37234 in the Institute for Microfilmed Hebrew Manuscripts of the Jewish National and University Library and were noted by Boksenboim, *Iggerot Melamdim*, p. 50. On Bologna see Isaiah Sonne, "On the History of the Jewish Community of Bologna at the Beginning of the Sixteenth Century" [Hebrew], *Hebrew Union College Annual* 16 (1942): 35–100. On R. Mordecai Canaruto see Rivlin, "Takkanot Hevrat Nizharim," pp.

358–359. Her transcription of a passage from R. Abraham's eulogy, however, is far from accurate.

25. This sermon should be added to the one earlier thought to be R. Isaac's "one extant sermon," cited by Bonfil (*Rabbis*, p. 305) from a different manuscript. On de Lattes, whose origins were in Carpentras and Avignon, but who had been in Italy since the late 1530s or early 1540s, see David Fränkel, "Toledot R. Yiẓḥak Yehoshua de Lattes," *Alim* 3 (1938): 27–33; the many citations in Bonfil, op. cit., index s.v. "Lattes, Isaac Emmanuel de"; Boksenboim, *Iggerot Melamdim*, pp. 20–21; and Idel, "Major Currents," pp. 246–248. On the Spanish congregations in Rome see, most recently, Ariel Toaff, "The Jewish Communities of Catalonia, Aragon, and Castile in 16th-Century Rome," in *The Mediterranean and the Jews*, ed. A. Toaff and S. Schwarzfuchs (Ramat Gan, 1989), pp. 249–270.

26. Note for example, the case of Abraham Colonia, a wealthy Jew of Viadana. When he died suddenly in 1556, the local rabbinic authorities ruled that his body should not be accompanied to burial since he did not confess publicly, and was therefore "akin to one who has no place in the next world." See Ya'akov Boksenboim, ed. (Responsa), *Mattanot be-Adam*, p. 393. I hope to discuss this theme more extensively in a future study.

27. Moreover, R. Abraham ha-Kohen, Bologna's leading rabbinical figure until his death in the late 1540s, had been his son-in-law, and R. Menahem Azariah of Fano was his grandson. On his wealth see Gedaliah ibn Yaḥya, *Shalshelet ha-Kabbalah* (Jerusalem, 1962), p. 153. For other details concerning R. Elhanan Yael and the members of his family, including a family tree of the Fano family, see Robert (Reuven) Bonfil, "New Information Concerning Rabbi Menahem Azariah da Fano and his Age" [Hebrew] in *Perakim be-Toledot ha-Ḥevra ha-Yehudit bi-Yemei ha-Beinayim uva-Et ha-Ḥadasha Mukdashim le-Professor Ya'akov Katz*, ed. I Etkes and Y. Salmon, (Jerusalem, 1980), pp. 99–101, 134–135, and the sources cited there.

28. The first to speak was R. Ishmael Ḥanina of Valmontone, in accordance with his rank as the first among Bologna's rabbis, after whom followed R. Abraham, then R. Elijah of Nola, and then R. Solomon Modena, uncle of the yet unborn Leon. On R. Ishmael Ḥanina, who was probably then the teacher of R. Elhanan Yael's grandson Menahem Azariah, see Bonfil, "New Information," p. 101, and the many sources cited there, n. 22. Of the two individuals bearing the name Elijah of Nola known to us in sixteenth-century Italy, the one here mentioned is probably the physician and rabbi Elijah b. Joseph of Nola, who is known to have spent time in Bologna. In 1536 he translated a medieval Aristotelian work (by the bishop of Lincoln) from Latin into Hebrew, and is later praised for his learning by both Moses Alatino and David de Pomis. See Moritz Steinschneider, *Die hebraische Übersetzungen des Mittelalters und die Juden als Dolmetscher* (Berlin, 1893), pp. 126, 476, and the sources cited there, as well as Harry Friedenwald, *The Jews and Medicine* (New York, 1967), pp. 47, 579, 582, and Cecil Roth, *The Jews in the Renaissance*, p. 84, who confuses him (p. 150) with the physician and copyist Elijah b. Menahem di Nola of Rome. The latter eventually converted to Christianity, and was known during his period of papal employ (after 1568) by the name Giovanni Paulo Eustachio Renato. On the distinction between the two

Elijahs of Nola see Friedenwald, *The Jews and Medicine*, p. 582 and earlier, Joseph Perles, *Beiträge zur Geschichte der hebräischen und aramäischen Studien* (Munich, 1884), p. 220. R. Elijah b. Joseph of Nola seems, like many others (such as R. Solomon Modena, concerning whom see below) to have left Bologna shortly before the expulsion of 1569, for we find him among the rabbis of Rome in Nisan, 1568. See Ya'akov Boksenboim, ed., *Parshiot* (Tel-Aviv, 1986), p. 49. It is likely that the *kinah* on the death of "the prince of physicians, R. Elijah of Nola of blessed memory," preserved in ms. Budapest Kaufmann A 539, is for this Elijah b. Joseph. On R. Solomon b. Mordecai Modena of Bologna, who was ordained in 1546 by R. Isaac de Lattes, see Bonfil, *Rabbis*, pp. 43, 102, 197, and the sources cited there, as well as *The Autobiography of a Seventeenth-Century Rabbi: Leon Modena's Life of Judah*, trans. and ed. M. R. Cohen (Princeton, 1988), pp. 76, 78–79, and especially the biographical sketch (by H. Adelman and B. Ravid) on p. 189. See also Ya'akov Boksenboim, ed., *Iggerot . . . Rieti* (Tel-Aviv, 1987), p. 11 for a list of letters to and from R. Solomon, and the index s.v. "Modena, Solomon."

29. On the later prohibition see Cecil Roth, *History of the Jews in Italy*, p. 384. On the use of torches in R. Judah Minz's funeral see Capsali (cited above n. 17), pp. 254–255.

30. Ms. JTSA, 174b. On Abraham as grandfather see Louis Ginzberg, *The Legends of the Jews*, trans. H. Szold (Philadelphia, 1909), vol. 1, pp. 298–299, 316–317. So far as R. Elhanan Yael's grandchildren are concerned, we know that he had at least two upon his death, since R. Menahem Azariah Fano, who was his father's second son (the first was Abraham Jedidiah), was born ca. 1548. His immediately younger brother Judah Aryeh was most likely born before the death of their grandfather, but the fourth and youngest of the brothers, Elhanan Yael, was probably born after the death of his namesake in 1562. On the date of R. Menahem Azariah's birth and the names and order of his brothers see Bonfil, "New Information," pp. 99, 134.

31. Ms. JTSA, 172b, where he quotes the rabbinic account (B.T. Baba Batra 91a–b) of the reaction of Abraham's leading contemporaries to his death ("Woe to the world whose leader is gone, woe to the ship whose helmsman is gone") and applies these to the deceased. Compare also the use of this nautical motif in Solomon ibn Gabirol's famous poem on the death of R. Hai Gaon. See Schirmann, *Ha-Shira ha-Ivrit*, no. 70.

32. See Boksenboim, ed., *Parshiot*, pp. 302, 305, 309, 312.

33. Ms. JTSA, 174b, and compare Ezek. 33:24. Although the straightforward meaning of the verse refers to Abraham's being only one man (as opposed to many) it was often understood in Jewish exegesis as referring to his uniqueness in his day. See, for example, *Midrash Bereshit Rabbah*, ed. J. Theodor and Ch. Albeck (repr. Jerusalem, 1965), p. 1171; *Midrash Tanhuma*, ed. S. Buber, 35b; *Zohar* 1: 65b.

34. The suddenness of his death is mentioned explicitly (177a) and its untimeliness may be inferred from the use of Gen. 29:7 ("Behold, it is still high day, it is not time . . . to be gathered"). The absence of male offspring is suggested by the reference to R. Mordecai's students among the Pisa family as being his spiritual

sons—"banav ha-ruḥaniyyim" (ibid.). The conclusion of the eulogy mentions R. Mordecai's devotion to and support of his parents, but nothing about a wife or children.

35. This is Boksenboim's conclusion (*Iggerot Melamdim*, p. 50) based on the fact that R. Moses Basola, who is thought to have died in 1560, is mentioned in the sermon with the blessing of the dead (181b). It should be noted, however, that the sermon refers to such 1550s events as the burning of the Talmud (1553), the papal bull which followed afterwards (apparently the 1554 *Cum sicut nuper* of Julius III), and the burning at the stake of the twenty-four martyrs of Ancona (1555), in such a way as to suggest that these wounds were still fresh (177a). None of these events are alluded to in the 1562 eulogy for Fano, and they would appear to point to a late 1550s date for the sermon.

36. "Like a loyal and loving father he policed you day and night, so that the designs of your hearts would take on wings like eagles (cf. Is. 40:31) and embrace the bosom (cf. Pr. 5:20) of those actions that are proper, good and honorable" (Ms. JTSA, 177a–b). The model of the resident tutor who was either unmarried or separated from his family and capable thus of devoting full time not only to the teaching of his students but also to the supervision and control of their behavior was common among sixteenth-century Italian Jewry. See my forthcoming article in the *Festschrift* for Shlomo Simonsohn. The words that I have translated as "policed you" appear in the Hebrew original, as far as I can tell, as "hishter etkhem" but have been transcribed by Rivlin (p. 359) as "haya meyasser otam." "Hishter" would appear to be a corruption of the "hiph'il" form "hishtir," concerning which see E. Ben Yehuda, *Milon ha-Lashon ha-Ivrit* (repr. Jerusalem, New York, 1959), vol. 8, p. 7060. On policing as part of a teacher's duty, even when teaching older students, see, for example, the 1557 letter appointing R. Isaac de Lattes as head of a yeshiva and study society in Pesaro, in Boksenboim, ed., *Iggerot Melamdim*, p. 259, and more extensively my forthcoming article mentioned above.

37. Ibid., 177b. The humble apology of the preacher was common in sixteenth-century Jewish sermons, and drew upon the rhetorical tradition of the "exordium." See David Ruderman, *The World of a Renaissance Jew*, pp. 16–17; Bonfil, *Rabbis*, p. 304.

38. See also R. Abraham's note at its conclusion (quoted by Boksenboim, *Iggerot Melamdim*, p. 50) where he refers to the sermon as having already been delivered.

39. See the statutes published by Rivlin, "Takkanot Ḥevrat Nizharim," par. 18 (pp. 365, 374–375).

40. Ms. JTSA, 181b, 182a, 183a–b.

41. Bonfil, *Rabbis*, p. 305. On the kabbalistic content in R. Isaac's sermons see further below.

42. See the instances cited by Nigal, "Derashotav," p. 83. Note there also the list of the other kabbalistic works cited (less frequently) by Katzenellenbogen in his sermons.

43. Note, in addition to his role (together with his father-in-law) in the publication of the Mantuan edition of the *Zohar*, their joint role in the spread of

Yohanan Alemanno's writings, mentioned by Idel, "Major Currents," pp. 246–247. Idel sees the two scribes as having influenced through their activity "the direction of kabbalah in Italy and elsewhere." For the perception in Italy of kabbalah as "exoterical wisdom" see ibid., p. 244. The curriculum followed by one of R. Abraham's students some years later included, according to the testimony of the latter's brother, "Halakha [Hebrew] grammar, kabbalah, and music." See Boksenboim, *Iggerot Melamdim*, p. 390. Note also R. Abraham's statements on behalf of spreading kabbalistic wisdom and against the opponents of its dissemination published by Kupfer, "New Documents," pp. 307–309.

44. Ms. JTSA, 188b.

45. See Simha Assaf, "La-Pulmus al Hadpasat Sifrei Kabbalah," *Sinai* 5 (1939–1940), pp. 362, 368 [= idem, *Mekorot u-Meḥkarim be-Toledot Yisrael* (Jerusalem, 1946), pp. 240, 246]; Tishby, "The Controversy," 133–135, 137, 150–151, 163–165; Kupfer, "New Documents," pp. 308–309. Among the sometimes hostile marginal comments by R. Abraham Sant'Angelo in his copy of R. Jacob Israel Finzi's letter published by Kupfer, one seems to relate directly to R. Meir. In response to Finzi's claim there that since "the rabbis of Venice, R. Meir [Katzenellenbogen] and his colleagues, had issued a decree on this matter, their voice must be heeded," according to the Talmudic teaching (B.T. Eruvin 21b) that "the words of the scribes were to be heeded more than those of the Torah," R. Abraham, after "the words of the scribes" wrote in the margin "but not one like him" (ibid., pp. 308–309). Was this a reference to R. Meir himself (whom R. Abraham was later to eulogize), or to Finzi, the author of the letter he was annotating?

46. Ms. JTSA, 190a. The term used by R. Abraham to describe the type of study through which Maharam reached the highest levels of wisdom is "ha-esek ha-toriyyi," by which he seems to mean the study of conventional, as opposed to esoteric, texts. On the term "toriyyi" see Klatzkin, *Thesaurus*, vol. 4, p. 186, where it is defined as religious, dogmatic, or relating to the Torah. The third meaning, however, suggests the possibility that the reference is to Maharam's involvement in meditations making use of the Torah text, perhaps of the ecstatic-theosophic variety described in the book *Berit Menuḥah* (concerning which see the following note). Compare the kabbalistic technique advocated by another Italian Ashkenazi, Yohanan Alemanno: "Once one has divested oneself of all material thoughts, let him read only the Torah and the divine names written there. There shall be revealed awesome secrets and such divine visions as may be emanated upon pure clear souls who are prepared to receive them." See Moshe Idel, "The Magical and Neoplatonic Interpretations of the Kabbalah in the Renaissance," in Cooperman, ed., *Jewish Thought*, p. 198. On Alemanno's influence see ibid., p. 229. The use of *Berit Menuḥah* by Alemanno was noted by Gershom Scholem, "Chapters from the History of Cabbalistical Literature" [Hebrew], *Kiryat Sefer* 5 (1929): 276 (I owe this reference to Moshe Idel). On the relationship between R. Abraham Sant'Angelo, who copied some of Alemanno's manuscripts and possessed autographs of others (see Idel, "Major Currents," pp. 246–247), and Maharam, see ms. JTSA, 189b, 190b.

47. See Altschuler's remarks in the Prague, 1610 edition of *Sefer Keneh Ḥokhma Keneh Binah* (a partial edition of the kabbalistic work *Sefer ha-Kanah*), 28a,

which are quoted extensively both by Tishby, "The Controversy," p. 165, and Siev, "Maharam," p. 191. On the *Berit Menuḥah*, which dates from the mid-fourteenth century but was not published until the mid-seventeenth, see Gershom Scholem, *Major Trends in Jewish Mysticism* (New York, 1961), pp. 145–146, and his entry on "Abraham b. Isaac of Granada," its putative author, in *EJ*, vol. 2., pp. 145–146, as well as the comments on the work in his entry on "Kabbalah," ibid., vol. 10, pp. 538, 632, where he writes that "this book, which contains lengthy descriptions of visions of the supernal lights attained by meditating on the various vocalizations of the Tetragrammaton, borders on the frontier between 'speculative Kabbalah' . . . and 'practical Kabbalah.' " On the essentially magical "practical Kabbalah" see Scholem's comments, ibid., pp. 632–638, as well as *Major Trends*, p. 144; idem, *The Messianic Idea in Judaism, and Other Essays in Jewish Spirituality* (New York, 1971), p. 263, and in his *Sabbatai Sevi: The Mystical Messiah*, trans. R. J. Z. Werblowsky (Princeton, 1973), p. 75, where it is defined as "the special use of divine mysteries to produce supernatural changes in the world" (see n. 52). On the mystical technique of combining the letters of the divine name see more recently the wide-ranging discussion of Moshe Idel, *Kabbalah: New Perspectives* (New Haven, 1988), pp. 97–103.

48. The first position is Tishby's (see the previous note) and the second that of Siev (ibid.) who does not mention him and appears to have arrived at his judgment independently. The responsum to Isserles is no. 126 in Siev's edition (p. 496, and see there also n. 14). Tishby calls attention to the fact that R. Elazar avoids stating unequivocally that the work was composed by Maharam, describing it rather as "nikra 'al shemo." I would see this, however, only as an indication of the recognition on his part that the work was largely derivative and that it drew extensively on other sources, especially the *Berit Menuḥah*. On the accessibility to Maharam of the *Berit Menuḥa* see the previous two notes. It should be noted also that the fifteenth-century manuscript of the work described in A. Neubauer, *Catalogue of the Hebrew Manuscripts in the Bodleian Library* (Oxford, 1886–1906), p. 635, as Spanish has now been identified as Ashkenazic. See card no. 19114 in the catalogue of the Institute of Microfilmed Hebrew Manuscripts in the JNUL.

49. As Meir Weiss has recently noted, "There is a distinct probability that Amos expressed himself in an exaggerated fashion." See his *The Bible from Within* (Jerusalem 1984), p. 105, and for rabbinic exegesis, p. 102, n. 3. For references to the *Zohar* in R. Samuel Judah's sermons see Nigal, "Derashotav," p. 83, n. 60. The entire sentence in his responsum reads, "I, in my affliction, am neither a kabbalist nor the son of a kabbalist, but I have [in my possession] a kabbalistic commentary on the Song of Unity [*Shir ha-Yiḥud*], not a comprehensive one, but fragmentary." If the testimony concerning himself and his father is as ironic as I suggest, the commentary alluded to by R. Samuel Judah may have been part of his father's own work on practical kabbalah, which according to Altschuler's description, contained more than five hundred entries and must have been rather fragmentary in character. On the "Song of Unity" in Ashkenazic kabbalah see Joseph Dan, *Torat ha-Sod shel Ḥasidei Ashkenaz* (Jerusalem, 1968), pp. 171–178.

50. It is possible that R. Samuel Judah was deprecating his own and his father's kabbalistic stature in relation to that of his correspondent (Isserles), who

has been recently described as "the most important Ashkenazi figure who was influenced by Italian philosphical-magical Kabbalah." See Idel, "Major Currents," p. 246. Although he chose not to stress it in his eulogy, this aspect of Isserles may have been well known to the younger Katzenellenbogen.

51. The suggestion in favor of emendation is that of Boksenboim, who has published the letter and established its approximate date. See *Iggerot . . . Rieti*, pp. 305–306. Boksenboim does not mention the evidence for Maharam's interest in practical kabbalah. The letter may possibly suggest, as he has noted, that a portrait of Maharam hung in the Rieti household. See ibid., p. 305 and compare Shulvass, *The Jews in the World of the Renaissance*, p. 235. If this is, in fact, what is intended by the cryptic words, "The likeness of the moon rising was engraved on the walls of our house, a throne to your great name, and upon the likeness of a throne, great love" (cf. Ezekiel 1:26, "and seated above the likeness of a throne was the likeness of a human form"), then the fact that R. Samuel Judah later posed for a portrait, thought by some to be the first portrait of a rabbi, would be yet another example of continuity in the Katzenellenbogen family. The allusions to Ezekiel's vision, however, may suggest that the reference is not to a portrait which hung in the Rieti home, but to a kabbalistic wall chart containing divine names which had been prepared either by Maharam or according to his instructions. This would dovetail, of course, with the reference to Maharam some lines later in the same letter as one in whom "those who know the names put their trust." On the knowledge of "names" see also the following note.

52. As Scholem has noted, *ba'al shem* was the title given, in both popular usage and literary works from the Middle Ages onward, "to one who possessed the secret knowledge of the Tetragrammaton and the other 'Holy Names,' and who knew how to work miracles by the power of these names." He has observed also that "there were large numbers of *ba'alei shem*, particularly in Germany and Poland, from the sixteenth century onward," some of whom were, like Maharam, important rabbis and scholars. See G. Scholem, "Ba'al Shem," *EJ*, vol. 4, pp. 5–6, and note also idem, *On the Kabbalah and its Symbolism*, trans. R. Manheim (New York, 1969), p. 200.

53. On R. Isaac's period of service in the Rieti household see Boksenboim, *Iggerot Melamdim*, p. 20, and idem, *Iggerot . . . Rieti*, pp. 33, 292. Note the letter sent to de Lattes in late 1557 by two sons of Ishmael Rieti congratulating the former on the marriage of his daughter to Sant'Angelo (referred to as "our brother and our flesh") published by Boksenboim, *Iggerot Melamdim*, pp. 269–270.

54. The age given by R. Abraham for Maharam Padovah at his death is considerably younger than that which has been traditionally accepted in scholarship (see the sources cited in n. 11 above), as Boksenboim (*Iggerot Melamdim*, p. 50) has already noted. It is thus less likely that Maharam's strange behavior at his deathbed (concerning which see below) can be attributed to senility.

55. Ms. JTSA, 190a. On the Messiah son of Joseph, "the dying Messiah who perishes in the Messianic catastrophe," see Scholem, *The Messianic Idea*, pp. 18, 97; idem, *Sabbetai Sevi*, pp. 53, 55–56, 70, 82; and David Tamar, "Luria and Vital as the Messiah Ben Joseph" [Hebrew], *Sefunot* 7 (1963): 167–177. On messianic

speculation in Ashkenazi Hasidism, which may have influenced Maharam, see Dan, *Torat ha-Sod*, pp. 241–245, and his comments in *EJ*, vol. 11, pp. 1414–1415.

56. Note also the great respect shown by the Italian scholar Sant'Angelo for the Ashkenazi rabbi, in contrast to the letter (written in late November, 1563) by R. Abraham Rovigo of Ferrara to Maharam in which he accused the latter of blatant favoritism toward Ashkenazim and questioned the basis of his authority to override the decisions of other rabbis. See E. Kupfer, "R. Abraham b. Menahem of Rovigo and his Removal from the Rabbinate" [Hebrew], *Sinai* 61 (1967): 162, and Bonfil, *Rabbis and Jewish Communities*, p. 108. Yet it should be noted that Maharam made it difficult for Rovigo to show him respect, calling him a madman (*meshuga*) twice in one of his rabbinical decisions, and referring there also to his "diseased mind" (Kupfer, "R. Abraham . . . and his Removal," p. 159). These words were not easy to take sitting down, even from the leading rabbi of the period.

57. This caused some consternation on the part of such fellow opponents as R. Jacob Israel Finzi. See Simḥa Assaf, "La-Pulmus," pp. 362, 368; Tishby, "The Controvesy," pp. 137, 163. On Finzi's opposition see also his letter, mentioned above, to R. Isaac Porto-Katz of Mantua, published by Kupfer, "New Documents," pp. 307–309.

58. See Tishby, "The Controversy," p. 164, who noted how strange it was that Italy's leading rabbinic authority would need Basola's approval to institute such a ban, and suggested pragmatic considerations on the part of the former. It should be noted that the two rabbis seem to have entertained similar messianic speculations. Maharam, in 1565, felt that the Messiah son of Joseph would soon be born, whereas Basola had in 1547 predicted that the final redemption would come between 1560–1588. See Isaiah Tishby, "Rabbi Moses Cordovero As He Appears in the Treatise of Rabbi Mordekhai Dato" [Hebrew], *Sefunot* 7 (1963): 129; "The Controversy," p. 150 [=idem, *Studies*, pp. 98, 139]. On messianic speculation in Italy during this period see also David Tamar, "The Messianic Expectations in Italy for the Year 1575" (Hebrew), *Sefunot* 2 (1958): 61–88.

59. As Boksenboim (*Letters*, p. 50) notes, at least one page (194) of the sermon is missing, but I do not share his certainty that the conclusion is missing as well. My suspicion is that the short section at the head of page 195a contains the brief notes that R. Abraham made for the conclusion of his eulogy on Maharam. As to why brief notes would suffice, see below. The use of verses describing a "woman of valor" concerning a man was technically facilitated by the fact that the Hebrew word for soul (here: *nefesh*) takes the feminine. For the earlier use of "Eshet Ḥayyil" as the basis for a lament on a woman see the poem written by R. Eleazar b. Judah of Worms (d. c. 1230) after the martyrdom of his wife Dulcia, published by A. M. Haberman, *Sefer Gezerot Ashkenaz ve-Zarefat* (Jerusalem, 1945), pp. 165–166. See also the English translation in Ivan Marcus, "Mothers, Martyrs, and Moneymakers: Some Jewish Women in Medieval Europe," *Conservative Judaism* 38, no. 3 (1986): 34–45. On exegesis of "Eshet Ḥayyil" as a separate unit see the commentary from late fourteenth-century Spain published by L. A. Feldman, "Exegesis of Proverbs XXXI: 10–31 by R. Abraham Tamakh" [Hebrew], in the *Samuel K. Mirsky Memorial Volume* (Jerusalem, New York, 1970), pp. 85–103. On

the use of the first verse of "Eshet Ḥayyil" in the *Ashkava* prayer for women according to the Sephardi rite, see *EJ*, vol. 6, p. 887. On the use of an alphabetical scheme, apparently as a mnemonic device, for eulogies, see S. D. Goitein, *A Mediterranean Society*, vol. 5, "*The Individual*" (Berkeley, Los Angeles, 1988), pp. 164–165.

60. Ms. JTSA, 186b.

61. Ibid. On this custom in sixteenth-century Italy note Moses Basola's advice, on explicitly kabbalistic grounds, to engage in Torah study after midnight, in a letter to a student published by Ruth Lamdan, "Two Writings by R. Moshe Basola" [Hebrew], *Michael* 9 (1985): 181–182. See also, for its actual practice, the 1579 letter of R. Mordecai Foligno in Boksenboim, ed., *Iggerot Melamdim*, p. 186.

62. Ms. JTSA, 195b. The eulogy was delivered during the week of the pericope of "Bo" in the year 5318, which was late 1557 or early 1558. For whom it was delivered is less clear, since R. Abraham writes cryptically that the eulogy had taken place in Pesaro upon the "fall from heaven of the shining star, son of dawn [cf. Is. 14:12], a cedar in Lebanon." The Hebrew, "hellel ben shaḥar," may possibly be a reference (if the first two words are reversed) to a son of R. Judah (Laudadio) de Blanis, the noted Pesaro physician and rabbi, who had been instrumental in bringing R. Isaac de Lattes to head the yeshiva there. The latter was referred to the previous year by Lattes (in a letter to R. Abraham) as "the physician R. Maestro Laudadio de Blanis," who, he claimed, had been his "shepherd" since 1538–59. See Boksenboim, *Iggerot Melamdim*, pp. 251, 257–258, 267–269, and, on the Blanis family in general, Ariel Toaff, *Gli ebrei a Perugia* (Perugia, 1975), pp. 149–150, 158, 162–163 (including a family tree). The deceased may have been Judah-Laudadio's son Mordecai (Angelo), with whom Lattes is known to have had a special relationship, and concerning whom nothing is known (to me) after June of 1557. See ibid., pp. 267, 391. In a letter of February 1557 to R. Abraham Sant'Angelo, Lattes refers to the sons of R. Judah-Laudadio as "cedars of Lebanon," (ibid., p. 251) precisely the phrase with which the deceased is described in R. Abraham's note!

63. Another instance in the written version is on the verse "She puts her hands to the distaff," (31:19) where the last word (*kishor*) is read punningly as a reference to the laws of *kashrut* and those of torts ("*ki yigaḥ shor*"). See Ms. JTSA 186b and compare ibid., 198a–b. Whether, as seems likely, R. Abraham borrowed further in the oral version, we cannot know for sure. His transcription of the sermon he delivered for R. Elhanan Yael Fano contains no hint, as noted above, of the "Eshet Ḥayyil" formula. R. Abraham may have decided against using it on that more public occasion, since some of those present, especially his fellow rabbis, may have already heard the "Eshet Ḥayyil" rendition straight from the horse's mouth—during one of his father-in-law's periods of residence in Bologna. R. Isaac de Lattes is known to have been in Bologna between February and June of 1557 and during the first half 1559 (see Boksenboim, ed., *Iggerot Melamdim*, p. 20), and may have delivered at least one eulogy there in which *he* used the "Eshet Ḥayyil" formula.

64. See *Zohar* 3:51a, 86b, and Isaiah Tishby, *Mishnat ha-Zohar* (Jerusalem, 1961), vol. 2, pp. 472–476. For wool and flax as symbols of divine justice and

divine mercy seee *Zohar* 3: 259b. For "Sh'atnez" as one of the commandments whose explanation was traditionally regarded as hidden, see, for example, B.T. Yoma 67b.

65. The translation is taken from Isaiah Tishby, *The Wisdom of the Zohar*, trans. David Goldstein (Oxford, 1989), vol. 3, pp. 1207–1208.

66. See Steinschneider, *CB*, pp. 1735–1736. His *Ta'amei ha-Miẓvot* was published in Constantinople in 1544. See also Efraim Gottlieb, "Recanati, Menahem" in *EJ*, vol. 13, p. 1608.

67. See Efraim Gottlieb, *Ha-Kabbalah be-Kitvei Rabbenu Baḥya ben Asher ibn Halawa* [Hebrew] (Jerusalem, 1970), p. 9, on the popularity of the work and on the five editions which appeared between 1492 and 1524. Note also the two editions published in Venice in the 1540s and that of Riva di Trento, 1559, mentioned by Steinscheider, *CB*, p. 779.

68. See *Rabbenu Baḥya: Beur 'al ha-Torah*, ed. C. Chavel (Jerusalem, 1974), vol. 2, pp. 527–528. The close correspondence between R. Baḥya's remarks on Lev. 19:19 and those of the *Zohar* was already noted and stressed by Gottlieb, *Ha-Kabbalah*, pp. 183–185.

69. Ms. JTSA, 195b. Note also the Zoharic identification of "Eshet Ḥayyil" with the "Shekhina," the female aspect of the divine presence and the lowest of the ten *Sefirot*. See Tishby, *Mishnat ha-Zohar I* (rev. ed. Jerusalem, 1971), p. 240; *EJ*, vol. 6, p. 887. The eulogy was evidently delivered for someone who combined a kabbalistic tendency with a philosophical inclination, a combination especially common in Italy and characteristic of the "school" of Alemanno (see Idel, "Magical and Neoplatonic Interpretations," pp. 188–189; "Major Currents," pp. 245–246). The gloss on the word *shalal* ("gain," Ps. 31:12: "he will have no lack of gain") plays on its similarity to the word *shelili* (negative), and states about the deceased that "when analyzing the divine attributes he would not fail to do so in negative terms." This might be an allusion to the demythicized philosophical view of the *Sefirot* in the negative kabbalistic theology favored by Alemanno and his followers in Italy. See Moshe Idel, "Bein Tefisat ha-Aẓmut le-Tefisat ha-Kelim ba-Kabbalah bi-Tekufat ha-Renesans," *Italia* 3 (1982): esp. p. 95 (Hebrew section); idem, "Magical and Neoplatonic Interpretations," pp. 219–227. De Lattes himself, who claims to have been for some time a teacher of the deceased, was, as was noted above, a follower of Alemanno in matters of kabbalah.

70. For the dates of publication see Tishby, "The Controversy," p. 131; Boksenboim, ed., *Iggerot Melamdim*, p. 268.

71. On Pesaro as a split community on the issue see Kupfer, "New Documents," p. 305; and on R. Judah's stand in favor of publication see ibid., pp. 305, 310, as well as Boksenboim, ed., *Iggerot Melamdim*, p. 271. On R. Judah's possession of a Zoharic manuscript which he put at the disposal of the book's publishers see Tishby, "The Controversy," pp. 143–144. For another kabbalistic manuscript in his possession see Toaff, *Gli ebrei*, pp. 149, 158.

72. See Kupfer, "New Documents," p. 305, 311–314. Significantly, R. Menahem, no opponent of kabbalah, was also in possession of a manuscript of the *Zohar* which he attempted to withold from those involved in its publication. See ibid., p. 312.

73. Note, for example, his letter in March of 1557 to R. Abraham, who was engaged but not yet married to his daughter, in which the language and allusions in which his praises for the former are couched move gradually from rabbinic to kabbalistic. See Boksenboim, ed., *Iggerot Melamdim*, pp. 256–257.

74. See the documents concerning R. Isaac's invitation to head a yeshiva and/ or study society in Pesaro, in Boksenboim, ed., *Iggerot Melamdim*, p. 258–269 (some of which were originally published by David Fränkel, "Shelosha Mikhtavim le-Toledot R. Yiẓḥak Yehoshua da Lattes," *Alim* 3 [1938]: 23–26). For the relative generosity of the contract see Bonfil, *Rabbis*, p. 162.

75. The events are narrated briefly by Roth, *Venice*, pp. 255–256, and in greater detail by David Amram, *The Makers of Hebrew Books in Italy* (Philadelphia, 1909, reprint London, 1963), pp. 254–263. See also Siev, "Maharam," pp. 183–190, and no. 10 in his edition of *She'elot u-Teshuvot ha-Rema*.

76. On this matter see Siev's edition of *She'elot u-Teshuvot ha-Rema*, nos. 18–19, as well as Leon Modena's responsum in his *Ziknei Yehuda*, ed. Shlomo Simonsohn (Jerusalem, 1956), no. 4. See also Boksenboim, *Iggerot . . . Modena*, no. 35. On earlier tension between *Ashkenazim* and *Italiani* on this issue see Bonfil, *Rabbis*, 258–260, and the sources cited there.

77. The glosses of Isserles to the *Shulkhan Arukh* were published as early as the Krakow, 1569–1571 edition of that work, and in subsequent editions which appeared there through the early seventeenth century. The first Venice edition they appeared in, however, was that of 1632, being conspicuously absent from those of the 1570s and of 1598. See H. D. Friedberg, *Bet Eked Sefarim* (2d ed. Tel Aviv, 1954), p. 1005. On Isserles and the *Shulhan Arukh* see Isadore Twersky, "The Shulkhan Arukh: Enduring Code of Jewish Law," *Judaism* 16 (1967): 145–155 [= Judah Goldin ed., *The Jewish Expression* (New Haven, 1976), pp. 325–334]. It is significant that in contrast to the dozen other Italian rabbis who composed poetic elegies (*kinot*) on the death of R. Joseph Caro in 1575 (among them, the virtuoso sermonizer R. Judah Moscato), the Ashkenazi Katzenellenbogen evidently felt culturally more at home with the prose genre of the *hesped* than the poetic one of the *kinah*. See the thirteen poems published by Benayahu, "Kinot Ḥakhmei Italia," pp. 302–359.

78. See de Lattes's responsum in the Mantua 1558 edition of the *Zohar*, where several Zoharic passages glossing the verse in Daniel are quoted. For the originals see, for example, *Zohar* 3: 124b; *Tikkunei Zohar* 1a. See also Tishby, *The Wisdom*, pp. 19, 1107, 1150.

79. *Shneim-Asar Derashot*, 34b. The passage, identified there only as coming from the *Zohar* on the pericope of "Pinḥas," is from *Zohar* 3:218a.

80. I follow the translation in Tishby, *The Wisdom*, p. 1495. Note also the translation in S. R. Driver and A. Neubauer, *The Fifty-Third Chapter of Isaiah According to Jewish Interpreters* (Oxford, London, 1877), vol. 2, p. 15.

81. Driver and Neubauer, *The Fifty-Third Chapter*, Preface, p. iii.

82. Note Yehudah Liebes, "Christian Influences in the *Zohar*," *Jerusalem Studies in Jewish Thought* 2 (1982–1983): 43–74 [Hebrew].

83. On Katzenellenbogen's intellectual eclecticism see Bonfil, *Rabbis*, pp. 309–311. I am somewhat more inclined to see this eclecticism in terms of the

preacher's need to meet the varied expectations of his audience than as a true reflection of his intellectual profile.

84. Modena, *Midbar Yehudah* (Venice, 1602), 67b. On the later use of Christological motifs by the kabbalist R. Moses Zacuto and the baroque implications thereof see Robert Bonfil, "Change in the Cultural Patterns of a Jewish Society in Crisis: Italian Jewry at the Close of the Sixteenth Century," *Jewish History* 3 (1988):21.

85. On Modena's polemical work *Magen ve-Ḥerev*, written shortly before his death, see Shlomo Simonsohn's introduction to his edition of that work (Jerusalem, 1960). On the comparison of Katzenellenbogen with Alexander the Great see Modena, *Midbar Yehudah*, 69a. On comparisons with Alexander the Great in Renaissance funeral orations see McMannamon, *Funeral Oratory*, pp. 47, 99, 103.

86. On the deliberate ambiguities which often puzzle the beholder of late sixteenth-century Italian mannerist art, "which not rarely reveals a hardly veiled licentiousness under the guise of prudery," see Rudolf Wittkower, *Art and Architecture in Italy 1600–1750* (London, 1986), p. 23. On the baroque sensibility and Jewish culture in Italy see now the remarks of David Ruderman, *A Valley of Vision: The Heavenly Journey of Abraham ben Hananiah Yagel* (Philadelphia, 1990), pp. 65–68.

NOTES ON CONTRIBUTORS

David B. Ruderman: Frederick P. Rose Professor of Jewish History, Yale University. Author of *The World of a Renaissance Jew: The Life and Thought of Abraham b. Mordecai Farissol* (Cincinnati, 1981); *Kabbalah, Magic, and Science: The Cultural Universe of a Sixteenth-Century Jewish Physician* (Cambridge, Mass. and London, 1988); *The Valley of Vision: The Heavenly Journey of Abraham ben Hananiah Yagel* (Philadelphia, 1990), and numerous essays on Jewish cultural history in early modern Europe.

Marc Saperstein: Gloria M. Goldstein Professor of Jewish History and Thought at Washington University in St. Louis. Author of *Decoding the Rabbis: A Thirteenth-Century Commentary on the Aggadah* (Cambridge, Mass. and London, 1980), *Jewish Preaching 1200–1800 An Anthology* (New Haven and London, 1989), and numerous essays on medieval and early modern Jewish history and literature.

Moshe Idel: Professor of Jewish Thought, Hebrew University, Jerusalem. Author of *Kabbalah: New Perspectives* (New Haven and London, 1988); *The Mystical Experience in Abraham Abulafia* (Albany, 1988); *Studies in Ecstatic Kabbalah* (Albany, 1988); *Language, Torah and Hermeneutics in Abraham Abulafia* (Albany, 1989); *Golem: Jewish Magical and Mystical Traditions on the Artificial Anthropoid* (Albany, 1990), and numerous essays on the history of kabbalah.

Robert Bonfil: Professor of Jewish History, Hebrew University, Jerusalem. Author of *Rabbis and Jewish Communities in Renaissance Italy* (Oxford, 1990; English translation of Hebrew original, Jerusalem, 1979), *Kitvei Azariah Min Ha-Adumin* (Jerusalem, 1991); *Gli ebrei in Italia nell'epoca del Rinascimento* (Florence, 1991; English translation to be published by

University of California Press, 1993), and numerous essays on medieval and early modern Jewish history.

Joanna Weinberg: Lecturer in Rabbinics and Jewish History, Leo Baeck College, London. Editor and Translator of Azariah de'Rossi's *Me'or Einayim,* to be published in the Yale Judaic series, and author of numerous essays on Jewish intellectual history in Italy.

Elliott Horowitz: Senior Lecturer in Jewish History, Bar Ilan University, Ramat Gan, Israel. Author of numerous essays on Jewish social history in early modern Europe and of a forthcoming book on Jewish confraternal piety.

INDEX

Designer:	U. C. Press Staff
Compositor:	Maryland Composition Company
Text:	10/12 Baskerville
Display:	Baskerville
Printer:	Edwards Brothers, Inc.
Binder:	Edwards Brothers, Inc.